The Slave Drivers

Recent Titles in
Contributions in Afro-American and African Studies
Series Adviser: Hollis R. Lynch

Black Ethos: Northern Urban Life and Thought, 1890-1930
David Gordon Nielson

The FLN in Algeria: Party Development in a Revolutionary Society
Henry F. Jackson

Old Roots in New Lands: Historical and Anthropological Perspectives on Black Experience in the Americas
Ann M. Pescatello, editor

Africans and Seminoles: From Removal to Emancipation
Daniel F. Littlefield, Jr.

American Socialism and Black Americans: From the Age of Jackson to World War II
Philip S. Foner

Black Academic Libraries and Research Collections: An Historical Survey
Jessie Carney Smith

The American Slave: A Composite Autobiography
Supplementary Series
George P. Rawick, editor

Trabelin' On: The Slave Journey to an Afro-Baptist Faith
Mechal Sobel

Revisiting Blassingame's *The Slave Community:* The Scholars Respond
Al-Tony Gilmore, editor

The ''Hindered Hand'': Cultural Implications of Early African-American Fiction
Arlene A. Elder

The Cherokee Freedmen: From Emancipation to American Citizenship
Daniel F. Littlefield, Jr.

Teachers' Pets, Troublemakers, and Nobodies: Black Children in Elementary School
Helen Gouldner

The Separate Problem: Case Studies of Black Education in the North, 1900-1930
Judy Jolley Mohraz

THE
SLAVE
DRIVERS

Black Agricultural
Labor Supervisors in the
Antebellum South

WILLIAM L. VAN DEBURG

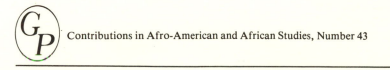

Contributions in Afro-American and African Studies, Number 43

GREENWOOD PRESS

WESTPORT, CONNECTICUT • LONDON, ENGLAND

E
443
V36

Library of Congress Cataloging in Publication Data

Van Deburg, William L
   The slave drivers.

   (Contributions in Afro-American and African studies;
no. 43 ISSN 0069-9624)
   Bibliography: p.
   Includes index.
   1. Slave labor—Southern States. 2. Elite (Social
sciences)—Southern States. 3. Agricultural
laborers—Southern States—History. 4. Slavery in the
United States—Southern States—Condition of slaves.
5. Plantation life—Southern States—History.
I. Title. II. Series.
E443.V36   301.44'93'0975   78-59261
ISBN 0-313-20610-4

Library of Congress Catalog Card Number: 78-59261
ISBN: 0-313-20610-4
ISSN: 0069-9624

First published in 1979

Greenwood Press, Inc.
51 Riverside Avenue, Westport, Connecticut 06880

Printed in the United States of America

10 9 8 7 6 5 4 3 2 1

FOR MARCIE AND TEDDY

contents

ILLUSTRATIONS   ix

ACKNOWLEDGMENTS   xi

INTRODUCTION   xiii

1 Who Were the Slave Drivers?   3

2 The Historians   31

3 The Planters   45

4 The Travelers   61

5 The Twentieth-Century Narratives   77

6 The Black Autobiographies   93

CONCLUSION   113

APPENDIX   117

NOTES   135

SELECTED BIBLIOGRAPHY   173

INDEX   195

illustrations

1 Uncle Tom   xvi

2 Afro-American ''Whipper''   13

3 Henry Bibb   101

4 Solomon Northup   107

5 Peter Still   108

6 J. W. Loguen   110

acknowledgments

I have arrived at my conclusions independently, but owe an obvious debt to other scholars whose pathbreaking, insightful, and in some cases provocative contributions are noted in the body of the text. I must also thank those members of the academic community who have, over the past decade, given this young historian something more personal and ultimately more valuable than a mere course syllabus or reading list. The most memorable of these individuals are: John Jefferies and Peter Schmitt of Western Michigan University and Frederick D. Williams, Peter Levine, and Douglass T. Miller of Michigan State University. Each should already know the specific reasons for my gratitude. Recognition also must be given to my parents, Lloyd and Cora Van Deburg; my wife, Alice; and my longtime friend, George Selement, for the tender care offered a sometimes tense and dispirited researcher. Staff members of the following institutions spent a good deal of time responding to my queries and providing necessary documents: Alderman Library, University of Virginia, Charlottesville; State of Alabama, Department of Archives and History; Barker Texas History Center, University of Texas at Austin; Library of Congress; Louisiana State University Libraries; William R. Perkins Library, Duke University; Southern Historical Collection, University of North Carolina Library, Chapel Hill; State Historical Society of Wisconsin; Tulane University Libraries; University of Wisconsin, Madison Interlibrary Loans.

I am especially grateful to John Page Elliott and Joseph F. Johnston for permission to reprint extracts from the letters of General John H. Cocke; to the Department of Archives and Manuscripts, Louisiana State University, Baton Rouge, for permission to reprint extracts from an August 20, 1834, letter by Boyd Smith to David Weeks; and to the Southern Historical Collection, University of North Carolina,

Chapel Hill, for permission to reprint extracts from the Pettigrew Family Papers and from the John Berkley Grimball Diary.

Mary Stark labored long hours to make certain that my pinched handwriting was converted accurately to typewritten copy. By their dedication to the teaching and recording of an accurate Afro-American history, my colleagues in Wisconsin's Afro-American Studies Department helped shape the emphases and overall tone of this study. The American Philosophical Society and the University of Wisconsin Graduate School Research Committee provided funds that greatly facilitated my attempt to reconstruct the life and times of the slave drivers.

introduction

> "I'll bring her to!" said the driver, with a brutal grin.
> "I'll give her something better than camphire!" and,
> taking a pin from his coat-sleeve, he buried it to the head
> in her flesh. The woman groaned, and half rose. "Get up,
> you beast, and work, will yer, or I'll show yer a trick
> more!"
>
> *Harriet Beecher Stowe's Sambo*

An accurate depiction of "leadership elites," in any society, can be obscured by the mind-set of outside observers who attempt to determine the nature of the elites' social influence, the practical limits to their power, and the basic motivating factors behind the elites' often seemingly contradictory actions. The term *elite*, derived from the Latin word *eligere* or "to choose," is itself possessed of various shades of meaning that can lead to damaging preconceptions. Originally serving to denote the choicest or most worthy of a certain type of product offered for sale, the word, as used by American social scientists, has come to refer to those persons who hold positions of eminence in specific areas of group life. Defined in this manner, elites do not have to be "choice" or "worthy," but simply have to "reach the top" in terms of education, wealth, power, or whatever personal attributes contribute most tellingly to the winning of high status.[1]

For the modern observer and interpreter of historical leadership elites, the separation of the qualifying condition of "worthiness" from confirmed social status has been encouraged by social scientists' aversion to Fascist, Nazi, and other nondemocratic ideologies that hold that *elites* are those who are fit to rule and thus *must* rule. Moreover, scholars have uncovered numerous situations in which societal leaders have become an *effete elite*, lacking in active courage and thereby failing to perform certain of the traditional tasks of leaders —in effect, refusing to represent the interests of the citizenry or to contribute to the formation of community values and social cohesion.[2]

The influence that modern conceptions of elites has had on the writing of history is readily apparent. Along with the Black Studies and "New Left" history boom of the mid-1960s to the late 1960s came a popular notion that elite groups were, almost by definition, corrupted and/or coopted by forces and institutions larger than themselves. Studies of the "underside" of American history were championed while examinations of once highly honored "movers and shakers" were considered unfashionable by historians who sought to be credited with having a "social conscience."[3]

The Slave Drivers is the first book to deal wholly with a slave elite, but as such, does not seek to turn back the historiographical clock to a time when the George Washington Carvers and Booker Washingtons ruled supreme in the world of Afro-American historiography. By examining hitherto shallowly researched antebellum events and historical visions, this study shows that the pressures of possessing both instrumental and expressive modes of leadership did not destroy the driver psychologically or turn him into a sadistic oppressor of his fellow bondsmen. Like the twentieth-century shop foreman who must concern himself with the instrumental needs of his employer (by setting work loads, supervising production, and maintaining machinery) even as he serves as the workers' expressive leader (by being concerned with their personal problems and participating in their social life), the pre-Civil War slave driver had to decide at times whether to follow the instrumental preferences of management to preserve his "elite" position or to side with his fellow slaves and thereby preserve the expressive leadership position he had attained. Although much of the available historical evidence appears, at first glance, to be filled with contradictory testimony, a critical evaluation of various types of source material has led me to conclude that drivers most often sided with "labor" as opposed to "management."[4] In so doing, the black supervisors served as role models both for other slaves and for those modern writers who are interested in reconstructing a more accurate picture of the Afro-American past. Perhaps with the image of a less than completely corrupted black leadership elite before them, scholars will be more willing to reexamine the character and life-style of other so-called privileged slaves, thereby increasing our understanding of the influences that shaped antebellum black society.

After making this apparent attempt both to predict and to influence the future character of Afro-American historiography, it must be noted that *The Slave Drivers* is not the "definitive study" of the black agricultural labor supervisors of the antebellum South. This assertion has not been necessitated by my modesty or by a lack of confidence in the research I have completed, but is given as evidence of my patent disbelief in "definitive" historical studies of any sort. By definition, *definitive* implies that an argument or an issue of some importance has been decided in a conclusive manner. Certainly the continued appearance of scholarly book reviews that pass judgment upon published works in relationship to this elusive pinnacle of public acceptance and professional esteem should lead no one to believe that America's historians are engaged in a lifelong quest for the "last word" in their respective areas of specialty. But through implied consent and scholarly neglect, statements and interpretations made by the historians of yesteryear often are allowed to remain unchallenged—thus remaining academically "sound"—for decades after closely related issues or fields of study have been subjected to vigorous rethinking and reinterpretation. "Reigning" interpretations that no longer mesh well with newer research done by scholars operating under more contemporary assumptions about man and society are no credit to the historical profession, but serve only as a sort of intellectual albatross encumbering the search for a history of the Afro-American experience that will be meaningful to the people of today.[5]

In recent years, as is more fully discussed in chapter 2, American Slave Studies have experienced a rapid development in terms of direction, focus, and purpose. Nevertheless, in the rush to reinterpret the patterns of life and thought within the plantation community, the slave drivers have been left behind. Often treated as an ill-fitting, scantily researched afterthought in published works, the drivers have been forced to retain a popular characterization remarkably similar to that forwarded by Harriet Beecher Stowe in her classic 1852 novel, *Uncle Tom's Cabin*. Mrs. Stowe's drivers, two unforgettably demonic minions named Sambo and Quimbo, were said to have been

1. **Uncle Tom.** Harriet Beecher Stowe's Uncle Tom after his "breakin'" by Sambo and Quimbo. From Harriet Beecher Stowe, *Uncle Tom's Cabin; or, Life Among the Lowly* (Boston: John P. Jewett & Company, 1852).

systematically trained in "savageness and brutality" by cotton planter Simon Legree. Through "long practice in hardness and cruelty," Legree succeeded in crushing and debasing the spirit of his two principal hands to such an extent that they would willingly do his cruel bidding. While they engaged in a kind of "coarse familiarity" with the slaveholder, the drivers "cordially hated each other" and likewise were feared and despised by the rest of the slave community. By continually "playing off one against another" Legree was assured of maintaining complete control of plantation affairs.[6]

As depicted by Mrs. Stowe, the drivers' appearance and behavior were closely matched in terms of savagery. Possessed of "coarse, dark, heavy features," and speaking with "barbarous, guttural, half-brute" intonations, Sambo and Quimbo were fitting examples of the antebellum axiom that "the slave is always a tyrant, if he can get a chance to be one." Legree's black supervisors participated in orgies of drunken debauchery with their master, treated the slave women as sexual toys, gloated with "fiendish exultation" at the brutal whippings they meted out to errant field hands, and jealously protected their coveted supervisory post from any and all potential usurpers. Certainly, to the abolitionists' eyes, the personality and behavior of Sambo and Quimbo were "in admirable keeping with the vile and unwholesome character" of the "peculiar institution."[7]

Apparently uninterested in removing this blighting stereotype from the historical personage of the driver, most historians who have written on the slave South have, by their silence, served to strengthen rather than to diminish various old, but still widely held, misconceptions regarding the black plantation surpervisors. This study offers a revised interpretation of the slave elite that is compatible with certain of the most recent historiographical developments in American Slave Studies. Chapter 1 outlines this new perspective and details the history, daily life, and duties of drivers. Chapters 2 through 6 "flesh out" the composite portrait while examining the various conflicting images of drivers that have appeared in the writings and commentaries of American historians, white southerners, antebellum travelers, ex-bondsmen, and fugitive slave narrators. A brief summary section and three appendixes containing background material on the sources used in the writing of chapters 4 through 6 complete the study.

The Slave
Drivers

1

WHO WERE THE SLAVE DRIVERS?

> The so-called "slave drivers" . . . were simply gang-bosses relieved from physical labor, armed with a whip, and set among the slaves to see that their tasks were performed. The drivers had to justify their being by urging their fellows to work, and were liked by neither side.
>
> *Albert Bushnell Hart*

According to the common understanding of the term, *slave driver* refers to "a harsh taskmaster," "a person in authority . . . who exacts extreme effort from his subordinates," or a boss who is "disliked for overworking those under him."[1] The "driver" portion of the term obviously lends itself to this sort of interpretation, but it is unnecessary to imply that the actual "driving" of the field hands was done with unfeeling severity. Throughout the years, observers of the plantation scene have compared the drivers to supervisory personnel employed in other segments of the economy. When likened to factory foremen, army troop captains, or permanent civil servants in a department of government where the bureau chief (that is, the white overseer) tends to change after each general election, the mental image formed in the mind of the reader is likely to be somewhat less harsh than when *driver* is the only word available to denote position, purpose, and authority.[2]

When used to designate a specific job category that existed within the agricultural South, *slave driver* is neither a very precise nor a consistently appropriate term. In antebellum parlance it could sometimes refer to a white overseer or slave trader as well as to the black supervisor of field labor. Moreover, titles such as *foreman, overlooker, leading man, head man, boss, whipping boss, crew leader, overdriver, underdriver,* and *straw boss* were also used to describe slaves who possessed supervisory and/or police authority over the field hands.[3]

To further complicate matters, not all slaveholders operated their farms on the assumption that there was a permanent slave driver post to be assigned. Some black supervisors held such positions only during specific periods, such as when the master was absent or during the Civil War years when white overseers were in short supply.[4] Other black supervisors performed many of the functions of a driver on a more permanent basis, but were not referred to by any particular title.[5] Still other slaves who provided supervisory services in the agricultural sphere also doubled as carriage drivers, wagoners, house servants, or artisans.[6] On occasion, disciplinary duties such as capturing and whipping misbehaving bondsmen would be forced upon randomly selected slaves or groups of slaves assembled in an ad hoc manner for the sole purpose of performing one of these driver-type tasks.[7] In a sense, it was possible for almost any bondsman to find himself "elevated" to driver status for an indefinite period.

Black freemen, too, could be found performing the tasks of plantation labor supervision.[8] Although they cannot correctly be termed *slave drivers*—since the term as it is used in this study denotes the legal status of the supervisor as well as the condition of the laborers working under his direction—the scattered use of free blacks in the supervisory machinery of the South gives evidence of the social and economic conditions that necessitated the creation of a driver class. Had their options been more numerous, it is unlikely that so many whites would have found it advisable to entrust a major share of the plantation "directorship" duties to Afro-American foremen. As it was, however, the long-term shortage of "satisfactory" white overseers, the mechanics and spatial division of plantation agriculture, and the ever-present quest for profit dictated that some blacks be assigned positions in the planter's "chain of command."

During the seventeenth century, few southern agricultural units were large enough to require an extensively specialized division of labor among the field hands. Those supervisory, skilled, or service occupations that were available tended to be awarded to English indentured servants whose language, prior experience, and race made them the obvious choice of the white planters.[9] Nevertheless, as the native-born slave population expanded and the concentration of black labor increased on the larger estates, more and more bondsmen were tapped for full-time domestic, craft, or supervisory duties.[10]

In the rice-growing regions of the South, this movement toward the use of black drivers was accelerated by the mode of crop production. Under the prevailing *task system*, rice fields were divided into half- or quarter-acre plots by a veritable checkerboard of drainage ditches. The individual plots not only provided the planter or overseer with convenient units by which to measure the performance of the hands throughout each successive stage of the growing process, but they also permitted the whites to delegate some of the routine supervisory duties on each plot to a black foreman. It was the duty of this slave to measure and stake off the "tasks" to be performed by each field hand. When the hands arrived at the plot, the driver would assign the duties for the day and thereafter periodically inspect their work. When a slave's task was completed, the chief hand would make a final inspection and, if the job had been done in a satisfactory manner, would dismiss the slave to the quarters or to other duties. At evening or the next morning, the planter or overseer could inspect the results of the day's labor and thereby keep a check upon both the driver and his squad.[11]

Agricultural operations in the cotton, tobacco, and sugar regions of the South were more often conducted under the *gang system* in which the field hands worked for a specific period each day under the general supervision of a white overseer. The main force on such plantations was usually divided into a plow gang and a hoe gang, each of which had its own black supervisor. Both of these men were responsible for the pace of their respective gangs and were often required to "set" this pace through their own labors. As ex-slave Mattie Gilmore recalled: "When dey's hoein' cotton or corn, everybody has to keep up with de driver, not hurry so fast, but workin' steady."[12]

Although there were many variations in these patterns of agricultural administration, by the antebellum period the chain of command on the plantations had become fairly well delineated. At the top of the whites' "pyramid of authority" stood the resident owner or the steward of the absentee planter's several estates. Directly below the planter or steward was the overseer of an individual plantation who might occasionally be assisted by a suboverseer or apprentice overseer. In the working of the slave force, the overseer could make use of one or more slave drivers. If there were several of these black supervisors, one of them would be designated "head driver" or "overdriver" and the others "underdrivers." Beneath, or at the same level of authority as the black field leaders, were slave foremen responsible for certain industrial or craft operations.[13] Less formally designated would be slaves assigned specific duties such as caring for the stock, ministering to young or sick slaves, or keeping the farm implements in good working order. Although various of these groupings of slaves could be considered—along with house servants, body servants, nurses, and mammies—as potential members of a "slave elite," it is only the bondsman who directed field labor and possessed supervisory and/or police authority over the field hands who truly can be termed *slave drivers* or *slave foremen.*[14]

Male slaves possessed a near monopoly of the driver post. In assigning the various plantation duties, slaveholders created a sex-related occupational structure that was very similar to that existing in the larger white southern society. Although men were virtually never spinners, weavers, seamstresses, or nurses, female slaves rarely rose to the rank of driver.[15] When women did appear as supervisors of field labor, it was usually as the leader of the *trash gang,* a tertiary laboring unit of "irregulars" formed from the ranks of children, the elderly, and female slaves in advanced stages of pregnancy.[16] On most occasions, however, even the foreman of otherwise all-female crews was a man.[17]

The individual planters responsible for the institution of these work patterns not only had to determine which of their chattels would make a good driver, but also had to decide—at an even earlier stage in their agricultural planning—whether to use black foremen as a part of their overall plan of labor supervision. Some seemed to treat the whole affair as a type of experiment, the progress of which was outlined in their self-congratulatory letters to farming journals of the day.[18] Several such adventuresome planters sought to combine the use of Afro-American foremen with systems of black-operated slave *courts,* or schemes for eventual colonization of the more "self-directed" slaves.[19]

Whatever their motives, planters who sought to elevate a slave to a high supervisory status were occasionally subjected to a good deal of criticism. Critics lamented the confidence the planters placed in their black supervisors and said that by doing so the slaveholders were undermining the position of the white overseer class, thereby further discouraging this group of men from taking an active interest in the improvement of southern agriculture. Tagged as members of a race of "juvenile darkies, or . . . the children of children," slave drivers were said to be incapable of exercising wisely the powers of authority invested in their office. Whether entrusted with the supervision of "mules, oxen, babies, or his fellows," the Afro-American as foreman was said to be "an unthinking and capricious tyrant" due to his alleged inferiority of intellect. In the spring of 1837, one unidentified Virginian even joined the "ill consequences" of the "driver regime" with a regional decline in farming prospects and blamed the increased use of black foremen for the agricultural depression.[20]

Much of this antidriver uproar was occasioned by the actions of certain slaveholders who turned over almost all aspects of daily plantation supervision to their slave foremen. When such authority was granted to a slave, the white overseer became "excess baggage" and was either relieved of his duties or assigned only a partial supervision of several estates. Those who sought to run their farms with only slaves as supervisors ran the risk of being brought before the courts on the charge of violating one of the various state laws that made it mandatory that at least one white person reside on each plantation. As early as 1712, South Carolina passed a law that provided for a forty shilling fine to be imposed upon any resident owning six or more "negroes or slaves" who refused to provide white supervision. In 1726 this provision was amended to require the employment of one white man for every ten Negroes used and for every two thousand acres of land held. Designed to open up jobs for white laborers and thereby to encourage white settlement, such laws had the further purpose of calming white fears that absentee plantations would become hotbeds of insurrection and harbors for runaway slaves.[21]

The number of slaves who labored under an individual driver or foreman differed from plantation to plantation. Despite the recent efforts of quantifiers, it is unlikely that historians will be able to agree upon a meaningful "conventional ratio" of drivers to slaves.[22] On Louisiana's New Hope sugar plantation in 1853, one driver was responsible for the supervision of sixty-eight field workers. At the

Alliance plantation in 1842 there was one *commandeur* for thirty field hands. According to traveler Frederick Law Olmsted, the owner of a "first-rate cotton plantation" in the lower Mississippi Valley with some fourteen hundred acres under cultivation, employed two black supervisors to direct the work of sixty-seven field slaves. In the inventory of personal property compiled after the death of Virginia's Robert "King" Carter in 1732, the various "quarters" of the Carter estate were listed as having a foreman to supervise slave settlements of from six to thirty-three bondsmen. During a twentieth-century oral history interview, one ex-slave noted that his former owner had appointed a "leading hand" to direct the work of "about ten grown people and their families." Such diversity in the size of the laboring population assigned to the black supervisors leads one to believe that in appointing drivers, slaveholders were influenced more by localized conditions and personal preference than they were by any prevailing "conventional ratio."[23]

Planters took various factors into consideration before they decided upon assigning a particular slave to the driver post. As described by North Carolina planter William Shepard Pettigrew, a slave foreman had to be "honest, industrious, not too *talkative* (which is a necessary qualification), a man of good sense . . ." In sum, he sought a "good hand" who had been "faithful in the discharge of whatever may have been committed to his care." Slaveholders placed varying degrees of emphasis on the individual components of this composite portrait of an "ideal" driver. South Carolina planter Robert F. W. Allston believed that the "first element in the composition" of a driver was his ability to obey orders and "conform to instructions notwithstanding the privations necessary." In addition, a good driver had to possess "energy, ready intelligence and satisfactory accountability." Other commentators listed strength, working speed, and real or potential leadership ability as key characteristics of a superior driver.[24]

As might be expected, slaveholders did not always succeed in locating bondsmen endowed with these ideal characteristics. Undoubtedly, many planters would have preferred their black supervisors to be men of impressive stature and great physical strength. To place such men in the driver's post would serve as a constant visual reminder of the force with which the driver's whip could strike the bare backs of misbehaving field hands. Although it is true that a large number of the available descriptions of black supervisors seem to show planters as being quite successful in finding prime specimens of Afro-American manhood, not all of the South's drivers could match the exploits of a "stout" foreman named Aaron Sidles who allegedly won a bet by hoisting the end of a seven hundred fifty-pound steamboat shaft.[25] A Kentucky foreman who directed the labors of ex-slave Harry Smith was unlikely to have performed any such feat because, as described by Smith, "Uncle Paul" was a "Guinea negro" of about "four feet in height." Joining "Uncle Paul" in the ranks of the nongiants were driver Solomon Northup, who was five feet seven inches tall, and North Carolina's "Uncle Philip," who was described as being of "small stature."[26]

Varying even more in age than in physique, the antebellum slave drivers were not, as some historians have assumed, "ordinarily . . . middle-aged" men. In announcing the appointment of a thirty-two-year-old bondsman named Glasgow to the foreman post, William Pettigrew explained that although the slave's "comparative youth" might "militate against him for a short while," he was encouraged by the fact that it would be many years before the "disqualifications for command that usually characterize old persons will overtake the man of 30." Moreover, a young slave placed in a position of authority had the advantage of growing up with the "business of the plantation." Hopefully, wrote the slaveholder, this would make it possible for the details of such "business" to become "incorporated in his very mind."[27] Other accounts give the ages of the black foremen as ranging from "twenty sompin'" to "de oldest slaves on the place."[28] Indeed, one South Carolina driver who was described as being "very black with a very white head" was said to be of such "extreme old age" that he was given an assistant to help him out with the day-to-day duties of his office.[29]

Slave drivers were so varied in their skin color that it is unlikely the possession of a certain quantity of "white blood" was a significant determinant of office. Ex-Mississippi bondsman Frank Cannon recalled that his former field supervisor was so "white looking" that he never did figure out whether "he was white man or nigger"; other observers described drivers who were "one-fourth white," "half Injun," "coal black," and "pure African, black as ace of spades."[30] When possession of light-colored skin was involved in the selection of a foreman, it was probably only of secondary importance to the planter-slave relationship that was the origin of the bondsman's fair complexion.[31] In general, a "typical" driver would probably more closely resemble the description given of South Carolina's "Daddy Joe" than he would the vivid word-portrait penned by Mrs. Stowe. According to ex-slave Sam Aleckson, Joe would not have answered to any of the descriptions usually given of the "plantation Negro." He did not have "a receding forehead, a protruding jaw, nor bandy legs." In fact, he "bore a striking resemblance to a well formed man."[32]

Often, the planter's driver-selection process was short-circuited by events that made careful evaluation of a "candidate's" credentials all but impossible. Illness or injury to the incumbent could make speedy replacement a necessity and white overseer fiat could result in the appointment of a foreman during the planter's absence.[33] Unsatisfactory performance of duties by an overseer could also result in the hurried appointment of a slave supervisor. Planters such as Virginia's Edmund Ruffin, who concluded that hired overseers seemed to take pleasure in "nothing else but thwarting their employer and abusing his negroes," often found it more satisfactory to assume a degree of personal control over their slaves and to appoint slave foremen as their assistants. On occasion, such decisions were made in the sudden heat of anger, rather than after a period of thoughtful deliberation. The autobiography of fugitive slave John Thompson contains an account of an incident in which an ambitious and hardworking planter became vexed with his overseer's lax behavior. Upon arriving at the field, master Richard Thomas noticed that instead of motivating the hands to increased activity, the overseer merely "stood with his whip under his arm, and his hands in his pockets, or sat under a shady tree and read the newspapers." After receiving an unsatisfactory response to his queries regarding the direction of the work at hand, Thomas seized a stick of wood and "aimed a violent blow at the overseer's head." Dodging the blow, the white supervisor ran from the field and was not seen on the plantation again. The supervision of the field hands was then turned over to John Thompson's father.[34]

The substitution of a slave foreman for a deposed overseer could also result from field hands' dissatisfaction with their white overlord. Ex-bondsman Sol Walton described how one disgruntled slave brought about a change in leadership through violent means. One day, while the hands on his master's plantation were engaged in "burnin' logs and trash," the lone white supervisor shoved an elderly slave to the ground and instructed several other slaves to hold him fast while the lash was laid on his back. Undaunted by the beating, the old man got up, knocked the overseer unconscious with a large stick, and then "took an ax and cut off his hands and feet." Upon hearing of this bloody incident, the owner of the plantation decided it would be unwise to replace the slain overseer. Instead, he appointed one of Walton's cousins to the supervisory post.[35]

No matter how they acquired the position, once in "office" the slave driver could be held responsible for the satisfactory performance of a vast array of tasks. From early morning until late at night, the black foremen were to serve as assistants to the master or overseer in directing the various parts of the complex mechanism that was the antebellum southern plantation. The initial role the driver played each day was that of "caller." While it was still dark, the foreman awakened the sleeping field hands by blowing a horn or ringing a bell. After the slaves had prepared a hasty breakfast for themselves and the working stock, a second signal was given for the field hands to assemble at some central spot. When the driver or overseer was satisfied that all hands were present—a determination that often required a quick cabin check of the slave quarters—the driver led the workers to the field.[36]

Upon arriving at the site of the day's labor, the driver would assign the tasks or begin to lead or to supervise his gang. Throughout the course of the morning, he might be called upon to administer punishment to a hand who was deemed to be falling behind in his work. The chosen instrument of correction was often referred to by contemporaries as the slave driver's "emblem of authority." This *driver's whip* differed somewhat in construction from plantation to plantation. On occasion, it might resemble the serpentine form of a horse or carriage whip. Other foremen carried a bundle of small, thin wands or switches. Still others were provided with the legendary *cow-skin*, a tool of punishment that, as noted by one observer, was certain to "make the woods ring" with the cries of suffering bondsmen. Where drivers were denied the right to certain discretionary powers, the overseer might be required to give or to supervise such correction. In

other cases, planters limited the number of lashes that field supervisors might administer. On one South Carolina plantation, drivers
were forbidden to carry their whips with them to the field. Thus, if the
overseer directed the punishment of a slave, the driver would be
obliged to embark upon a mile or two journey back to his cabin to
secure the necessary instrument. Such a system of discipline was an
obvious deterrent to hasty decisions involving the possible disfigure-
ment of the slaveholder's human property.[37]

As the assigned work of the day progressed, the black foreman was
responsible for various types of time and account keeping. When he
determined that the hour of the midday meal had arrived, the driver
called a halt to the work and directed the feeding of the field hands and
their draft animals. As the slaves devoured the provisions they had
carried from home or that were brought to them from a common
plantation kitchen, the driver would survey the condition of the plows
and make note of any equipment that might need to be taken to the
blacksmith for repairs.[38]

On some plantations, the foremen were not only held accountable
for all implements used by the slave laborers, but were also directed to
keep track of the number of calves marked and branded, the fluctua-
tions in the planter's livestock holdings, and the quantities of farm
products gathered by the bondsmen. Not necessarily requiring a great
deal of literacy or extensive experience with higher mathematics, the
task of weighing the various agricultural crops at harvest time was
sometimes assigned to the foreman. As "crop weigher," the driver
was then in a position to make decisions regarding the punishment or
nonpunishment of field hands who "came up short" at the scales or
who were found to have rocks secreted in the bottom of their baskets.
In addition to tallying crop weights, foremen were often authorized to
weigh and to distribute the weekly allotments of rations granted each
slave family.[39]

In carrying out their assigned duties, drivers sometimes served as
their master's agents in dealings with merchants, tradesmen, and
suppliers. While away from his estate, William S. Pettigrew instructed his foremen in these matters of provisioning and trade. "I
hear nothing from you respecting the lime that was to be brought by
Capt. Carson & Capt. Belanga," he wrote from Virginia's White
Sulphur Springs in the summer of 1856. "If you remember, I said in

2. An **Afro-American "whipper"** applies the lash under white supervision. From Mrs. A. M. French, *Slavery in South Carolina and the Ex-Slaves; or, the Port Royal Mission* (Westport, Conn.: Negro Universities Press, 1969 [New York: W. M. French, 1862]).

one of my last letters that it was my wish that they continue bringing lime . . . until the lime-house was full & that I wished you to say this to Capt. Carson when you saw him, in order that there might be no disappointment in getting the quantity I wanted.'' On other occasions, the planter responded favorably to specific requests contained in the letters dictated by his foremen and authorized them to obtain other types of supplies from area merchants.[40]

When the day's agricultural, correctional, and commercial activities were completed, the drivers took on the responsibility of policing the quarters. After the hands had prepared and eaten their evening meal, the foreman would once again blow a horn, ring a bell, or simply yell ''Oh, yes! Oh, yes!' Ev'body in an' do's locked''—thus signaling the end of both the slaves' physical labors and the brief period of time available for family and social life. If a member of the slave community was found to be missing during the subsequent evening cabin check, it was the responsibility of the driver to report the absentee to the master or overseer. Should the slaveholder order that a search be made for the runaway, the driver might also be directed to participate in the ''sweep'' of the neighborhood. Even if all appeared to be well on the estate, the foreman was often required to turn in a nightly verbal report of the preceding day's activities and accomplishments.[41]

Although the slave drivers performed a number of important services for their masters, they were not without roots in the quarters. The roles they played here did not revolve around their assigned task of labor supervision, but instead gave free rein to their own personalities, specialities, and interests. Within the slave community, the drivers could be respected for their own accomplishments or shunned for their personal failings. As members of this community, the foremen participated in the family, religious, and social life of enslaved black America.

The families of the drivers were a varied lot. Many times the wives, mothers, or children of the driver also occupied ''favored'' positions in the whites' pyramid of authority and status. Although the holding of such jobs did not guarantee a correspondingly high status within the quarters, mere possession of the cook, house servant, or Mammy posts within the driver's family was probably sufficient to generate the type of acceptance, however grudging or laced with jealousy, that "aristocratic" clans in free society have been known to possess.

Through the possession of household assignments, it was possible for the driver's family to acquire certain privileges normally denied to "common" slaves. Ex-Georgia bondsman Henry Bland recalled that his father, Sam Coxton, not only had been hoe gang foreman during the slave era, but also had been taught the blacksmithing trade by white artisans who were employed occasionally on the plantation. At the same time, Henry's mother was the cook in the Big House. Because of her position, the treatment of mother and son was said to have been "considerably better" than that received by those slaves who worked in the fields. Even though their basic allotment of food was identical to that of the field hands, her proximity to the kitchen assured that "choice morsels" from the planter's table would appear occasionally in the young slave's diet. Also, due to the nature of her work, Henry's mother was given clothing of a "better quality" than that normally supplied to field laborers. Other children of driver-house servant parents reported that they were fed "right from the [master's] table," were taught to read and write by the whites, and were allowed to play with the planter's children—seldom mixing with the other slaves on the plantation.[42]

Nevertheless, not only were such privileges minor, but there were also definite disabilities and hardships experienced by children of drivers and house servants. As in Henry Bland's case, when each of the slave parents supervised a separate department of plantation activity, their living quarters were likely to be separated—the driver father staying in the quarters while the house servant mother and young children resided in the Big House. For the Coxton's, living with the "white folks" may have afforded mother and son more pleasant surroundings, but it also meant sleeping on the planter's hard wood floor. Young slaves raised in this somewhat "sheltered" household environment could not count on maintaining their position forever. At the age of nine, Henry was relieved of his light childhood duties of picking up chips, driving the cows to pasture, and cutting stove wood. Thereafter, he began to be trained in the duties of the plow hand. Having thus passed into an early manhood, it is likely that he would have agreed with ex-South Carolina slave Harriet Gresham's estimation of the perquisites granted her fellow "house niggers." Despite her position as a daughter of the plantation seamstress, her close relationship with the master's children, and her father's driver status, it seemed that "somethin allus happened . . . to remind me dat I was jist a piece of property."[43]

If the slave driver and his family were united under one roof, the homestead was more likely to be located in the quarters than in the neighborhood of the Big House. When he did not live in a randomly assigned cabin, the slave holding the driver post usually occupied a dwelling at the head of the "street" formed by two facing rows of slave cabins. Should there be two foremen assigned to the agricultural unit, they might live "across the street" from one another. If the white overseer was assigned a cabin in the quarters area, it would be at the opposite end of the street to provide for "total supervision" of the slave community. Although it is sometimes assumed that the driver's residence was generally "a little larger and somewhat better than the rest," the descriptions of such dwellings given by those who lived in them show that the cabins were actually quite "common" and, at times, extremely uncomfortable. Richard Macks, son of a black foreman from Charles County, Maryland, recalled living with his parents and one sister in a log and mud, dirt-floored cabin composed of one room and its adjacent loft area. Each "room" had two unpaned windows. Bed frames for the driver's family were constructed by Richard's father and made tolerable by straw-filled mattresses. As for the black foreman, Macks remembered that "dad slept on a bench beside the bed and that he used in the day as a work bench, mending shoes for the slaves and others." Fellow bondsman Jim Gillard, son of a slave supervisor in Georgia, condensed Macks' comments when he described his former plantation home by noting simply: "No'm, our houses wasn't nothin' to brag about."[44]

Although accounts exist that tell of various sexual "privileges" being granted to members of the slave elite, drivers who were assigned to stud duty or were allowed to have more than one wife cannot be said to typify the foreman class. Wide-ranging sexual freedom on the plantation was not reserved exclusively for black field labor supervisors, nor was such activity always authorized by the planter.[45] Other accounts tell of the strong bonds of familial attachment possessed by those who shared the driver's cabin. A typical example of the ties that bound the driver to his kin was given by ex-slave Frank Bell. As plantation foreman on the John Fallon farm near Vienna, Virginia, Frank's uncle, Moses Bell, directed the labor of most of his relatives. Working in family groups rather than in randomly assigned gangs, the Fallon slaves coordinated the activities of each family member with the overall daily goal set for the entire group. Working in close proximity to one another so each slave "could help de other when dey got behind," the Bells often combined their efforts to "pitch in and help Momma who warn't very strong." Although overseers on neighboring plantations refused to allow families to work together in this manner because "dey ain't gonna work as fast as when dey all mixed up," Uncle Moses refused to pattern his operation after that of the surrounding estates. According to Frank, "he always looked out for his kinfolk, especially my mother."[46]

As with other black families during the era of slavery, driver families lived under a constant threat of temporary or permanent separation occasioned by forces over which they had little control. Whether hired out to a nearby planter for a season, employed at the city residence of the slaveholder, or auctioned off to cover the whites' debts, the member of the driver's family thereby separated from his or her loved ones presented a sad commentary on the exigencies of the "system." Antebellum traveler Basil Hall described the sale of one such family at Charleston, South Carolina, in 1828:

> The principal person was a stout well-built man, or as the auctioneer called him, "a fellow, who was a capital driver." His wife stood by his side—a tall, finely proportioned, and really handsome woman, though as black as jet. Her left arm encircled a child about six months old, who rested, in the Oriental fashion, on the hip bone . . . two little urchins clung to her knee, one of whom, evidently much frightened, clasped its mother's hand, and never relinquished it during the sale which followed. The husband looked grave and somewhat sad; but there was a manliness in the expression of his countenance which appeared strange in a person placed in so degraded a situation. What struck me most, however, was an occasional touch of anxiety about his eye as it glanced from bidder to

bidder, when new offers were made. It seemed to imply a
perfect acquaintance with the character of the different parties
competing for him—and his happiness or misery for life, he
might think, turned upon a word![47]

Although the group described by Hall was purchased by a single
slaveholder and thus may have been able to maintain their household
intact, other drivers and their close relatives were not so fortunate.
Jermain Loguen's sister Maria and her three young children were
snatched from their plantation home by slave traders—"incarnate
devils" who were "eyeing their gains" amidst the "unutterable
agonies" of the helpless slave community. After this forced parting,
Loguen never saw any of his family again. Archer Alexander, a man
described by his biographer as possessing a "manly, patient character" had his patience tested when several of his children were sold
because they had "behaved badly." Even though the foreman bore
the "inevitable burdens" of this separation for a season, he eventually fled the plantation and then went to great lengths in an attempt to
lead the remainder of his family to freedom.[48] Other drivers were
allowed only infrequent visits with relatives who lived on neighboring
estates or on separate farms owned by the same planter. Frank Bell's
Uncle Moses, for example, was separated from his wife and two
children as a result of their status as chattel property belonging to two
different owners. Only on Sunday was Moses allowed to visit his
family. Each of these trips must have been eagerly anticipated and
deeply cherished for, as Bell's nephew recalled, sometimes the foreman did not return to the Fallon farm until "early Monday morning
just in time to start de slaves working in de field."[49]
    Although their contact may sometimes have been fleeting, mem-
bers of the drivers' families seemed, in later years, to maintain fond
memories of their relatives who served in the ranks of the slave elite.
Will Adams, who experienced slavery in Harrison County, Texas,
recalled that his father would come home from the fields after it was
dark, rouse the young slave from bed, get him dressed, fix him
something to eat, and then play with the youngster "for hours." As
noted by Adams, this pattern of father-son "togetherness" was
necessitated by the fact that father Freeman Cavin was "leader" on
the farm and was "gone from 'fore day till after night."[50] In like

manner, Peter Randolph could overlook the harsh duties his father was occasionally forced to perform and was thereby better able to evaluate the driver as a parent. During his childhood, Randolph often overheard conversations in which his father described how the white overseer had forced him to whip one of the slaves "until the blood ran down to the ground." Initially, the young bondsman was led to "think very hard" of the driver, concluding that he was "a very cruel man." But as his understanding of plantation life increased, Peter realized his father "could not help himself." As Randolph later wrote, after gaining this understanding, he "could not but alter my views and feelings in regard to his conduct."[51]

As a parent living within the slave community, the drivers not only had to discipline their own offspring for violations of family mores, but often helped settle various disputes that would otherwise disrupt everyday life in the quarters. The driver might be called upon to intervene to prevent possible trouble between two rivals for a particularly desirable young woman; to collect testimony from the various parties engaged in intraquarters disputes; or to provide protection for slaves who were particularly vulnerable to the wiles of quicker witted bondsmen.[52] In dealing with such matters, drivers were imaginative enough that they did not have to resort to the whip each time correction of an ill-behaving family member or other misbehaving slave was made necessary by the severity of the infraction. One former slave from Virginia told of an instance when she was punished by her driver-father in a rather unusual, but effective manner. It seems that young Nancy Williams had played a "sinful trick" on her parents by attempting to cover up the loss of some money that had been entrusted to her father. After he discovered that she had "tole a black lie" to hide her guilt, the driver marched Nancy to the smoke house and, as she vividly remembered, "put me in a guana bag, an' push all de hams back an' hung me up to de wall. Den he sweep up some baccy on de flo' an' tookin' light it an' smoke me til Ise drunk." When his incredulous and greatly disturbed wife asked the reason for this unusual punishment, the driver shot back that he would "rather die an' go to hell an' burn den to live agin in heaven roun Christ robe an' leave a passel o' tongue tied niggers here to steal." Perhaps not fully understanding the concern her father felt for the proper upbringing of his children, Nancy Williams nevertheless remembered the punishment in the smoke house. As she noted, "I ain' never forgit dat an' I ain' never stole from nobody else."[53]

Although Nancy Williams's father approached the problem of disciplining his offspring in a rather unorthodox manner, other drivers evidenced their concern for the proper moral development of young slaves by entering into the duties of the plantation preacher. On estates where such activities were tolerated—or where they were effectively concealed from the eyes of the whites—members of the slave community conducted religious services that combined elements of Euro-American Christianity and traditional African religious belief. Despite restrictive laws pertaining to slave-led gatherings, black preachers heeded "the call" and directed the others in Sunday worship. Where such preachers were also foremen, the slaves' acceptance of their driver as a spiritual guide showed him to be a "natural leader" chosen by his fellows rather than an imposed, impotent figurehead selected by the master.[54]

In her reminiscences of life on the John Linguard Hunter plantation in Alabama, Victoria Clayton described the activities of Uncle Sam, a slave foreman who was also a Methodist preacher. Standing beside his cabin in the quarters was a small building that served as a chapel. Each Sunday morning, with the permission of the planter, Sam would gather the slave children together in this structure and proceed to "teach them their duty to God and man." Later in the day, the adult members of Sam's congregation would assemble for worship. According to Clayton, the black preacher could read the Bible, but his formal education did not extend much beyond that. The only other occasion upon which he had an opportunity to display his literacy was during the cotton harvest when he was responsible for weighing the cotton as it was brought from the fields and recording the weights in the plantation log. Nevertheless, his achievements and his "Christian walk" were sufficient for Clayton to note that the slaves "looked up to him with almost reverence."[55]

A black foreman did not have to be a formally designated preacher to be credited with possessing a deeply held Christian faith. During a visit to her husband's family home near Camden, South Carolina, in 1861, Mary Boykin Chesnut observed a black church service at which a driver displayed a particularly fervent approach to worship. As the Sunday services progressed under the direction of a white Methodist minister, driver Jim Nelson was asked to lead in prayer. Facing the congregation on his knees with his eyes closed, the bondsman became increasingly excited as his petition to God took verbal form. Clapping his hands at the end of each sentence, his voice "rose to the pitch of a shrill shriek." Moved by Nelson's example, the slave audience sobbed and shouted, swaying back and forth, clapping their hands and responding in rhapsodical tones, "Yes, God!" "Jesus!" "Savior!" "Bless de Lord, amen." When the fury of their collective entreaties had subsided, Nelson rose from his knees, trembled, and "shook as one in a palsy." Unable to stand, the driver sank back on his bench. It was obvious, as Mrs. Chesnut noted, that "the ecstasy had not left him yet."[56]

For other antebellum blacks, the "ecstasies" of the Christian faith were made unattractive by their method of presentation. Alienated by the whites' "use" of religion as a disciplinary tool, countless slaves throughout the history of the "peculiar institution" rejected the "servants, obey in all things your masters" theology—a skewed and incomplete interpretation of scripture that slaveholders forwarded in the hope that meek, dutiful, and faithful servants would be created by "unconscious" religious means. When the whites attempted to drown out the autonomous voice of Afro-American religion, drivers joined with "common" slaves in rejecting "white" Christianity as a viable mode for personal religious expression.[57]

Maryland head man Bill Cole was led to reject the whites' religion as a consequence of the cruelties he experienced at the hands of his church-going owners. Even though his master was a trustee and his "Old Missus" a leading member of the local Methodist Episcopal church, Cole was unimpressed with their displays of piety. Describing the slaveholder's wife as "a very large, rough, Irish-looking woman, with a very bad disposition," the head man claimed that she was "always wanting her husband to have some one whipped." Certainly, at times it seemed as if she hated even "to see a 'nigger.'" The unfavorable Christian testimony offered by this woman prompted Cole to shun all worship services, to term the slaveholders' religion "a pretense," and, eventually, to "disbelieve in the Protestant faith altogether."[58]

Although Cole probably never confronted the whites directly over the "religion issue," Charles Morgan, head man for South Carolina minister John Bailey Adger, boldly stood up to his master's efforts to have the slaves attend the local Presbyterian church on Sundays and to join in Adger's family prayers at the close of each working day. According to the white minister, Morgan one day informed his master that he was capable of obeying direct orders, but that he would refuse to be forced into attending church services. Taken aback by this unexpected behavior, the slaveholder replied that he certainly did not intend to "take a stick to force him to pray, or to drive him to church." Crediting Morgan with the possession of "as many and as astute objections to the revealed word as any infidel philosopher ever produced," Adger apparently surrendered to the slave's determined opposition to formal religious instruction. As the defeated slaveholder remarked in his autobiography: "Of course, no compulsory methods can be employed in bringing religion to Negroes, or to any other men."[59]

In taking their version of religion to the bondsmen, southern slaveholders failed to convert still another type of driver—the slave who resolvedly continued to cling to West African Islamic beliefs. The most famous of these Muslim slave supervisors was Bu Allah, head man on Thomas Spalding's Sapelo Island estate. Born in Africa and nurtured in the Mohammedan faith until he was captured and enslaved, Bu Allah continued to practice the tenets of his religion on the New World plantation. Three times daily the black foreman would kneel on his sheepskin prayer rug, turn his face to the east, and pray to Allah. Although both he and his family eventually learned how to speak English, they continued to use an African dialect when conversing among themselves. One account of the life of this unusual slave supervisor even asserted that he kept Spalding's plantation record books in Arabic. It is also said that this man of "unusual intelligence and character" was a rather haughty being—thinking himself superior to the plantation's non-Islamic residents. When, in 1813, a British fleet lay off Sapelo Island, Spalding armed and drilled his slaves to better repel an enemy invasion. Bragging that he, Bu Allah, and the newly armed slaves would give a good account of themselves if attacked, Spalding must have been chagrined when his head man responded by declaring: "I will answer for every Negro of the true faith, but not for the *Christian dogs* you own." Despite his somewhat uncharitable nature, the legends surrounding Bu Allah were so persistent and widespread that during the 1890s they inspired Joel Chandler Harris to pen two works of fiction based upon the exploits of the Islamic head man and his family.[60]

Some drivers shared their Christian faith with the residents of the quarters while others were so critical of the "white man's religion" that they rejected the proffered gospel or adhered to previously adopted forms of worship, and there were still other slave supervisors who combined a strong Christian profession with an equally potent critique of the whites' "use" of religion. Tennessee head man Jermain Loguen, who succeeded in escaping to the North in 1837, was a determined exponent of this type of Afro-American Christian militancy. In his published narrative, Loguen described a conversation he had with a poor white friend while still a slave. His commentary is a vivid example of the degree to which a chattel could correctly distinguish between the "wheat" and the "chaff" of antebellum southern religion. As the two men discussed the nature of "true religion"—that eternal "rule of goodness and truth"—the slave remarked:

> If I ever get to a free country, I mean to get learning and preach that religion, as the means of putting down the religion of the slaveholders. What a wicked thing it is, that our mothers, brothers, and sisters cannot be delivered until this religion is put down. They make a great fuss about religion, as if it required much learning and study to get at it. The truth about it is, it requires skill and study to give it a false face and cover it up.[61]

By concluding that the "bawling hypocrites" of the slaveholding South practiced and forwarded a false religion, Loguen showed that even though the driver gained his position of authority through the auspices of the white planter, he was not necessarily bound by those instruments of intellectual coercion through which the whites hoped to control the slave community.

Planter selection and approval was not a universal prerequisite for a slave to rise to the heights of recognition and esteem in the quarters. Within the cluster of slave cabins, the planter's hand-picked black elite had to be respected, but they did not have to be liked. When the drivers were selected by their fellows to "lead" in various community activities, the slaves gave evidence that their field supervisors were not simply the agents of the whites, but were also the chosen leaders of the enslaved.

Through elevation to the honorary post of "corn general," the black foreman had an opportunity to combine the dual roles of field labor and community social leader. *Corn generals* presided over the harvest time corn-shucking activities and were generally selected by the slaves rather than by the slaveholder. Various observers have noted that the post tended to be held by a male member of the slave community who not only possessed a powerful voice, but who was also known to be "original" and "amusing" in the leading of the customary corn songs. Considerable debate might precede the final selection of the general with strong arguments being introduced by various factions for and against the different leaders proposed. The slave who was finally chosen by this informal caucus would then begin the evening's festivities by ascending to the "place of honor" atop the pile of unshucked corn.[62] As described by Garnett Andrews of Georgia:

> The "General," sticking a corn-shuck in his hat, by way of distinction, would mount the corn-pile and frequently, in his recitative, address the ring as his children, his soldiers or his army. Sometimes he would, in the enthusiasm of the occasion, fall on his knees and clap his hands above his head, then rise, holding them, clasping a ear of corn, in the same attitude, then with legs in the form of the letter V inverted, and his left arm akimbo—all the time "giving out"—he would wave his right, in his rhapsody, gracefully—as if monarch of all he surveyed.[63]

As the work proceeded, the general would continue to lead the singing, pass the jug around, and cheer the hands on to new corn-shucking heights with encouraging remarks such as: "Dat's de lick, little Ellick!" "You kin beat yo' daddy, young York," "Gentermen, des look at big Frank!" or "Hol' onter Lonzer dar, don' let him kill hizse'f." After the corn was shucked, the driver-general would lead his "army" in devouring the harvest feast that awaited them. As master of ceremonies, he might direct the servers, organize various races and games, or play the fiddle or banjo as the slaves danced.[64] Although some ex-slaves believed that corn shuckings better served the economic interests of the planters than they did the recreational needs of the slave community, others seemed to recall only the festive spirit with which they entered into their labors.[65] As supervisor of these activities, the foreman-general continued to "drive" the field hands, but at the same time he entered into the life of the quarters in a way that showed where his sociocultural roots lay. Rather than merely being looked upon as the "planter's man" who was to rule over them, he was considered by the slaves to be "one of them."

In many cases, the final disposition of the driver's loyalties was manifested most clearly as the advance of the Union armies signaled the imminent destruction of the plantation regime. Even as some slave supervisors were coaxed or bullied into remaining faithful to the whites' interests during the war years, others perceived the rapidly moving events of the 1860s as heralding a new day of freedom.[66] Although certain drivers found it expedient to remain on their master's estates, directing the hiding of valuables and the harvesting of what were to be the South's final slave-produced crops, foremen such as Jordan—the stepfather of Tennessee slave Henry Pyles—"run away wid de Yankees" and contributed to the Union war effort.[67]

Disobedient drivers, released from the close scrutiny of white overseers who had gone to war in defense of the Confederacy, led the hands in depredations against their masters' estates. In a series of letters written to a fellow Louisiana planter in 1863, John H. Ransdell told of how the slaves had been "turned . . . crazy" by this lack of white supervision and by the close proximity of his estate to the advancing Union troops. According to the owner of Elmwood plantation, the bondsmen of the area were having "a perfect jubilee," refusing to perform their normal plantation tasks, slaughtering livestock, and, in one instance, forcibly placing a Confederate soldier in the stocks. Confused and angered over the flow of events, Ransdell raged: "Counfound them, they deserve to be half starved and to be worked nearly to death for the way they have acted . . . The *drivers* everywhere have proved the worst negroes." Displaying his shock over the dereliction of duty evidenced by both driver and field hand, the planter told of his new-found conviction that "no dependence is to be placed on the negro . . . they are the greatest hypocrites and liars that God ever made."[68]

Other drivers were more restrained in their actions, but no less filled with a sense of great joy over the prospect of freedom. Ex-Arkansas slave Mittie Freeman told of how one such foreman reacted to the demise of the "peculiar institution." She recalled that her father, Harry Williams, was a "stern man, and honest." Although assigned to the post of plantation "manager" by his often-absent physician owner, the slaveholder's death decreed that Williams' family be "passeled . . . out" among the doctor's children. Placed upon a farm that was presided over by a white overseer who seemed to be "the meanest devil ever put foot on a plantation," Williams rebelled when the overseer whipped him "for sompin' he never done." As a penalty for striking his supervisor, the slave was sent down to New Orleans to be sold, but was returned to Arkansas when the auctioneer could find no suitable buyer. On "the day freedom came" to their plantation, Harry Williams and his daughter were fishing. Then, as Mittie Freeman later noted:

> All a-suddent cannons commence a-booming, it seem like everywhere. . . . Pappy jumps up, throws his pole and everything, and grabs my hand, and starts flying towards the house. "It's victory," he keep on saying. "It's freedom. No we 'es gwine be free."[69]

No matter how they reacted to or "took" their freedom, all of the antebellum slave supervisors eventually had to make important adjustments to the new era the northern victory had thrust upon them. For some, these adjustments were delayed by the fact that their owners were unwilling to give up the antebellum way of life. Smith County, Texas, bondsman Andrew Goodman was placed in charge of his master's estate during the Civil War, but later recalled that the information given him by the planter was somewhat incomplete. "We didn't know what the war was 'bout," he noted, "but master was gone four years. . . . We never heard tell what the war was 'bout." In like manner, Jane Montgomery, daughter of Louisiana foreman Edmond Beavers, complained that her master was less than completely candid with his "onliest overseer." According to the ex-slave, the whites "never did jest come out and tell us we was free."[70]

Although some drivers and their families had to postpone the celebration of their new freedom due to attempts to thwart the inevitable, others were forced to scour the South in search of loved ones who had been torn from them by the events of the war years. Ex-slave Morris Sheppard described how the relatives of "Uncle Joe," black foreman of a small farm labor force, were scattered during the civil conflict of the 1860s. Fearing the loss of his chattel property, the Sheppards's owner had liquidated most of his slave assets in 1862. At that time, Morris's mother, three of her children, and Joe's wife were sold because "old Master seen he was going into trouble." At war's end, the slaveholder further divided Morris's family by sending him to a Freedmen's Bureau encampment where he was bound out on a labor contract. As the ex-slave noted, it took considerable effort during the Reconstruction years "to git de family all together agin." In a similar case, the family of South Carolina head man-preacher Abraham Brown had to be reunited at the close of the Civil War. Brown's master had given son Henry to a relative "for a Christmas present" while several other members of the foreman's household were "refugeed" during the war in an attempt to remove them from the path of the Union advance. While Abraham carried out his assigned duties on the main plantation, two other members of the Brown family were "drafted" into the southern war effort and wife Lucy Brown died on the farm where she was taken as a "refugee" slave. Hoping to gather up the scattered pieces of his family at the end of the war, the driver located at least four of his children and brought them "home."[71]

The immediate post-Civil War period was an especially trying time for the slave foremen. Had they been a true slave elite, accustomed to working hand-in-glove with the planters in the often brutal business of disciplining the field hands, the drivers might have expected their adjustment to freedom to have been made easier through the aid and encouragement of their former employers. As it was, however, while some were given jobs by their masters, others complained that the arrival of freedom was followed immediately by an order to "git off the plantation." As John Goodrum, son of a black overseer in Des Arc, Arkansas, noted, sometimes driver and field laborer alike were "just turned out like you turn a hog out the pen and say go on I'm through wid you."[72]

Those drivers who stayed with their masters often did so under the pressure of necessity and then sometimes only for a short while. During the postwar period, both southern whites and their former slaves had to decide—often on rather short notice—how to proceed within the region's new socioeconomic climate. Writing to his wife, Ellen, a bankrupt Benjamin Allston described one planter's search for stability during the Reconstruction years:

> I feel rather nervous about trying the Rice again, but I do not exactly see how to do otherwise. Should all things go smoothly I would do well at it, but should there be again a failure, lackaday, it would be hard indeed. I have Sam Benjamin for Foreman, he was my old Driver, and in this I am better off than heretofore. You will be apprehensive of the result, and may fear the result, even as I feel, but we must trust to Providence. . . .[73]

If a member of the once-powerful Allston family was forced to seek the aid of a former field supervisor in his attempt to once again bring regularity and prosperity to the plantation, it is wholly understandable that ex-drivers might try to obtain whatever "shelter" their former owners could offer them during this confused period of southern history. As Arrie Binns, daughter of Georgia foreman Jordan Sybert explained, her family continued to work for the whites following the war because "us didn't know whar to go an' what ter do." Nevertheless, tiring of working cotton under white supervision, the Syberts, like certain of the other families headed by former drivers, left their white employers after a brief two-year term of service.[74]

Released from the immediate control of their former masters, the drivers-as-freedmen engaged in a fairly wide variety of occupations. During the postwar years, ex-drivers could be found throughout the South and Midwest serving as hired hands, teamsters, hod carriers, sharecroppers, renters, and landowners.[75] By 1868 former foreman Henry Clay Bruce had been able to save some $500 out of his earnings and had opened a small mercantile business in Leavenworth, Kansas. James H. Johnson's father, a former South Carolina foreman, garnered sufficient profit from his farm and his store in Camden to provide for James's public school and college education. Benjamin T. Montgomery, who had served as plantation manager for Joe and Jefferson Davis, leased and later purchased the Davis holdings in Warren County, Mississippi. According to a neighboring landholder, Montgomery soon gained the reputation of being the "best planter in the county and perhaps in the state." In 1867 the ex-slave was appointed to the post of justice of the peace at Davis Bend. Foreman Jim Hanover also served in a public capacity during Reconstruction, but was less fortunate in his officeholding than was Montgomery. According to his granddaughter, Hanover was chosen mayor of the small Arkansas town of Powhatan,—"an' he made a good mayer too"—but, unfortunately, "de Ku Klux'ers said dey wuz en' gonna have no 'nigguh' mayor. So dey tuk him out an' killed him."[76]

The experience of other drivers during the postwar years shows that some were "killed" in other ways. Discrimination, proscription, lack of education and saleable skills, combined to destroy the hopes of many ex-slaves. In battling these societal forces, members of the slave elite often held little advantage over their field hand brethren. The case of Rufus Dirt exemplifies the sad fate that could befall driver and "common" slave alike. When the ex-driver was located by an oral history interviewer during the depression years of the 1930s, he was living on the south side of Birmingham, supporting himself by begging for coins. As noted in the transcribed account, the driver now had sparse white hair, "glazy" red-rimmed eyes, and a useless hand and arm that had been crippled "in de mines." Dirt told the interviewer how he had struggled to make ends meet ever since the demise of slavery. "When de war was finally over an' I was free," he recalled, "my family went to Vicksburg, Mississippi where we made a livin' first one way an' den de other." Then, apparently embarrassed by being discovered in such dire straits, Dirt, in a brief, but poignant affirmation of his manhood, assured his interrogator: "An' boss, I ain't beggin' 'cause I'se too lazy to work. I'se worked plenty in my time. . . ."[77]

The slave drivers of the plantation South did indeed "work plenty" both during and after slavery. Should modern-day students of antebellum black America wish to remain faithful to the legend of the callous, dehumanized driver, they must, of necessity, reject the idea that such work encompassed more than a leisurely supervision of the field hands and the all-too-frequent "laying on of stripes." To uphold the ancient Sambo-Quimbo stereotypes, one must refuse to believe that an existing diversity of plantation tasks, contexts, opportunities, and hazards greatly affected the demeanor of individual foremen. To continue to paint the drivers with the colors of the past, one must accept as valid the outdated view of Afro-American personality that portrays blacks as "wax in the hands of a stronger race" and denies them a fellowship with the people of the quarters.[78] To posit a wide gulf of motivation, experience, and feeling between driver and field hand, it is necessary to reject wholly the testimony of the ex-slave who wrote, with much wisdom: "Slaves were much truer to one another in those days than they have been since made free. . . . There were no Judases among them during those exciting times."[79]

THE HISTORIANS

It would be interesting to know more about the drivers—
their ages, type of Negro, methods used to get work from
the slaves, and the attitude of the other Negroes toward
them—for it must be apparent that the driver occupied a
position of considerable importance in the production of
the crops.

J. Carlyle Sitterson, 1943

Yet despite this evidence of his obvious importance to the
slave scene, the driver has not received much attention
from scholars. . . . On large plantations the driver's influence in slave affairs was often of such importance as to
alter many perceptions we have about the total slave
community. He has to be an integral part of our examination of slavery.

Leslie Howard Owens, 1976

Historians have been inordinately slow to recognize the complexities
of the slave driver's position within the plantation community and to
credit the "driver elite" with the ability to maintain a large measure of
its humanity even while participating in the coercive disciplinary
system of the antebellum South. This long-term historiographical
lethargy can be traced to what social historian J. C. Furnas has termed
the "American intellectual block" on the subject of American race
relations and related issues. Although perhaps not as enamored with
Mrs. Stowe's vivid portrait of driver brutality and dehumanization as
the general public, professional historians have been, until recent
years, ensnarled in a societal and scholarly "climate of opinion" that
has limited their ability to conceive of black slaves as being capable of
responding to other than planter-sponsored stimuli. Deemed to pos-

sess a "humanity" less well developed or at least far less interesting to study than that of the antebellum planter, it is not surprising that blacks as drivers, as portrayed in early accounts, were rarely credited with resisting the blandishments of the planter's world.[1]

Ulrich B. Phillips, the Georgia-born and educated historian who came to be the reigning interpreter of the American Negro slave experience during the first half of this century, set the tone for subsequent discussions of the "plantation elite." Filled with erroneous, inaccurate, and dangerous preconceptions about blacks in America, Phillips's writings described slaves as "notoriously primitive, uncouth, improvident and inconstant" workers who possessed such unenviable traits "because they were Negroes of the time." Contentedly enjoying their status as chattels, the antebellum slaves "ruled not even themselves." With "hazy pasts and reckless futures" they "lived in each moment as it flew" and left "Old Massa" to provide both physical sustenance and mental direction for his black wards. According to Phillips, most planters contented themselves with the meager level of achievement to which such a labor force might attain because they considered it a hopeless task to transform the slaves into "thorough workmen or full-fledged men."[2]

To aid in ordering the daily affairs of this sluggish lot of laborers, southern planters developed a "whole hierarchy of administration," which might include slave foremen or drivers at the head of the various gangs or a *trusty slave* who was charged with keeping the storehouse keys. Phillips likened slaves holding such positions of authority to sergeants in the planter's "conscript army," termed them "exceptional" in relation to the "talents and vigor" of the majority, and noted that their skills were fostered by "special training and rewards" doled out by their owners. Even though this acquisition of status was not of their own construction, the foremen reveled in the fact that they had become "men of position and pride."[3]

Phillips accounted for the relative scarcity of such co-opted drivers not only by citing the legal requirements regarding the employment of overseers, but also by noting that there was a definite shortage of "sable paragons" in the agricultural South. It seemed that even the chattel elite stood perilously close to the ineptitude of the masses—a body of dependent beings whose achievements and progress during the antebellum period were "restricted by the fact of their being negroes."[4]

In any evaluation of the impact that Phillips's views had on his contemporaries, consideration must be given to his voluminous publication record, his status as a pioneer in the use of plantation records in the writing of agricultural history, and the importance of the teaching posts he held at well-known northern schools such as Wisconsin, Yale, and Michigan. One must also make special note of his claim that many of the "Negro traits" described in his writings on slavery were carried into the twentieth century largely unmodified by the altered social conditions of the postbellum South. As Phillips wrote after visiting a Camp Gordon, Georgia, army camp in 1918, the blacks seemed to "show the same easy-going, amiable, serio-comic obedience and the same personal attachments to white men, as well as the same sturdy light-heartedness and the same love of laughter and of rhythm, which distinguished their forbears." Black noncommissioned officers evidenced "a punctilious pride of place" that matched that of the "plantation foremen of old." To Phillips, the Afro-American-as-free citizen remained a dependent, malleable being whose general personality makeup and laboring abilities could be considered nothing less than inferior commodities.[5]

Influenced both by Phillips's persuasive prose and by the fact that many were entrapped in similar or mutually compatible "climates of opinion," white academics long accepted the Georgian's portrait of slave life and his hazy assumptions about black personality. Like others of their profession, historians of the Negro reflected the society in which they wrote, and during the Phillips era blacks were adjudged to be in many respects "inferior." Phillips merely mirrored these tendencies in American thought more fully and with somewhat more academic flair than did many of his colleagues.[6]

Of the few "nonbelievers," only black historian Carter G. Woodson spoke out against Phillips's "inability to fathom the negro mind" and his tendency to portray the bondsmen more as "goods and chattels" than as human beings. Had this "human dimension" been more in evidence during these years, perhaps historians would have found it possible to credit the slave drivers with the possession of a humane nature sufficiently well developed to resist the temptation of the "special rewards" offered by the planters.[7]

Following the publication of Phillips's *American Negro Slavery* in 1918, most white historians of slavery chose to elaborate upon the patterns of slave life as set down by Phillips rather than to formulate new and contrasting interpretations. The implications of this trend for the study of slave driver historiography are two-fold. Some writers began to practice a variation of what Idus A. Newby has termed "Spook History." Accepting Phillips's views on the poor quality of black labor, they credited white overseers with the performance of practically all jobs requiring some degree of supervisory skill or judgment. In certain accounts of this nature, the reader, armed with a degree of historiographical hindsight, can only marvel at the overseers' capacity for work and their mastery of plantation tasks. The driver's presence may have been acknowledged in such accounts, but he remained a nebulous, ghostly figure, always in the background because of his racially determined inabilities.[8]

During this same period, in a logical development from Philips's references to the driver's "pride of place," Mrs. Stowe's memorable Sambo and Quimbo stereotypes, and Albert Bushnell Hart's early pejorative remarks about the hatreds black foremen engendered within the plantation community, other historians focused on the perquisites of the driver's office and concluded that "the position of driver would naturally please most slaves." Relieved from much of the laborious work of the common field hand, their appetite for material goods fairly well sated by "Christmas presents and other bounty," the "favored few" could scarcely escape the curse of becoming disgustingly haughty. This trait of the driver's personality seemed to be particularly evident to those historians who were positively convinced that even the modern-day Afro-American had "a tendency to be boastful and to parade his authority." Academics concluded that the driver "must generally have been unpopular among the other slaves" due to this unseemly personality flaw.[9]

Although the interpretations of the driver's office penned during the Phillips era were largely elaborations upon a common theme, a period of revitalizing reinterpretation was destined someday to arrive. This period of "new beginnings" for the study of American Negro Slavery broadly corresponded with the upsurge in civil rights agitation during the early 1950s. Acknowledging that the scholar's "knowledge of the present is clearly a key to his understanding of the past," Berkeley historian Kenneth M. Stampp replaced Phillips as the chief interpreter of the slave experience. Reflecting the influences of a vastly changed "climate of opinion," Stampp's 1956 book *The*

Peculiar Institution exposed both the historical misconceptions and the racist underpinnings of much of his predecessor's work. Unfortunately, Stampp's method of attack left the dehumanized driver stereotype a wholly viable construction.[10]

In contrast to Phillips's assertion that there was "clearly no general prevalence of severity and strain" in the slave regime, Stampp sought to show that one of the planter's major goals in managing slave property was "to make them stand in fear." No longer was it acceptable for students of slavery to believe that the plantation was a "chapel of ease" or a "school" for the training and control of improvident Africans. Slavery was above all a labor system in which the master class sought to bring "maximum efficiency" to the organization and exploitation of labor. According to Stampp, to achieve the desired level of efficiency, the slaveholders depended upon the services and the "willing cooperation" of those slaves who would "be loyal to him and take his side against the others." Encouraged to feel superior to the field hands by grants of material goods and privileges, foremen soon "identified themselves wholly with the master class" and became "notoriously severe taskmasters" who might "whip more cruelly than white masters." From being described as a co-opted and racially inferior dependent of a benevolent master, the driver had now become a co-opted and brutal tool of the oppressive plantation regime.[11]

Stampp's historiographical rejection of Phillips's apologetic portrayal of planter benevolence was carried even further by Stanley M. Elkins. In his pioneering work *Slavery: A Problem in American Institutional and Intellectual Life,* first published in 1959, Elkins posited the idea that a peculiarly American brand of "unopposed capitalism" had resulted in the creation of a harsh and psychologically damaging "closed" system of slavery that left the typical southern chattel a broken, "infantilized" being best described by the stereotype of "Sambo."[12] Believing that Kenneth Stampp had underestimated the impact of social institutions on human behavior, Elkins sought to convince his readers of the truth of the maxim that "granted sufficient power you could do terrible things to personality." The vehicle he used to demonstrate his thesis was a dramatic analogy between the Nazi concentration camp and the antebellum United States plantation. Admitting that his purposes were limited and his analogy inexact, Elkins held that the Nazi camps were "a special and highly perverted instance of human slavery."[13]

In seeking to delineate the common psychologically corrosive features of these two social systems, Elkins relied heavily upon the published studies of those sociologists and social psychologists who had described the psychological changes affecting concentration camp inmates. Chief among his sources were the writings of Dachau and Buchenwald survivor Bruno Bettelheim. Not only did Bettelheim provide Elkins with the raw materials used to construct his "infantilization" analogy, but he also described a somewhat singular type of inmate whom certain of those who evaluated Elkins's work equated with the antebellum slave driver.[14]

In Bettelheim's interpretation of the Kapos, those inmates who served as labor foremen and liaisons to the concentration camp control apparatus, were "slave drivers" indeed. Attracted to the post by "what seemed like irresistible chances for power, safety and privilege," Kapos fell prey to the coercive pressures of the institution and sought to maintain their privileged position "at all cost." Since the Kapos were often punished for what the SS considered to be shortcomings in the productivity of the labor gangs, the "prisoner elite" attempted to protect themselves by anticipating any demand that the SS might make—often "outdoing the SS." According to Bettelheim, only the exceptional Kapo escaped identification with the values of his ruling overlords and used his position to better the lot of common prisoners.[15]

Elkins agreed with this portrait of camp life, believing that the Kapo was the "final quintessence" of prisoner identification with the SS. These "creatures," as he termed them, behaved with "slavish servility" to the German troops and more than matched them in terms of "sheer brutality." For those historians who saw the Kapo as a latter-day incarnation of the driver, Elkins provided an intriguing reinforcement of an old image.[16]

Although it would be unfair to the purposes of Elkins's methodology to posit the idea that the Kapo was directly analogous to the antebellum driver, it must be noted that other and more recent interpretations have viewed the Kapo in a much more sympathetic light than did Elkins's major source of reference. Studies by Eli Cohen, Erving Goffman, and Terrence Des Pres have been especially helpful in pointing out that the camp inmates may actually have suffered "infantilization" and identification with the SS to a much less critical degree than Bettelheim assumed. Des Pres, for example, cited the case of a Kapo employed in an SS storeroom at Auschwitz who, each day, discovered that various crates of food had been "accidently" dropped and had to be reported as "shipment damage." He then routinely distributed the "damaged goods" to his fellow prisoners, all the time maintaining a gruff external demeanor when under the scrutiny of his SS superiors. As our understanding of the concentration camp experience is modified, perhaps our interpretation of the antebellum plantation should also be corrected to include the presence of a more humane Kapo-driver figure. To quote Des Pres, it seems likely that men and women have the capacity to "live beneath the pressure of protracted crisis, to sustain terrible damage in mind and body and yet to be there, sane, alive, still human."[17]

Although both Elkins's and Stampp's studies seemed to solidify the "harsh driver" image within the profession, each work also contained new and liberating tendencies that would soon be more fully developed by other scholars. Although Elkins was adamant in his belief that the United States' slave system was "closed and circumscribed" compared to its Latin-American counterpart, he did feel it was likely for an "underground" of sorts to have existed alongside the main body of "infantilized" slaves. Since all social systems were, in practice, less able to produce consistently a desired personality type than they theoretically appeared capable of doing, it was possible for certain slaves to escape the full impact of the system and thus to mitigate the system's "coercions upon personality." Even though he listed only urban slave mechanics, house servants, and slaves who had won the right to "hire their own time" as primary components of the "underground," Elkins hinted that "even among those working on large plantations, the skilled craftsman or the responsible slave foreman had a measure of independence not shared by his simpler brethren." Certainly it was possible for such "independence" to lead to a situation where the system's authority structure claimed the foremen's bodies, "but not quite their souls."[18]

Stampp's contribution to the modern reinterpretation of the slave driver was an important component of his revision of Ulrich Phillips. In detailing the characteristics of a brutal slave system, he made note of the significant fact that the chattels remained "a troublesome property" who were capable both of group resistance and of individual endurance. Not even the cruelties inherent in the harsh antebellum plantation regime could prevent its intended victims from running away, shamming illness, continually evidencing the most perplexing "rascality," and, in general, putting up a determined resistance against those forces that sought to crush the human spirit.[19]

Before the theme of the bondsmen's spiritual liberation could be developed fully enough to be applicable to the drivers as well, one further historiographical development was necessary—historians had to explore more fruitfully the writings of the slaves rather than merely to remain in sympathy with their assumed strivings.[20] John W. Blassingame of Yale University provided the major thrust in this direction with his 1972 book *The Slave Community*. Rejecting those insights gained through the use of psychological theory that were "applied to stereotypes and restricted to traditional sources," he chose instead to rely upon autobiographies and other personal records left by the slaves themselves. In so doing, Blassingame sought to discredit the prevailing picture of plantation life, derived largely from studies based upon planter accounts, which characterized the antebellum slave system as a monolithic institution eminently capable of systematically stripping the bondsmen of any "meaningful and distinctive culture, family life, religion, or manhood." As a black American, Blassingame sought to balance the views of white planters and travelers with representative voices from the antebellum Afro-American community. By constructing a freshly focused interpretation of the plantation as a more "open" system and by positing the existence of many different personality types within the vital, extensively self-directed slave community, Blassingame allowed the driver to shed his monochromatic image.

Like the rest of the slaves, whose behavior "ran the whole gamut from abject docility to open rebellion," Blassingame's "elite slaves" included unprincipled individuals who curried the favor of the whites as well as those who attempted to protect their fellows from the harshest rigors of bondage. Certainly the same range of personality types existed in the quarters as in the mansion. With the participation of sympathetic members of the slave elite, the bondsmen developed a group solidarity that enabled them to unite in a battle of wits and nerve against those who would strip them of their manhood.[21]

Blassingame concentrated so intensely upon slave personality types that he could devote little space to occupational categories. Although it was not his purpose to enter into an extensive argument seeking to revise the commonly accepted stereotypes of house servants, mammies, or drivers, historians had been urging, ever since 1943, that a thorough examination be conducted of the last named plantation type.[22] At the 1966 Socialist Scholars Conference, historian Eugene Genovese revived the call for intensified research into the formation and character of "class leadership" within the slave community. Having conducted research for his *Political Economy of Slavery* (1965) in southern manuscript collections, Genovese had come to doubt the legend that held that drivers and house slaves "arrayed themselves on the side of the master against the field hands." In an article that appeared in the *New York Review of Books* in late 1970, he again lamented the profession's lack of precise knowledge about the slave foremen. As he reminded his readers that there were no books and only a few scattered articles available on life in the slave quarters, Genovese noted that there had not been a single study done of the slave driver—"the most important slave on the larger plantations." Unlike earlier, perhaps less inquisitive scholars, Genovese did more than simply complain about the lack of published material on the drivers. He researched the topic and incorporated the black foremen into his overall conception of the slave South.[23]

In *Roll, Jordan, Roll* (1974), the culmination of Genovese's years of devotion to the study of southern plantation society "in its paternalistic aspect," the theme of blacks struggling to "survive spiritually as well as physically—to make a liveable world for themselves and their children"—composed a major theme of the overall interpretation. According to Genovese, it was due largely to the "elaborate web of paternalistic relationships" existing on the plantation, as well as to the slaves' insistence on defining paternalism in their own way, that the bondsmen were so able to resist the psychological aggressions of the "peculiar institution."[24]

To illustrate the workings of plantation paternalism, Genovese focused upon the upper echelons of the slave community—craftsmen, mechanics, house servants, mammies, and drivers. Terming the latter group "the men between," he presented the first significant revised interpretation of the overall character and function of the black foreman class. To Genovese, the drivers occupied a rather precarious position within the southern labor system. Forced to maintain their own position by keeping the field hands working at a pace that would satisfy the slaveowner, drivers were also compelled to respect the demands of their fellow bondsmen to proceed "according to reason" —to maintain an evenhanded approach to discipline. Since the black supervisory personnel were Afro-American slaves who lived in the same quarters and experienced many of the same deprivations as the laborers they supervised, it is not at all surprising that their definition of "evenhanded" often included winking at curfew violations, faking "brutal" whippings, neglecting to report poor work performance, and even conspiring against the master class. By behaving in this manner, a driver not only asserted his manhood vis-à-vis both the master and the other slaves, but since "at least two-thirds of the slaves in the South worked under a black man who had direct access to the master with no white overseer between them," he also served as a strong role model for younger blacks, rescuing them from the dehumanizing tendencies of the slave experience.[25]

Based upon a wide variety of sources—planter records, fugitive slave autobiographies, traveler accounts, and the narratives of ex-slaves recorded during the depression era of the 1930s—Genovese's interpretation and approach had an immediate impact upon those students of plantation life who were concerned with resurrecting a more realistic picture of the black foremen.[26] Nevertheless, the difficulty one encounters when attempting to view objectively *Roll, Jordan, Roll*'s twenty-four pages of driver material apart from its author's overall conception of the Old South as "a historically unique kind of paternalist society" that encouraged "kindness and affection," but simultaneously "encouraged cruelty and hatred," leads one to believe that Genovese's account is not the "last word" in driver historiography. Interpreted as being "the men between," drivers could not only promote accommodation while accepting "the ambiguity of their role," but could in effect suffer portions of their own individual personality and humanity to be erased in the social tug-of-war between the quarters and the Big House. Being all things to all members of the plantation community left the drivers with precious little time to be themselves.[27]

Both Genovese's and Blassingame's studies evidenced the increased scholarly use of long-neglected literary source materials in the construction of new interpretations of antebellum plantation society. This should not be understood to mean that a veritable treasure trove of wholly new sources had been discovered. Both the accounts of bondage penned by fugitive slaves and the depression-era oral history interviews had been available for years—albeit somewhat difficult to obtain. What made these two works so important was the extent to which the "new" sources were used in their construction and the degree of emphasis placed upon various portions of the "raw data" contained in the sources.

Demonstrating the interpretive nature of the discipline, other scholars during the past decade have used the new sources, but have come to significantly different conclusions regarding the nature of the driver's office. One such interpreter was Stanley Feldstein, whose *Once a Slave* sought to delineate the emotional and physical effect of slavery on the slaves "from within, through the words of slaves themselves." Basing his brief section "The Black Driver" on materials obtained from less than a dozen antebellum autobiographies and scattered portions of the depression-era accounts, Feldstein concluded that the employment of slave foremen was "perhaps the most invidious method" of labor control used by the planters. The purposeful turning of black against black was "one of the most degrading and dehumanizing aspects of the institution." The portrait of the driver drawn by Feldstein was not at all an attractive one.[28]

A second study that made use of the less traditional literary sources, but retained the picture of the brutal driver, was George Rawick's *From Sundown to Sunup*, a work that served as an introduction to an eighteen-volume collection of reprinted black oral testimony from the 1930s and the 1940s. Speaking out boldly against those who would deem the slaves to be "dehumanized victims, without culture, history, community, change, or development," Rawick's book nevertheless portrayed the drivers as "instruments of superbrutality" towards the slaves under them. Although he admitted that the slave personality was "an ambivalent one," there was little ambivalence evidenced regarding the personality of the driver. Supporting his views by the use of selected portions of the narratives, Rawick concluded that foremen "often were the meanest blacks that the master or overseer could find."[29]

The late Robert Starobin's exploratory work on the mechanisms of accommodation affecting privileged bondsmen constituted the third major body of material produced during the 1970s that used new literary sources and yet diverged significantly from the interpretive findings of Blassingame and Genovese. Basing his study upon the relatively scarce letters penned or dictated by members of the "upper crust of slave society," Starobin characterized the drivers as men of great responsibility and superior privilege. Possessing "awesome disciplinary powers," the black foremen served their owners obediently, identified with the planter's interests, and attempted to transmit proper standards of behavior to the rest of the slaves. Compelled to control their fellow bondsmen for the benefit of their masters, the drivers were so completely "trapped in their onerous role" that they sometimes punished errant slaves more severely than did whites. They were seldom found in the vanguard of resistance movements within the quarters.[30]

When speaking of the recent studies that have incorporated supporting data from previously little used literary-based sources, it must not be assumed that these traditional types of historical sources—autobiographies, letters, recollections—are the only kinds of evidence available for interpretive use in the search for a better understanding of the duties and characteristics of slave drivers. Cliometricians, that newly "discovered" group of historians who seek to supplement the use of traditional literary sources with a more data-based, quantitative approach to the study of the past, have also claimed a large slice of the "interpretive pie."

Striving to demolish the idea that black Americans were "without culture, without achievement, and without development for their first two hundred and fifty years on American soil," Robert Fogel and Stanley Engerman, in their controversial 1974 cliometric study *Time on the Cross: The Economics of American Negro Slavery*, stressed the degree to which successful antebellum planters relied upon black supervisory personnel. According to the cliometricians, over 25 percent of male slaves were either managers, professionals, craftsmen, or laborers who held such semiskilled positions as teamster, steward, gardener, coachman, or house servant. Drivers and slave overseers alone composed roughly 14 percent of the adult male slave population on the larger plantations.

Not only were the black managers "ubiquitous," they were also extremely able. Indeed, this high degree of competence helps to

explain why so many slaveowners came to rely upon the black foreman more than the white overseer. Seeking to create a labor force
composed of "devoted, hardworking, responsible slaves" who identified their fortunes with those of their masters, planters hoped to
"imbue slaves with a 'Protestant' work ethic" and to transform that
ethic from a state of mind into a high level of production. Through an
elaborate system of rewards and bonuses, the slaveowners accom-
plished their goal in a surprisingly humane manner. Sufficiently
flexible to allow upward mobility, the planters' incentive system
provided hardworking field hands with the opportunity to move up to
assistant driver, head driver, or overseer status. By successfully
climbing this "economic ladder," the slave invariably gained not
only higher social status and "more freedom," but also obtained
"significant payoffs" in terms of better clothing, improved housing,
and increasingly generous cash bonuses. For their outlay of time,
money, and inventiveness, the planters gained a force of "diligent
workers, imbued like their masters with a Protestant ethic." The
"superior quality of black labor" made the large slave plantations
about 34 percent more efficient than free southern farms and contributed importantly to making southern agriculture, as a whole, significantly more efficient than northern agriculture.[31]

Like the other "principal corrections" of the traditional characterization of the slave economy contained in Fogel and Engerman's
self-styled "disturbing book," the interpretation of the black managerial class contained in *Time on the Cross* spawned a good deal of
critical comment. Several critics went to great historiographical and
mathematical lengths to revise downward the percentage of slaves
occupying the driver and overseer positions.[32] Other historians vigorously attacked the Protestant work-ethic concept as applied to slave
labor. Feeling that although Fogel and Engerman had succeeded in
"turning Elkins on his head," they had unwittingly laid the foundation for their own "undoing" by using Elkins's "oversimplified and
one-dimensional" model of slave socialization, Herbert Gutman accused the cliometricians of placing the bondsmen in an interpretive
Skinner Box. With the "sanctions of the system" determining their
character, slave belief and behavior could be little more than pro-
grammed responses to planter-sponsored stimuli. Seemingly, self-
definition was sacrificed to the gods of efficiency and productivity.[33]

Although *Time on the Cross* presented a graphic portrait both of slave driver presence and competence on the antebellum plantation, the book was, in actuality, what Gutman correctly termed an "old-fashioned work." Even though Fogel and Engerman vigorously flayed the forces of bigotry—blaming the operation of racism upon the historical mind for the creation of the "myth of black incompetence in American historiography"—their own conclusions remained remarkably supportive of Ulrich Phillips's terse comment that the slaves "ruled not even themselves." After viewing the black managers of *Time on the Cross*, one must ask, in paraphrase of Mark 8:36: For what shall it profit a slave if he shall gain the Protestant work ethic, lucrative bonuses, and foreman status, and lose his own soul?[34]

Whatever one's individual reaction to the methods and conclusions of those who have contributed to the "cliometric revolution," it is clear that historians will continue to use and thereby to develop further the quantitative modes of investigation. In addition, the new literary sources have by no means been exhausted. All avenues of investigation should be used in the quest for a more accurate view of the black past and of the slave driver's contribution to the forming of that past. Since they are importantly influenced both by events of their own day and by the types of source material they select as being most useful to their quest for interpretive insight, it is vital that modern interpreters of the black past struggle mightily against any new "intellectual blocks" that might arise on the American scene. There has been too much promise evidenced in the variety and direction of the recent interpretations of the driver's character to abandon the antebellum foremen to any single historiographical mind-set. During the Phillips era the drivers were seen as something less than "full fledged men." Lacking a full quotient of humanity, they were said to have been easily co-opted by the planters and thereafter served as perquisite-seeking tormenters of their own people. It would be a tragedy for any future era of "historical consensus" to permit a reversion to such an "understanding" of the driver. To do so would be to dehumanize an important figure in the history of Afro-America, thereby making us all a little less human.

THE PLANTERS

> Our ancestors performed a great work—the work allotted
> them by God, civilizing and elevating an inferior race in
> the scale of intelligence and comfort. . . . Never again
> will the negro race find a people so kind and true to them
> as the Southerners have been.
>
> *Page Thacker (Letitia M. Burwell)*

In their search for an understanding of antebellum plantation life,
historians have found a wealth of information in the correspondence,
personal records, and random jottings of southern whites. The writings of farmers, planters, and overseers have, for many years, been
used to provide information on the nature of the slave community and
its relationship to the residents of the Big House. Historical interpreters in their own right, the whites typically characterized slave drivers
in a manner that was wholly compatible with the Phillips era view of
slave docility, malleability, and incapacity. Nevertheless, with the
passing of the years and the emergence of a "slave-oriented" history
of antebellum black life, the published writings and recollections of
the planters must be regarded as sources that tell us little about the true
personalities and inner strivings of the slaves relative to the amount of
information they contain about the planters' *perceptions* of their black
charges.

Although white antebellum southerners had often tended toward
the romantic in viewing themselves and their labor system, it is
probably not an exaggeration to say that the Civil War made them the
most sentimental people in history. The memory of a disastrous
military defeat, the sense of suffering intolerable wrongs under the
heel of the enemy, and the heightened loyalty and the nostalgia for the
past created an atmosphere in the South that gave free rein to those

erstwhile literati who would paint the portrait of the lost cause, the benevolent master, and the good slave in resplendent colors.[1]

Many of the postbellum reminiscences penned by members of the former slaveholding class were little more than lengthy treatises defending the prewar southern way of life. Some accounts sought to vindicate the entire South from the accusations of wrongdoing that had been forwarded by abolitionists and other smugly victorious northerners. Seeking to "rescue from oblivion" the story of the plantation, James B. Avirett, son of a North Carolina planter, wrote with pride of "the blessed days of the old South" and hoped to teach a younger generation of southerners to cherish the memories and to emulate the virtues of the bygone civilization. Writing in superlatives, the elderly minister claimed that in no other portion of the world had there ever been, or would there ever be again, "such happy social conditions as formerly existed in the old South on the old plantation." In his opinion, history had never before seen "a peasantry so happy, and in every respect so well to do," as the black slaves of antebellum America.[2]

Other writers chose to defend one particular region or state against the barbs of northern critics. Former Confederate General Basil Duke, for example, was raised in the bluegrass region of Kentucky and thus sought to divorce the state of his birth from those areas of the deep South that practiced a "sterner" version of the black bondage system. According to Duke, Kentucky chattels were not only well cared for and kindly treated, but were also "the most contented and jolliest human beings I ever saw." Profiting from their close association with kindly masters, slaves from the bluegrass region were "kind-hearted, docile, and, in their way, quite honest."[3]

Still others who penned accounts of the Old South seemed to be more concerned with uplifting the image of an individual planter family—most often their own. Fearing that her father's grandchildren would grow up hearing only of the wickedness of the slaveholders, Susan Dabney Smedes memorialized Mississippi planter Thomas S. Dabney. She hoped the children would be able to learn of a good master, "one who cared for his servants affectionately and yet with a firm hand, when there was need, and with a full sense of his responsibility." In like manner, Andrew Phelps McCormick defended the methods used by his father to encourage the slaves in their labors.

Although most of the business of the elder McCormick's Brazoria County, Texas, plantation was handled by a white overseer, the slaveholder took personal charge of all disciplinary matters to insure that "no overseer's or slave-driver's whip was ever used on that place." According to son Andrew, McCormick never used the lash as a prod to work, but only to "conserve the peace and secure decorous deportment" on the plantation. The slaveholders were apparently so fond of "their Negroes" that Duncan Clinch Heyward, great grandson of a prosperous South Carolina rice planter, could boast that the planters of his acquaintance "even refrained from hurting their feelings by speaking of them as *slaves*."[4]

Along with praise for the planters, the postbellum writings contain vivid stereotypes of antebellum slaves and black drivers. In explaining how and why the slave South functioned as it had, slaveholders and their descendants described blacks as "naturally lazy" people who were lacking in both "fixed principles" and moral sense. "It should be remembered," wrote Belle Kearney, daughter of a planter from southwestern Mississippi, "that a race, like an individual, has its period of youth. The African in America has not yet advanced beyond that age." To Kearney's mind, whoever sought to evaluate the Afro-American without considering the thickness of his skull, the length of his underjaw, and the relative smoothness of his brain would surely underestimate the time needed to "perfect" the southern Negro.[5]

Those writers who sought to describe slaves who had been placed in positions of trust and authority had a difficult time in divorcing the figure of the "exceptional" bondsman from his racial connection with the "backward" masses. In an account of daily life on her family's Penultima estate, Anna Hardeman Meade described a foreman named Austin whose leadership abilities failed completely when a springtime flood threatened the plantation. According to Meade, the black supervisor's response to this crisis was one of disorientation, panic, and fear. In reporting the situation to his owner, Austin was clearly without plan or direction: "Marster! Marster!" he called up to the Big House; "For Gawd's sake, Marster, come! De levee done broke, an' de water's runnin' 'cross de turn row in de upper fiel' jes' dis side de gin! Oh, Gawd A'mighty! Gawd A'mighty!"

After sternly but hopelessly urging his foreman to "be a *man*,"

Mrs. Meade's grandfather was forced to take matters into his own hands. As the slaveholder directed the removal of people and live-stock to higher ground, the bondsmen "gathered around him, in their helplessness, trusting implicitly in his judgment, receiving his rapid, comprehensive orders. . . ." When calm had been restored to this confused scene, Austin attempted to reassure his master that he would be better prepared for future emergencies: "Lord, Marster," said the foreman, ". . . I *boun'* I'll be ready fer de nex' overflow, mun, ef I has ter staht on dat levee no sooner en dis water go offen us. I lay hit ain't er gwine ter ketch me wid my breeches down *no* mo'!" By excusing his behavior in a manner more befitting an early-day Stepin Fetchit than a supervisor of field laborers, Austin proved himself to be at one with his fellow bondsmen. To Mrs. Meade's mind, all of the blacks were "April-hearted children of Nature."[6]

If certain of the slaves described in the post-Civil War accounts were deemed to be directionless and immature, others possessed the redeeming quality of faithfulness. John Clinkscales's reminiscences of his plantation childhood contain an engaging description of the ever-dutiful foreman, "Unc' Essick." Striving mightily to be "de bes' nigger on de place," Essex was diligent in his labors and always demanded first-class work from his crew. Clinkscales's father was often in poor health and thus counted himself fortunate in having a foreman of "such fine judgment and one in all respects so absolutely trustworthy." When the slaveholder was on his deathbed, Essex was summoned to the dying man's side and entrusted with the care and protection of the white plantation family. "Trembling like a leaf and sobbing like a wounded child," the black foreman dropped to his knees, pressed his master's hand to his lips, and said between his sobs, "Gawd bless you, Marster; ef Gawd spar me, I'll tek kere Missus an' dese chillun. Gawd knows I will." According to Clink-scales, Essex was true to his word. Many a night he slept on the piazza of the Big House in order to protect his white charges from intruders. Certainly, Clinkscales asserted, the trusty slave "would have died before any man, black or white, could have entered that door uninvited."[7]

Faithful drivers such as Essex were said to have worked closely with their owners in implementing workable plans for the operation of the plantation and the disciplining of disobedient field hands. The postbellum reminiscences contain numerous references to close friendships that supposedly developed between the planters and their field supervisors. According to the whites, drivers were "greatly attached" to their owners while many slaveholders considered their foremen to be "valued and trusted" friends.[8] Often, this "mutual bond" of companionship was said to have begun in childhood, as black and white youth played together in the plantation barnyard, or as a young slave was assigned to perform the duties of body servant to the planter's children.[9] When they reached adulthood, white children raised in such an atmosphere could scarcely help but exercise "a kind and well-nigh paternal oversight" over their former playmates, sometimes selecting these "boon companions" as drivers or foremen. Certainly, from the slaveholder's perspective, such long-standing interpersonal relationships would be helpful both in bridging the gap between the Big House and the quarters and in instilling principles of discipline in the black labor force. As one elderly white survivor of the slave regime recalled, the foreman was a "most useful man" to have on the plantation. Confidence placed in him was seldom betrayed because the feeling between master and slave supervisor was one of "kindliness and friendship, tho the black man never 'forgot his place.' "[10]

A prime example of this driver-master compatibility was given in Varina Davis's memoir of life on the Brierfield plantation in Warren County, Mississippi. Until his death in 1850, a slave named James Pemberton served as personal servant, bodyguard, and manager for master Jefferson Davis. When Davis was absent from the plantation, the black supervisor "took charge" of the place and directed the work of the field hands "according to his master's and his own views." A "dignified, quiet" slave of "fine manly appearance," Pemberton was always referred to as James rather than Jim because the planter felt that "it is disrespect to give a nickname." According to Ms. Davis, the slaveholder and the foreman were "devoted friends" who always observed the utmost ceremony and politeness in their personal dealings. When Pemberton came to report on the day's labor, he would not take a seat without being asked. Davis always requested that his manager be seated and frequently brought a chair for him. At each parting, the planter presented Pemberton with a complimentary cigar. With memories of such marvelous interracial decorum to ponder, it is understandable that Ms. Davis would regret the passing of the slave era. Those were the days when "love was law" to the bondsmen, when whites "nursed their children and they ours, and there was entire mutual confidence."[11]

If such mutual trust did indeed exist on some antebellum plantations, it was no accidental occurrence. A second type of documentary source left by the planters describes the mechanisms used by the whites in their attempt to turn their drivers into well-oiled "cogs" in the plantation's disciplinary machinery. The plantation rules, overseer contracts, and essays on management found in the planter's records and in antebellum agricultural papers often portrayed the black supervisory elite as the soul-less automatons the slaveholders *hoped* to create through the use of various "incentives."

From these sources, one learns that the first order of business in the training of a driver was to gain his complete confidence. In an article directed at white overseers, F. G. Ruffin noted that both master and overseer were often benefited by consulting with their head slaves or drivers. Not only could "a great deal of useful experience" be gained by conferring with them, but at the same time such a conference would serve to win their "confidence and esteem."[12]

Once the prospective driver had become convinced that "the happiness and prosperity of all will be in proportion to the fidelity with which each member discharges his part," it was the further task of the slaveholder or his agent to boost the image of the black supervisor in the eyes of those he was to superintend. Considering the head driver to be the "most important negro on the plantation," South Carolina planter James Henry Hammond required that the slave who occupied this post be dealt with more gingerly than the other bondsmen. At no time was the white overseer to allow the driver to be "treated with any indignity calculated to lose the respect of the other negroes." Should an action of the head slave require correction, only Hammond was to decide upon and administer the punishment.[13]

Other southern whites were also aware of the important role a well-conditioned "black trustee" could play in the disciplinary system of the plantation South. They, too, sought to divorce the driver from his prior state of "commonality" with the field hands. Roswell King, Jr., overseer of the Butler's Island plantation in Georgia, believed it was to the overseer's advantage to have as principal drivers men who could "support their dignity." To insure the continued flowering of this valuable character trait, he urged that "a condescention to familiarity should be prohibited." In like manner, another overseer, writing in the *Farmers' Register* in 1836, asserted that "the more the driver is kept aloof from the negroes, the better." The driver could not possibly maintain too much pride in his conduct toward the "common" slaves. Once he weakened and allowed the field hands to believe they were his equals, all control would be lost and he would become useless.[14]

Apparently in agreement with planter J. H. Bernard, who believed that "avarice, combined with pride and vanity" were "strong principles even in the breast of a negro," some slaveholders urged that rewards and privileges be granted the slave elite to strengthen their loyalty to the whites' interests. Hammond's plantation manual stated that drivers were to receive extra allowances of meat and molasses, use of a cart in which to ride into town, and a $5 bonus on Christmas day. Other planters advised that their foremen should be allowed to dress better than the other slaves, to live in "more pretentious" cabins, and to cultivate extra-large garden plots—advantages calculated to instill in the driver "a pride of character . . . highly beneficial" to the smooth functioning of the plantation.[15]

To planters such as J. Hamilton Couper of Georgia, a smoothly functioning agricultural unit meant that "daily accountability" had been introduced in each department of plantation activity. By doing so, everything—including the actions of the black foreman—could be reduced "to system."[16] A third variety of planter-oriented source material, the relatively rare correspondence between absentee slaveholders and their black managers, seems at first glance to show that the planters succeeded remarkably well in implementing their plans. This planter-driver correspondence, the black component of which was sometimes dictated to an amanuensis who actually penned and read the letters, is remarkable for the insights it provides into the ways in which slaveholders sought to control the activities of their foremen through the mails. When "out of sight" the black supervisors were definitely not out of their master's minds.

Often absent from his Belgrade and Magnolia estates while vacationing at the Virginia mineral springs or visiting relatives in various parts of the South, North Carolina planter William S. Pettigrew entrusted the management of his properties to his two black foremen, Moses and Henry. Pettigrew's instructions were transmitted to them by letter and they in turn made weekly reports to him by means of letters dictated to a neighboring white farmer. In his correspondence, the slaveholder continually sought assurances that plantation affairs were progressing at an adequate and orderly pace. Indeed, it could be said that Pettigrew veritably "pestered" his black supervisors until he received notice of such progress. "Notwithstanding the two letters written to you last week," he wrote from Virginia in the fall of 1858, "I will address you another today to remind you of the fact, that my mind frequently dwells on my home & business & people." On another occasion, fearing that his initial letter might become lost in the mails, Pettigrew penned a second epistle to Moses and Henry containing identical instructions as to the proper procedure to be followed to prepare for his imminent homecoming. The planter seemed always to be "feeling anxious on the subject of my people & business."[17]

To calm this anxiety about being so far away from his plantations, Pettigrew sought to convince his foremen that they were partners in a great agricultural enterprise. By encouraging them to join with him in commonality of purpose, the slaveholder hoped that Moses and Henry would uphold his interests while he was away. In a June 1856 letter, Pettigrew reminded the slaves that they must do all that was in their power to "promote the welfare and credit" of Belgrade. "I have placed much reliance in your management, industry & honesty by thus leaving the plantation & all on it in your charge," he wrote, "nor have I any fear that you will fall short of the confidence I have placed in you."[18]

While playing the part of a paternalistic friend, advisor, and confidant, Pettigrew nevertheless presented the slaves with a vision of the ill consequences that would befall them should they decide not to play *their* roles in an acceptable manner. Disguised in terms appropriate to the form and intent of the correspondence, the "wages" of disobedience involved the withdrawal of the whites' friendship and goodwill. On several occasions Pettigrew told his foremen how "distressing & mortifying" it would be for him to return home and discover that the field hands had not been "industrious and obedient" during his absence. Seemingly, even those whites who did not have a direct economic interest in the success of the Belgrade and Magnolia crops were certain to be upset over any inattention on the part of the foremen. During the summer of 1856, Pettigrew informed Moses that he had shared one of the slaves' letters with his close friend James C. Johnston. Pleased that the work at Belgrade was proceeding in a satisfactory manner, Johnston hoped the slaves' letters would continue to be filled with "good news." But as Pettigrew warned, should his friend hear "bad reports"—should things take an "unfavorable turn" in consequence of the planter's long absence—both Johnston and Pettigrew would be "distressed." According to their master, Moses, Henry, and all the hands "would not only be disgraced in my estimation, but also in his."[19]

Moses and Henry, for their part, seemed willing to abide by Pettigrew's rules and appeared to do everything in their power to please him. They dutifully answered his queries, filling their correspondence with words of comfort about the state of the crops and the disposition of the hands. As Henry reported in the fall of 1856, "The people is quite well master an veary well behaved an wishes thare love to master hoping that master is well. the crop at magnolia is veary good master." Indeed, the correspondence of the black foremen contained so many laudatory details of agricultural progress and proper slave deportment that one suspects that instead of reporting "all the news" of the plantation, Moses and Henry selectively told Pettigrew the type of things he wanted to hear and reported field hand indiscretions only when they were forced to do so by the magnitude of the offense. When viewed in this manner, it is possible to see the black supervisors as self-directed men rather than merely as obedient "cogs" in the slaveholder's agricultural machinery.[20]

When, in their letters, the foremen noted that the hands had "conducted themselves well an has worked hard," they were not serving as "agents of accommodation" for their owners, but rather as protectors of their own and their black brothers' best interests.[21] The slave correspondence contains numerous requests by the foremen for goods that would ease the lot of the field hands. "Our molasses has almost gave out. our tobacco has give out all. ef master pleases to send some pleas send a grind stone ef master pleases for Magnolia," wrote Henry in the fall of 1857. At other times, the foremen requested "casteroil" and "shirten for the people" because they felt the slave

community would soon be in short supply of those important commodities. On still another occasion, Moses reported that he had not
yet required the hands to haul timber from the woods as it had been so
wet that he could not accomplish the task without "damaging the teem
an the people wading."[22]

When planters such as Pettigrew had to deal repeatedly with such
requests, it is likely that they would eventually come to the realization
that their drivers were actually serving both a white and an Afro-
American constituency. Although few former slaveholders would
admit to the fact in published reminiscences, it is apparent from their
private diaries and correspondence with similarly afflicted planters
that, for good reason, the whites feared their drivers were more
faithfully serving the black constituency than they were the residents
of the Big House. Unlike the postbellum recollections, the master-
driver correspondence, and a large percentage of the antebellum
writings on proper plantation management, planter diaries and correspondence openly portray the slaveholders' relationship with the
supervisory elite as something other than one of mutual trust and
comradeship.[23] Robert F. W. Allston of Chicora Wood plantation in
South Carolina was not expressing an unusual sentiment when, in an
1859 letter to his nephew, he described a slave named Orinoca as "a
smart intelligent Driver but tricky." It is unlikely that the dual personality traits mentioned by Allston were possessed by all members of
the supervisory elite, but when a slaveholder found himself to be the
owner of a driver who evidenced a marked tendency toward both
intelligence and deception, he could be certain that any hope of
maintaining a consistently smooth running agricultural operation
would, sooner or later, be frustrated by the actions of his field
captain.[24]

Perhaps the most famous slaveholder to be afflicted by the wiles of
a black foreman was a Virginia farmer by the name of George
Washington. The president-to-be had inherited a dozen or so slaves
from his father and purchased additional servants as circumstances
and financial wherewithal allowed. By 1787 he possessed some 216
slaves, including a large group of "dower Negroes" owned by his
wife. Washington divided his slaves between the five "farms" that
constituted the Mt. Vernon estate. The work on each unit was directed
by an overseer with a steward supervising the whole. At Muddy Hole

Farm, a 476-acre piece of property set back from the Potomac, Washington placed 30 slaves under the direction of a black overseer-foreman named Davy. In letters to his steward, Washington told of his general satisfaction with the way in which Davy "carries on his business" and asserted that "with proper directions he will do very well." Nevertheless, since he was writing in the hope that certain "abuses" that had "crept into all parts" of his agricultural enterprise could be remedied, the scion of Mt. Vernon found it necessary to give voice to his suspicions regarding Davy's negligence in the care of livestock. The foreman's accounting for missing Muddy Hole sheep apparently did not completely satisfy Washington's orderly mind. "If the lambs had been poisoned, or had died a natural death, or their deaths had been occasioned by any accident, their bones would have been forth coming," he wrote from Philadelphia in 1795. "His not being able to produce them, is an argument both of his guilt, and of his not expecting to be called upon for that evidence of the truth of his assertion." Thus, Washington urged that the steward "watch him a little closer." The president feared that if the black foreman was prone to this type of underhanded behavior nothing on the farm would be safe from his "Rogueries."[25]

Even more distrustful of the plantation elite than Washington was Landon Carter, son of Robert "King" Carter of Virginia. The master of Sabine Hall was sufficiently skeptical about the good intentions of his foremen that he ordered his white overseer to keep a constant check on the amount of work done by the black supervisors. Considering the trouble Carter had with slave overlooker Jack Lubbar, it is not surprising that he would be less than completely trusting in his relations with such men. In the spring of 1766, Carter wrote in his diary that Jack's plea for an additional supply of feed corn at the Fork quarter sounded extremely suspicious. "He made 33 bushels. Measured in February," noted the planter, ". . . 40 would have kept the plantation a whole year; therefore he must be a rogue. He pretends the Cattle and sheep eat it. He has but 6 calves and 15 lambs." Discouraged over this and other incidents of slave pilfering, Carter exclaimed, "I must get an overseer at my fork quarter. Old Jack is both too easy with those people and too deceitfull and careless himself. A negroe can't be honest . . . it will be better to have more eyes than one over such gangs."[26]

Jack Lubbar was not the only member of the supervisory elite deemed to be "too easy." Planter diaries and correspondence contain numerous complaints about the slowness of the work pace under the black supervisors. Following an 1834 visit to one of his employer's Louisiana plantations, steward Boyd Smith complained to master David Weeks that he could not get the resident driver to "take sufficient interest" in the business of the plantation. Moreover, he noted that the driver had committed "several acts of inexcusable carelessness." In 1847 William P. Gould's overseer filed a similar complaint against a driver named Stewart. According to the Alabama overseer, the field hands worked "verry well" when under white supervision, but as soon as he left the field, Stewart acted as if he were incapable of prodding them into any additional exertions. "I have tried talking to him," complained the overseer, "but it does no good." Other drivers were said to be "indolent scoundrels" who idled the hours away taking "double the time [necessary] to do any one thing."[27]

In general, then, the most common complaint voiced about the drivers in the antebellum diaries and correspondence concerned their failure to live up to the planters' behavioral expectations. Certainly, slaves who were being properly "educated" in the manner suggested by the agricultural press of the day should not give evidence of such inveterate pilfering and laziness. But, according to the planter's pen, this was exactly the type of activity in which some drivers continued to engage each time white supervision was eased. "Rascality" was not confined to the more adventurous field hands, but seemed to infect even the highest echelons of the slave community. Southern whites complained that their drivers were lax in supervising the quarters at night, violated plantation rules regarding the use of passes, created friction with white overseers, and misused plantation liquor supplies.[28]

Virginia temperance crusader John Hartwell Cocke discovered in 1848 that such disturbing behavior could thrive even on a so-called model plantation. Hoping to prepare his chattels for eventual manumission and settlement in Africa, Cocke sought to encourage upright behavior within the slave community. Beginning in 1829, he substituted soup and molasses for the customary sixty to eighty gallons of spirits he had previously furnished the slaves at harvest time. One year later, he participated in the establishment of a local Temperance Society for Colored People and prevailed upon some sixty of his slaves to abstain from drink except for medicinal purposes. To all joining the society, the slaveholder promised a medal, made from a coin and stamped with a "T," that, when worn around the neck, signified one had taken "the pledge." By the summer of 1833, Cocke could claim 90 percent of his laboring force as Temperance Society members.[29]

Leading the field hands in their "swearing off" of strong drink was Cocke's black foreman George Skipwith. When Cocke decided to establish a new plantation in Greene County, Alabama, it was Skipwith to whom the slaveholder looked for both managerial and moral leadership. As Cocke wrote to one of the white supervisors of the slave resettlement project: ". . . remind George & the other professors of religion how much depends upon them . . . and don't omit to remind them all again & again of their pledges to abstain from every sort of drink that can affect their reason or intoxicate them." Despite this encouragement, Skipwith proved a great disappointment to the planter. During a winter 1848 visit to his Alabama holdings, Cocke found that although there had been satisfactory improvement in the agricultural sphere, a "shocking state of moral depravity" prevailed on the plantation. Blamed with engaging in "indiscriminate sexual intercourse" and plagued by venereal disease, the slaves were said by Cocke to have brought "disgrace upon themselves and scandal upon my plantation." Instead of becoming a moral leader, foreman Skipwith had turned the estate into a "plantation Brothel." Not only was the foreman, a member of the Baptist Church with a wife and ten children, "keeping a young girl on the place," but his two eldest daughters had become "kept mistresses" of two area white men. His plans for the establishment of a temperate, moral slave community blighted, Cocke charged Skipwith with contributing to the delinquency of the young women and understandably confided to his diary that his "hopes of elevating the character of these people . . . were deeply depressed." The driver's "rascality" could indeed have a telling effect upon the expectations of even the most high-minded and benevolent master.[30]

Not all drivers who were described as "rascals" in the planter diaries and correspondence broke plantation rules because of their fondness for strong drink or illicit liaisons. Other disturbingly disobedient members of the supervisory elite "went against orders" because they sought to protect their black brothers from harm. During the summer of 1771, one of Landon Carter's foremen was found to have been hiding a fugitive slave in the loft of his cabin. His "rascality" brought to light, foreman George sought to escape censure by taking "Wench Lydy" to the Big House and pretending that "he had just catched her." Unwilling to believe the foreman's tale, Carter recorded the chicanery in his diary, tersely describing his black supervisor as "An old Sun of a bit[c]h indeed."[31]

Although breaking no specific rule in the course of his actions, a Florida foreman named Prince also sought to protect one of his fellows. In the fall of 1854, planter George Noble Jones received a letter from his Chemonie estate describing an incident in which one of his overseers was confronted with an angry axe-wielding slave. Seeking to prevent the whipping of his sister, a mill hand named Aberdeen attacked the overseer, but was seized and prevented from harming him by the black foreman. As a result of Prince's quick response, young Aberdeen received "a genteel Flogging" rather than the more severe punishment that would almost certainly have resulted had the axe found its intended target.[32]

In September 1823 a South Carolina driver named Fenmore used his position within the plantation chain of command to uphold the interests of the field hands in a somewhat different manner. Having witnessed the brutality of a neighboring overseer, he described to his white supervisors how one of the Waverly slaves was "most dreadfully beat . . . by Swinton, Genl. Carr's overseer, so much so that he had not been able to work since." Realizing the feeling of outrage such a revelation would generate in the breast of planter Robert F. W. Allston—a man who valued highly the territorial and judicial integrity of his estate—Fenmore was undoubtedly pleased when Allston's nephew Joseph joined him in urging that Swinton be prosecuted for his unjustifiable act. With such sympathetic eyes and ears resident in the quarters, the slaves were, to a degree, protected against arbitrary incursions by local whites.[33]

Unfortunately, should a driver be caught engaging either in advocacy or "rascality" to an extent deemed excessive by the whites, *he* would likely find himself subjected to the arbitrary nature of his master via demotion to field hand status. The diaries and correspon-

dence of the planters describe not only the "sins" of the black
foremen, but they also tell of the "wages" paid for the commission of
such persistent breaches of plantation decorum. Tiring of his
foreman's "libidinous & adulterous propensities," John Hartwell
Cocke eventually decided that George Skipwith could not adequately
be reformed. Concluding that Skipwith's disruptive behavior was
"too much to be borne," the planter reluctantly removed the slave
from his position of authority, shipped him to Mississippi, and returned to "the execrable Overseer-system as the least evil."[34] On
another occasion, an overseer on Cocke's Hopewell plantation demoted a driver in response to a collective act of "laziness" on the part
of the field hands. "After finding himself in the grass," overseer J.
Walter Carter stripped his head man of authority, put him to work with
a hoe, and took over the immediate supervision of the gang. Angered
at this usurpation of the driver's post, the field hands attempted to
discredit Carter by further slighting their work on the cotton crop.
Thereafter, conditions on the plantation became so tense that Cocke's
steward had to step in and do some "plain talking" to all parties
involved in this incipient battle of wills. Thus, as these incidents
reveal, even in their fall from power, strong-willed drivers could be
very disruptive of the whites' attempts to conduct "business as
usual."[35]

Perhaps a brief comment recorded in the diary of South Carolina's
John Berkley Grimball, another planter who was plagued by the
problem and necessity of demoting a driver, could serve as a bench
mark from which interested scholars might proceed in their attempts
to understand the true, nonromanticized nature of the relationship
between the slaveholders and their black managers. If trust and comradeship entered into the planter-driver equation, it was only at the
whites' hopeful insistence. If the relationship between master and
slave supervisor seemed to be cordial, it was likely to be a cordiality
born of necessity and fraught with tension and uncertainty. As Grimball noted in describing the "breaking" of his driver Richard,
"Negro property is certainly the most troublesome in the world."
The multitudinous day-to-day problems of slave management were
certainly sufficient to elicit comments of this nature and must have
greatly complicated the lives of men such as Grimball. For good
reason, the slave drivers were often included in the antebellum planters' definition of "troublesome Negro."[36]

THE TRAVELERS

> Bananas, negroes, and negro-songs are the greatest re-
> freshments of the mind, according to my experience,
> which I found in the United States. And to every one,
> whether in Old or New England, who is troubled by
> spleen or dyspepsia, or over-excitement of brain or
> nerves, would I recommend, as a radical cure, a journey to
> the South to eat bananas, to see the negroes, and hear their
> songs.
>
> *Fredrika Bremer*

Accounts of the agricultural South penned by travelers from the
North, Great Britain, or various parts of Europe have been used by
many scholars in reconstructing the life and times of the plantation
community. Such travel accounts are no less "interpretations" of the
southern way of life than are the formulations of professional historians or the recollections of the planters. Nevertheless, the characteristics of the outsiders' commentaries are of a sufficiently singular
nature as to warrant a separate study designed both to find out how the
travelers viewed the slave supervisory elite and to determine the social
factors that influenced their judgment.

One major problem the harried antebellum traveler faced was the
difficulty in getting a more complete view of the southern countryside
than that which could be seen from the deck of a steamer or the car of a
passenger train. Although rail and river transportation sped the visitor
on his way, it also separated him from the land and the people he had
presumably come to observe. As Alexander Mackay noted after his
1846-47 tour, misrepresentations of southern society were most likely
to flow from the pens of those who were satisfied with "depicting life
as they saw it in the railway carriage, on the steamer, and in the
bar-room."[1]

Travelers who were limited to such a narrow perspective did indeed produce some incredible inferences based upon their "view from the steamer." As he gazed from the hurricane deck of a ship making its way down the Mississippi to New Orleans, Thomas Nichols marveled at the difference between the scenery he was observing and that of his native New Hampshire. "I cannot describe the appropriateness of everything on these plantations," he noted. "These creole planters look as if nature had formed them for good masters. . . . The negroes, male and female, seem made on purpose for their masters, and the mules were certainly made on purpose for the negroes." Only by disembarking and making a concerted effort to find out more about the individual components of this "harmonious" relationship could Nichols have hoped to give his readers a more realistic view of slavery.[2]

Other voyagers were separated from life on the plantations by lodging in urban, "civilized" areas of the South. As with tourists of any era, it took some degree of inventiveness and determination for antebellum travelers to step aside from the hotel, the railway, and the steamer and attempt to live with the people, instead of merely observing them from a comfortable distance. As clergyman-traveler Philo Tower observed, little confidence would be placed in the reports of Americans returning home from Ireland who had formed their opinion of the condition of the Irish peasantry solely from the "appearance of the waiters of a Dublin hotel." Yet, this was the kind of testimony that was often forwarded by northerners who had toured the slave South.[3]

Even if the travelers succeeded in getting off the boat and out of the hotel, there were other forces of influence waiting to mislead them about the true character of southern plantation life. When the northern and overseas visitors slowed their pace and journeyed into the rural South, they often came under the sheltering wing of a resident southerner. Although the overall level of hospitality in the Old South may have been exaggerated by later romanticizers, there were many travel accounts that described the warm reception and gracious treatment that was afforded visitors to the great plantations.

In recounting her 1849-50 American tour, Lady Emmeline Stuart-Wortley described a most splendid reception at the Zachary Taylor plantation near Natchez. With the late President's son serving as a guide, she reviewed the "well fed, comfortably clothed, and kindly cared for'' servants who had been ''mustered and marshaled for us to see,'' observed the field hands picking cotton, and peered into the interior of a slave ''dwelling-house.'' Lady Emmeline described the cabin as being a ''tastefully decorated and an excellently furnished one; the walls were covered with prints, and it was scrupulously clean and neat.'' After such a marvelous tour of the grounds, she could not help but conclude that the slaves were ''thoroughly happy and contented.''[4]

Other travelers were given the same type of ''package'' tour by resident whites. After being shown a ''first-rate'' Mississippi Valley cotton plantation by the resident overseer, Frederick Law Olmsted remarked that this was the only large agricultural unit he had visited where his tour ''was not chiefly conducted by an educated gentleman and slave owner, by whose habitual impressions and sentiments my own were probably somewhat influenced.'' Such planter control over the visitor's itinerary, and thus his impression of the slave South, was roundly condemned by northern abolitionists. As Theodore Weld noted in 1839, travelers were destined to see only the ''least repulsive parts'' of slavery inasmuch as it was wholly at the option of the master what parts to show them.[5]

Whether they deemed such information to be ''repulsive'' or not, slaveowners were eager to fill the travelers in on the nature of the slaves' character. In this way the southerner could hope to provide his northern guest with a ''complete'' explanatory picture—and justification—of the ''peculiar institution.'' While touring South Carolina, one antebellum visitor was informed by an Episcopal clergyman that Negroes could never be trusted with any responsibility involving the exercise of authority because they invariably abused the privilege. They tended to treat animals ''with positive brutality'' and sometimes whipped their children so unmercifully that the whites had to interfere in their domestic relations. Given this same basic description of slave personality in a different portion of the South, Lady Emmeline Stuart-Wortley remarked that instances of slave brutality were easily understood when one recalled that the bondsmen were ''universally ignorant and uneducated, without any proper moral training to teach them to restrain and subdue their naturally violent and inflammable passions and tempers.'' Lady Emmeline had learned her ''lessons'' well.[6]

Buffeted by unfamiliar sights and strange experiences, the traveler had to wrestle with the moral implications of his new role as interpreter of the southern social system. Many told of tremendous mental strivings toward objectivity and the desire to "judge dispassionately" what passed before their eyes. After examining the evidence at hand, some were converted from their prior antislavery leanings and became willing supporters of the slaveholding way of life. Finding that there was not one-fifth of the "real suffering" on the cotton plantations that he had witnessed in England's factories, William Thomson was forced, in this manner, to revise his estimation of slavery. Although there were cases of brutality, slavery in America was certainly not the "horrid system of cruelty and oppression" described by the abolitionists. Having witnessed slaves "laughing at the jokes of the auctioneer" while they were being sold on the block, Thomson could claim that the bondsmen laughed and sang "more than any class of men on earth."[7]

Nehemiah "South-Side" Adams was perhaps the most famous "convert" to a pro-southern stance. Adams told the readers of his travel account that his eyes, rather than southern propaganda, had taught him that certain aspects of the slave system were wholly different from his expectations. "I saw it," he wrote, "and received instruction." Expecting to witness a scene of "hopeless woe" in which each chattel would have the expression that said "I am a slave" indelibly stamped upon his countenance, Adams was relieved by the sight of Savannah's black nurses tending infants in the parks and of the seemingly good humored stevedores working on the docks. To the northern visitor, it seemed as though he had been let down into a cavern he had imagined to be "peopled with disagreeable sights," and then, upon touching bottom, found "daylight streaming in, and the place cheerful."[8]

One likely reason for such "conversions" was that few travelers witnessed punishments being dealt out to the slaves. After one of his many tours through the South, agricultural journalist Solon Robinson claimed that during the entire trip he "did not see or hear of but two cases of flogging"—one for stealing and the other for "running away from as good a master as ever a servant need to have." In 1817 a visitor to Georgia told the readers of the *National Intelligencer* that although he had traveled far and had observed numerous gangs of slaves, he had yet to hear the "lash of the whip" or the "torturing cry of a suffering slave." Even a traveler such as Nehemiah Adams, who claimed to be actively looking for instances of southern brutality, could write that he had been at the South for over a month before "anything presented itself to my mind that excited painful feelings."[9]

Critical readers of travel accounts that expressed such sentiments quite rightly pointed out that the temporary guests of southern planters probably had little opportunity to learn fully the everyday habits and caprices of their hosts. Antislavery critics of the plantation regime found it impossible to believe that "power so despotic, so utterly uncontrolled," would never degenerate into violence. As one northern skeptic wrote, travelers staying in the homes of nonslaveholding families undoubtedly never witnessed the father or mother whipping their children because well-bred parents usually did not discipline their offspring in this manner "in the presence, or within hearing of their guests." But it was asked, "are we hence to infer that they never do it *out* of their sight and hearing?"[10]

If few travelers were privy to the mechanisms of plantation discipline, many were introduced to a venerable plantation figure—the "display" slave. During their stay at southern estates, visitors were often escorted by or shown selected "representatives" of the slave community. The much-traveled Frederick Law Olmsted, for example, observed that there was "always at hand some negro mathematician," who was not merely held to be far in advance of the native Africans, but who was also touted as being able to surpass most white men in his "quickness and accuracy in calculation." At the same time such a slave was considered to be so thoroughly trustworthy that he was employed by his master as an accountant and collecting agent. Slaves said to possess these characteristics were meant to serve as pieces of visible human evidence that would hopefully move the planters' unwary visitors to believe that an "institution, productive of so much mutual appreciation, *must* be excellent."[11]

Quite often, "display" slaves were drawn from the ranks of the black foreman class. Olmsted told of planters boasting that they had promoted certain slaves to managerial posts—deferring to their agricultural judgment since it was "superior to that of any overseer or planter in the county." Other visitors reported the pride that slaveholders evidenced in the diligence and intelligence of their drivers and recalled the "touching instances of faithfulness" that were related to them about the black supervisory elite.[12]

Although it is likely that travelers came into closer contact with "display" slaves than common field hands, it is doubtful that many received a significantly different impression of plantation life from the bondsmen than they had already gained from the master. Great shrewdness and tact had to be exhibited by those slaves who served as attendants, guides, or carriage drivers and by those who were interviewed by visiting whites. When closely questioned by strangers as to their treatment, common sense dictated that they formulate their answers with an eye to keeping themselves out of difficulty. As one traveler who claimed to have spoken with hundreds of slaves noted, "not one man—not even one Northerner—in ten who speaks with the slaves on the subject of bondage ascertains their sincere opinions."[13]

Some travelers, such as actor Louis Tasistro, were taken in by the slaves' tactful and uncritical comments. Following his 1840-41 tour of the South, Tasistro claimed that the planters had been "most grossly misrepresented" in regard to the treatment of their slaves. Basing this conclusion on his observations of southern conditions and on conversations he had had with the bondsmen, the actor noted that he had not only found the chattels to be "extremely contented with their lot," but also to be "generally disposed to reject the boon of freedom, should it be offered them." In the plantation South, role playing was certainly not restricted to professional theatrical performers.[14]

Despite their unfamiliarity with the components of southern society, the time and distance pressures experienced while touring, and the confusion that resulted from listening to so many competing voices of authority, the antebellum travelers did, for better or for worse, leave to history their impressions of the slave drivers, foremen, and managers of the agricultural South. As with interpretive reminiscences penned by outside observers of other eras, when the antebellum traveler viewed his surroundings with an uncritical eye, he was likely to leave an account that was filled with stereotypes and generalizations drawn from a few isolated, perhaps atypical incidents. In terms of the "outsider's" view of the black foremen, such an approach invariably resulted in a patently dehumanized type of creature being forwarded to the reading public as *the* slave driver. Possibly endowed with some degree of imperfectly developed intelligence, yet possessing a cruel, debased spirit, this species of driver fit in well both in accounts antagonistic to and those sympathetic with the slave regime. Whether southern bondage was held to degrade a human being to the level of a brute or to raise a barbarian to the stage of civilization where he could usefully and willingly serve as a pliant lackey of the master class, the dehumanized driver could be seen as a representative product of America's slave labor system.

Many travelers who characterized drivers in this manner observed the dealings the black foremen had with southern whites and concluded that all supervisory elements of the plantation South were leagued together in an unholy conspiracy to uphold the slave system. Those visitors who managed to penetrate the veil of southern propriety and either to witness or to hear descriptions of the whipping of disobedient slaves often assumed that the driver who carried out the master's orders was as eager as the slaveowner to exact a painfully harsh and long-remembered punishment. Claude Robin, a naturalist who lived in Louisiana for four years at the opening of the nineteenth century, vividly described a cruel whipping given by a Negro "executioner" of the day. After the offending slave had been stripped naked and spread-eagled, face downward, between four stakes that had been driven into the ground, the driver acted upon the master's orders and lashed the victim like "an angry cartman beating his horses." While Robin was so upset that his "agitated hand" could hardly bear to "trace the bloody picture," the whip continued to crack and the blood kept flowing "without softening either the hand of the executioner or the heart of the master." Recalling the terrible scene, Robin recounted how he had "shuddered at the faces of those barbarous monsters"—master and driver—upon which he "saw inscribed the number of victims sacrificed to their ferocity."[15]

Other travelers not only placed the order-giving master and the order-taking driver in a common cesspool of inhumanity, but went even further and claimed that the black supervisory elite was *more* depraved than the white planter class. Fredrika Bremer, for example, described the driver as being the cruelest and most severe man on the plantation. Such supervisors became "the worst torment of the negroes" largely because of an unfortunate racial flaw. It seemed to be common knowledge at the South that "when the negro is unmerciful, he is so in a high degree."[16]

Another traveler in the Mississippi Valley during the winter of

1829-30, overseas visitor Simon O'Ferrall, elaborated upon the drivers' supposed lack of mercy in his published observations on the region's sugar and rice plantations. Along with "ill fed, ill clad, truly wretched" field hands, O'Ferrall viewed drivers armed with long whips—which they could use "at discretion"—overseeing the other slaves. Although it might be assumed that slaveowners would severely punish a slave only to establish disciplinary norms useful to the profitable functioning of the plantation, O'Ferrall's drivers were motivated by less crass, but certainly far less honorable, considerations. He found that punishments meted out by the black supervisors were more frequently inflicted to "gratify the private pique or caprice" of the driver than as a painful recompense for crime or neglect of duty.[17]

Although modern readers of these and similar statements made by antebellum travelers may wish to agree with psychohistorian Earl Thorpe that the basic concept of the corrupt, "Savage Negro" has been purposefully used by generations of whites to soften the guilt engendered by their "systematized exploitation, humiliation, and oppression" of blacks, it must also be remembered that the travelers really did believe in the image of the driver that their overworked senses and underused powers of perception conjured up.[18]

Certain of these "truthful" travel accounts that seem to describe a stereotypical "debased driver" can, however, with a closer look and the application of a bit of interpretive insight, be used to formulate a more modern, considerably more reasonable portrait of the slave foreman class. A case in point is George Featherstonhaugh's account of a group of slave traders leading some three hundred Virginia chattels to new homes on the Louisiana sugar plantations. Aware that slaves in such circumstances were "always watchful to obtain their liberty," the traders attempted to mitigate their discontent by feeding them well on the march and by encouraging them to sing "Old Virginia never tire" to the strains of banjo music. Aiding in this program designed to calm any disposition toward mutiny were other blacks who had been specially trained by the slave dealers to "drive the rest." Amusing the shackled bondsmen through the telling of "lively stories" and boasting of the fine warm climate to which they were going, and of the "oranges and sugar which are there to be had for nothing," these black supervisors seemed to be well-oiled parts of the interstate slave trade's sordid mechanism of exploitation. Nevertheless, farther on in the account, the careful reader discovers that Featherstonhaugh later came into close contact with one of the slave trader's right-hand men, a personable slave named Pompey. Out of sight and hearing of his master, Pompey acted like anything but a dehumanized cog in the trader's machinery. Carrying on at some length about his owner's inordinate fondness for onions and brandy, the slave drew a rather unfavorable picture of the trader's character. As the traveler noted, Pompey told him a great many things that "served to confirm my abhorrence of this brutal land-traffic in slaves." In so doing, the slave showed both Featherstonhaugh and later readers that a role cleverly played was not necessarily a role deeply internalized.[19]

Even though they are certainly not free from biased comments about the various social components of the plantation South, there are three travel accounts in particular that contribute importantly to a modification of the pejorative "brutal driver-slavish Negro" stereotype found in so many of the travelers' writings. Frank, the intelligent head man observed by actress Fanny Kemble, the rebellious Isaac described by James Redpath, and Charles Grandison Parsons's tragic Dread are examples of drivers whose recorded experiences and whose apparent, albeit somewhat romanticized, characters contradict many hackneyed truisms regarding the slave elite.

In June 1834 Frances Anne Kemble abandoned her theatrical career and married Pierce M. Butler of Philadelphia. During the winter of 1839 the couple visited Hampton Point and Butler's Island, the two Sea Island rice plantations that had been in the family since the 1790s. During her three and one-half month stay on the two small islands at the mouth of the Altamaha River, Fanny kept a journal in the form of letters meant for the eventual perusal of a northern friend. Following her return to the North, her divorce from Butler, and the start of the Civil War, she published her journal in the hope that its passionate denunciation of the oppressive southern system of bondage would spur the Union forces to victory and help rally British public opinion to the side of the North.

At Butler's Island, Fanny Kemble observed the various human and mechanical components of the task system of rice production and seemed to pay particular attention to the family of head driver Frank.

Unlike the underdrivers, who were limited to twelve strokes, Frank's status enabled him to administer up to three dozen lashes to errant field hands. In addition, the head driver was deemed to be second in command on the estate and "second to none" whenever the overseer visited plantations on other islands or fled the area entirely "during the pestilential season, when the rice swamps cannot with impunity be inhabited by any white man." On such occasions he became the "sole master and governor of the island" and was responsible for the administration of discipline, the assignment of tasks, and the granting of passes. In addition to these responsibilities and privileges, Frank was entrusted with the keys to all storerooms, was responsible for the correct allotment of the weekly rations and other provisions, and was even allowed to supervise the labors of the slave workers in the plantation's threshing mill.[20]

Housed at the head of a row of slave cabins adjacent to the residence of the white overseer, recognized as the "most intelligent and trust-worthy" of Butler's slaves, and deemed by a former overseer to possess "quite the principles of a white man," Frank seemed to be fit material for the "debased driver" stereotype. The apparent powers and perquisites of office were, however, insufficient to prevent Kemble from describing him as a "grave, sad, thoughtful-looking man" who kept himself "a good deal aloof from the rest" by spending his leisure hours "looking, with a countenance of deep thought . . . over the broad river, which is to him as a prison wall, to the fields and forest beyond, not one inch or branch of which his utmost industry can conquer as his own."[21]

In addition to describing a type of melancholy that was rooted in the commonality of experience the driver shared with other slaves—a shared experience acknowledged by few other travelers—Kemble pinpointed an individualized source of sadness affecting Butler's head man. Frank's wife, Betty, who was described as being "a most active, trustworthy, excellent woman, daughter of the oldest, and probably most highly respected" of all Butler's slaves, had been taken from her husband by overseer Roswell King, Jr., and had borne a son by him. By the time of Kemble's visit to the Sea Islands, husband and wife had been reunited, but the "outrage upon this man's rights" remained "perfectly notorious" within the slave community.[22]

Also remaining all too obvious, from Frank's point of view, was the mulatto offspring of this forced union—a particularly obnoxious young man named Renty. Said to bear witness to his "Yankee descent" by his troublesome, discontented, and insubmissive disposition, Renty, on one occasion, attempted to gain permission to keep a gun even though the generality of slaves were not allowed firearms. In what must have been a cruel blow to the ego of Betty's husband, Renty sought this special permission not on the basis of his close relationship with head man Frank, but on "account of his color."[23]

Capable of exercising "all functions of undisputed mastery over his fellow slaves," Frank was nevertheless "just as much a slave as any of the rest" in that his own marriage relationship was not a stable, contractual one. Instead, it was an "institution" of convenience for others—one that could be interrupted or terminated by outside forces. Even though she expressed her sentiments in a manner compatible with her antebellum view of racial capacities, Fanny Kemble was more "modern" than she realized when she wrote that the "disgrace of such an injury" was felt and appreciated by Frank "much after the fashion of white men." From being credited with reacting to tension-producing situations in much the same manner as whites, it would be only one small interpretive step for the drivers to advance to the next higher stage of development—one in which the nature of their humanity could be described in terms of equality with that of their masters.[24]

Claiming for himself an allegiance to a variety of "humanity and human rights" that would speedily abolish slavery and drive the "Legrees of the plantations . . . into the sea, as Christ once drove the swine," James Redpath made three extended tours of the South during the mid-1850s. Redpath sought through his journeyings to see the slave institution with his own eyes, to learn what the bondsmen thought of their situation, and then to report his findings to the northern reading public. To accomplish this task, he talked with numerous slaves—taking "stenographic notes" as the bondsmen responded to his queries—or recording their responses as soon after the interview as was convenient. Redpath found the slaves' testimony to be uniform. "They all pant for liberty," he concluded, "and have great reason to do so. . . . Wherever I have gone, I have found the bondsmen discontented, and the slaveholders secretly dismayed at the signs of the times in the Northern States."[25]

The slave driver Redpath described fully evidenced these tendencies toward rebelliousness and mirrored the traveler's own militant leanings. Head man Isaac presided over a plantation owned by a family intimate with John C. Vaughan, one of Redpath's acquaintances. Vaughan, who first told the story to Redpath, recalled that in the days of his youth a terrific stir had resulted from the discovery that Isaac was the leader of an extensive insurrection plot. To the planters of the region, this particular slave had seemed to be a very unlikely conspirator. Implicit confidence had been placed in him not only by his master, but also by the local minister and by "everybody who knew him." The boys of the plantation affectionately called him "Uncle Isaac" and even the patrol "would take his word and let him go his way." Even though possessed with a fine muscular physique and "great strength," Isaac was seemingly "kind and affectionate, and simple as a woman." He never tired of doing things for others, was an "exemplary husband," a wise and kind father, and was said to be second to none in terms of "clear-headedness and nobleness of will." Richly "gifted" in intellect, Isaac was considered by Vaughan to be "born to make a figure."[26]

His plot betrayed by a fellow servant, the driver had a chance to evidence his superiority of character on the witness stand. Refusing the counsel of his young masters, Isaac boldly admitted his leading role in the conspiracy. With "no hesitation in his manner—no tremulousness in his voice" the driver announced to the court: "I am the man, and I am not afraid or ashamed to confess it." Despite this ready admission of guilt, "no ingenuity, no promises, no threats," could induce him to reveal the names of those who had agreed to participate in the planned uprising. To the white minister who went to the slave's cell in hopes of eliciting such testimony, Isaac described the motivation behind his insurrectionary efforts. Although he loved "old master and mistress" and would normally hurt "no living thing," his reflection upon the religious teaching that God was no respecter of persons had caused him to realize fully the implications of his slave status. Although his young masters could aspire to a formal education, set their own goals in life, and reap the profits of their toil, his fellow bondsmen could do nothing but that which others directed them to do. With this realization, Isaac concluded that "there was and could be no help for me, for wife or children, for my race, except we were free." Thus, he preached freedom to the slaves, and bid them "strike for it like men."[27]

Even on the gallows, Isaac continued to exhort his fellows toward full manhood. When one of the other condemned slaves began to evidence his fear of imminent death, the driver spoke out. "Be men," he counseled, "and die like men. I'll give you an example." Then, after saying a few final words to his brother and to his young masters, he shouted "I'll die a freeman," sprang up from the platform as high as he could, and fell heavily as the knotted rope pulled tight around his neck. As Vaughan noted in concluding his tale, Isaac the head man would be remembered on earth as an insurrectionist, but the "record above" would contain his virtues. In heaven, the good would know and love him—"for Isaac was a MAN."[28]

A third, possibly less glamorous, but no less human, driver was described in C. G. Parsons's *An Inside View of Slavery*. Like the story of Isaac, Parsons's account of Dread allows the reader to view a member of the black supervisory elite who stepped outside of the institutionalized role for which slavery had "trained" him. Like the account of Frank's heartbreak, Dread's story reveals the personal tragedy that was often hidden from the casual observer by the facade of perquisites and "special privileges" granted to the driver.

Parsons made his 1852-53 tour of Georgia, Florida, Alabama, Tennessee, and the Carolinas with the object of entering into a "thorough investigation" of the southern labor system. Not only did he have "influential friends" among the slaveholders—a circumstance he claimed provided him with better access to the institution's "secret operations" than had ever been enjoyed by "any one not supposed to be in favor of it"—but he also sought to obtain a more "correct knowledge" of the manners and customs of the southerners by traveling as an agent for a Savannah commission house and by taking a job as superintendent of a lumbering operation. The notes Parsons recorded in his journal during his stay in the South later formed the basis of a series of lectures he gave in several of the New England states.[29]

Parsons's Dread was, both in mind and body, a man of superior strength. One observer well acquainted with the slave told Parsons that he regarded Dread as both the stoutest and the most intellectual man he had ever met. "Dread had the largest head I have ever seen," the southerner remarked, "—and I have seen Daniel Webster; and his natural abilities were not inferior to those of that statesman." After one year of service on a South Carolina plantation, the abilities of the

nearly seven-foot-tall slave were recognized and he was made overseer of a gang of forty field hands. Soon, the management of the entire
plantation was left in his care. Instead of abusing his fellow slaves to
endear himself further to the whites, Dread got the job done by taking
a reasoned approach to the labor requirements of the plantation. If a
feeble woman became ill or was for some reason unable to complete
her assigned task alone, the driver allowed her husband or brother to
assist her. If a male slave could not keep up with the gang, his friends
were permittted to help him. Despite this humanitarian flexibility, the
crops produced by Dread's gang became the envy of neighboring
planters— so much that they sought him out for advice and deferred to
his opinion in matters pertaining to the management of their farms.[30]

Although he seemed to have quite handily won the respect and high
esteem of the slaveholders, Dread nevertheless made some powerful
enemies. Refusing to go through life behaving in the approved "me-
nial and timid" manner of the chattel, the driver made it a point to
thumb his nose at convention by refusing to doff his cap to whites he
passed on the street and by neglecting to carry it under his arm when he
entered a white-occupied dwelling. Jealous of his success in plantation management and angered over his "arrogance," white overseers
from surrounding plantations began to whisper that, if he was so
disposed, Dread might become the leader of an insurrection. Convinced by the overseers that such fears constituted a viable issue of
some concern to the plantation community, area slaveholders held a
conference and decided to conduct an experiment to "test the manhood of the giant slave." By doing so, they hoped to ascertain whether
he could "be made as submissive as all slaves should be made."[31]

In working out their experiment, the slaveholders first demoted
Dread to field hand status and placed a white overseer in his place.
Hoping that such treatment would anger the ex-driver and give them an
excuse to "whip him severely, and 'break him in,' " the planters were
surprised at the calm manner in which he accepted the demotion.
Without expressing "the least surprise or regret" at his loss of place,
Dread carried on his field work as usual.[32]

Frustrated in their attempts to crush the man's pride, the slaveholders decided to prefer false charges against Dread and to punish him if
he complained of suffering wrongfully. Even though he continued to
perform his task well—hoeing the corn "as neat as a garden"—his

master one day went to Dread's cabin and accused him of turning in a shoddy performance. Cognizant that he had done better work than the other bondsmen, the ex-driver replied, "How do you know that, Master!" Unwittingly, even in this rather mild response, Dread had exceeded the prerogatives granted to the type of slave the local planters sought to create. "Ah! you have got above yourself, boy," the slaveholder raged, "You shall be flogged, you impudent, black rascal!" Dread was rightfully indignant at his master's deception and refused to submit to a flogging. Instead, he armed himself with a butcher-knife and stood "in an attitude of conscious innocence, moral courage, physical strength, and bold defiance" until a blast from the planter's shotgun quelled his "insurrectionary spirit." Mortally wounded, the former driver staggered a few yards to a hillside "crying to Heaven for vengeance" on his murderer and uttering in deep, painfully strong tones, "I'm killed! I'm killed!! I'm killed!!!" Then, as Parsons noted, the proud bondsman "fell a sacrifice to the slave system."[33]

Although drivers such as Dread, Isaac, and Frank did indeed fall victim to certain of the physical coercions of the "peculiar institution," they nevertheless left a legacy to the slaves who knew them or who eventually heard their stories. The drivers' legacy was one of suffering, enduring, and sharing a common bond of human experience with their fellow blacks. Such lives and such experiences could usually be seen only in an imperfect and clouded manner from the deck of the steamer.

THE TWENTIETH-CENTURY NARRATIVES

> In all the books that you have studied you never have studied Negro history, have you? You studied about the Indians and white folks, what did they tell you about the Negro? If you want Negro history you will have to get [it] from somebody who wore the shoe, and by and by from one to the other you will get a book.
>
> *Reed, ex-Tennessee slave*

In an article that appeared in the spring 1974 issue of *Daedalus*, Yale historian David Brion Davis described what he considered to be "five major turning points" in the ongoing debate over the character of American Negro slavery. In addition to the appearance of Kenneth Stampp's *Peculiar Institution*, Stanley Elkins's *Slavery*, and Philip Curtin's *The Atlantic Slave Trade: A Census*, Davis cited the emergence of cliometric studies of slavery and the "availability in published form of the evidence of slaves themselves" as major contributions to the development of an ever more complex historiographical picture of black bondage. In recent years, historians such as Norman Yetman, George Rawick, Julius Lester, and John Blassingame have turned to the oral-history testimony of ex-slaves in their quest for sources that would expand, and perhaps modify, the picture of slavery as drawn by the planters and travelers of the Old South.[1]

The acceptance of the former slaves' testimony as a viable research tool that could be put to use in reinterpreting the drivers' role has been a painfully slow historiographical development. Following the lead of Ulrich Phillips, who considered such evidence to be "generally unsafe" for use as a documentary resource, most early interpreters of

American Negro slavery neglected to consider available black
"reminiscences" and placed their faith in plantation records, diaries,
and travelers' tales rather than in the materials of recorded black oral
history.[2]

Persisting beyond the end of the Phillips era, this frustrating skepti-
cism has persuaded countless historians to shun the testimony of the
chattels in favor of that offered by other, lighter skinned contemporaries. Scholars of the stature of George Fredrickson, Christopher
Lasch, and Bennett Wall have viewed the documentary materials
available to them and have asserted that slavery was largely an "unre-
corded experience, except from the masters' point of view." Even
Kenneth Stampp became discouraged over the "hopelessly inadequate" nature of the materials left by the slaves and concluded that the
large number of oral accounts collected during the 1920s and 1930s by
the Federal Writers' Project (FWP) as well as by several independent
investigators came "too late to be of much value to historians."[3]

Certainly, not all of the narratives transcribed by post-Civil War
interviewers were likely to inspire confidence. As the number of
slave-era survivors dwindled, popular interest in the remaining wit-
nesses increased markedly. One former bondsman who took advantage of this newfound notoriety was Mark Thrash, who lived in a
one-story, unpainted log cabin in Chickamauga (Ga.) National Park.
After he had passed one-hundred years of age in 1920, Thrash became
a favorite subject of feature articles in Sunday newspaper supple-
ments. On April 23, 1943, he was featured in Robert Ripley's "Believe It or Not" column as the "oldest person, oldest voter and oldest
pensioner in the United States." When social scientist Roscoe Lewis
of Hampton Institute journeyed to the park to interview the ex-slave,
he found a willing subject awaiting him on the porch of the cabin. Not
only did Thrash recall the days of bondage, but he already had his
"story" printed up for sale to the numerous tourists who had made his
cabin something of a side attraction to the park's Civil War bat-
tlefields. One leaflet carried "Uncle Mark's" picture as well as what
Lewis termed "the printer's version of his life." It told of how the
elderly Afro-American never appeared without his white apron, feeling undressed when it was not securely tied around his waist. Supposedly, he had acquired this unusual habit in childhood when his
owner ordered all of the slaves to don white aprons so they "could be

distinguished from others' servants.'' When Lewis brought up the subject of the apron and asked if Thrash really wore it all the time, the old man laughed heartily and said, ''Well, son, I reckon so. Specially during visiting times. I reckon I got used to it by now.'' After having stayed some time at the Thrash cabin, listening to the ex-slave tell several groups of white tourists his life story in a ''mechanical, sing-song voice, as though it had been memorized,'' Lewis undoubtedly left the park with the realization that he knew the inner workings of the ''peculiar institution'' no better than when he had first arrived.[4]

Cases such as this must give scholars working with the narratives some degree of concern and should logically stimulate them to sharpen their powers of discrimination in the evaluation of primary source materials. Most assuredly, the care with which historians have handled the fruit of the early oral-history projects is evidence of the profession's collective desire to produce, as Kenneth Stampp has suggested, studies of black American slavery that would be ''based upon no assumptions whose validity cannot be thoroughly proved.'' But the conscientious researcher still must ask why the memoirs of famous, near famous, and infamous members of white antebellum society have been used in constructing modern accounts of that society to a far greater extent than has the testimony of the ex-slaves.[5]

Perhaps a brief commentary made by Howard Zinn, one of the ''New Left'' historians who called for a more humanistic approach to the writing of American history during the late 1960s, can aid in answering this perplexing question. In his collection of essays, *The Politics of History*, Zinn asserted that the creation of a history of slavery drawn from slave narratives was ''especially important.'' Available histories of the southern labor system seemed to be written either from the standpoint of the slaveholder or from that of the ''cool observer,'' the liberal historian who condemned slavery, but did so ''without the passion appropriate to a call for action.'' Rejecting both of these approaches, Zinn insisted that a slave-oriented history would fill out the historiographical picture in such a way as to ''pull us out of lethargy.''[6]

It is indeed likely that a type of lethargy has been largely responsible for the lack of credence given to the testimony of the former slaves. This slowness of the historical mind to grasp and to use the narratives may be a symptom of the same malady that caused Ulrich

Phillips to dismiss the ex-slave accounts by tersely noting that the
"lapse of decades" had "impaired inevitably the memories of men."
For those researchers influenced by either Phillips's approach to the
narrative accounts or by his societally approved approach to race
relations, it would certainly not be difficult to come to the conclusion
that among the "impaired" memories of humankind, the Negro's was
by far the most debilitated.[7]

Even with the modern-day lifting of most of this irrational, obscur-
ing fog of racism from Clio's shoulders, the question remains: How,
when, and to what extent and purpose should the ex-slave accounts be
used? C. Vann Woodward has noted that the FWP narratives "can be
mined for evidence to prove almost anything about slavery," which is
simply to say that they are to be treated with the same degree of
caution that one should use when examining the collected papers of an
important historical figure or when weighing the conflicting scraps of
information found in the correspondence and internal communication
of any major historically important organization. The choice of when
to use or when to disregard the narratives, as well as the care and
circumspection with which they are accepted as valid historical evidence, rests with the individual interpreter. Given this freedom of
interpretation as well as a freedom from the racial "mind-set" of an
earlier era, it would be instructive to know how the materials collected
by the interviewers of the 1920s and 1930s can be used to construct a
newer, more accurate interpretation of the life and times of the slave
supervisory elite.[8]

Initially, it must be recognized that many of the available narrative
accounts do, in fact, seem to describe brutal, sadistic, dehumanized
drivers. "Uncle Big Jake," the overseer on a plantation near West
Columbia, Texas, exhibited these unfavorable traits to such a degree
that he became a living representation of his owner's cruelest authoritarian tendencies. According to Sarah Ford's account in the
Texas FWP narratives, Jake was so mean that it was likely "de devil
done make him overseer down below long time ago." Wherever the
end point of Jake's spiritual existence, while in earthly employ, black
overseer and white master conspired to deprive the field slaves of any
"rights" or "privileges" that might disturb the status quo. On one
occasion, an elderly slave preacher named "Uncle Lew" made the
mistake of openly proclaiming his belief that "De Lawd make

everyone to come in unity and on de level, both white and black.'' The following morning Jake routed Uncle Lew from his cabin and ''put him out in de field with de rest.'' Here, it seems, master and overseer held certain of the same beliefs regarding proper plantation decorum. They also harbored the same hatreds. Sarah Ford recalled that both ''Massa Charles'' and Uncle Jake were hostile to her father '''cause he ain't so black, and he had spirit, 'cause he part Indian.'' In his hatred and through his actions—which eventually caused Sarah Ford's father to run away—the black overseer epitomized ''de bad part of Massa Charles.'' Indeed, by allowing Jake to ''whip de slaves so much'' the slaveholder created a situation in which the bondsmen were inescapably led to ''forgit de good part.''[9]

In addition to the slave foreman who closely matched his owner in cruelty, there is a type of driver described in the narratives who was apparently even *more* inhuman than the whites. ''De owners always tuk care of us, and when us got sick dey would git a doctor, an' ole Miss was all right,'' noted ex-slave Henry Cheatam, ''But dat oberseer was a debil.'' The ''nigger oberseer'' employed by Cheatam's owner attempted to prevent the slaves from attending worship services both in the ''white folks church''—a privilege granted to other slaves in the area—and on the plantation itself. He did so, according to Cheatam, ''so's us couldn't learn nothin'.'' The ex-slave described how he had witnessed the overseer beat his mother as well as his pregnant Aunt—''beat an' beat her for a half hour straight till de baby come out right dere.'' So bestial was this black authoritarian that, as a youth, Cheatam vowed to ''kill dat nigger iffen it was de las' thing I eber done.'' When asked why his former owner allowed the overseer to treat the slaves in this manner, Cheatam replied: ''A heap of times ole Miss didn't know nuthin' 'bout it, an' de slaves better not tell her, 'case dat oberseer whup 'em iffen he finds out dat dey done gone an' tol'. Yassuh, white folks, I'se seed some turrible things in my time.''[10]

Henry Cheatam's account of the bestial foreman is repeated many times in the narratives. Jenny Proctor, who experienced slavery in Alabama, had her back cut ''all to pieces'' by a cruel driver. When the master returned and asked the reason for this severe chastening, the driver explained that young Jenny had eaten an unauthorized biscuit while going about her duties as a house girl. Angered by his response, the slaveholder stormed at the driver: "She can't work now for a week, she pay for several biscuits in dat time." In the master's eyes, the driver had used poor judgment and an unnecessarily sadistic approach to plantation discipline. According to Jenny Proctor, the bondsmen "might a done very well if de ole driver hadn' been so mean. . . ."[11]

A further example of a slave foreman exceeding his master's requirements for stringent disciplinary measures is found in Ben Horry's FWP account. According to Horry, every year when the whites left their South Carolina plantation to summer in the mountains, they instructed Fraser, the black overseer: "Don't treat them anyway severe. Don't beat them. Don't maul them." But with the master gone, Fraser was, in Horry's words, "TURNED LOOSE." Disregarding his instructions, the overseer brutalized those of his fellow bondsmen who would not obey his every command. After refusing Fraser's sexual advances, Horry's mother was taken to the barn, strapped to a "pony," and given fifty lashes. Recalling this incident, Horry noted: "If Marse Josh been know 'bout that obersheer, the oberseer can't do 'em, but just the house servant get Marse Josh an' Miss Bess' ear." The ex-slave reasoned that Fraser was so exceedingly cruel because, unlike a white overseer, he did not have to worry about overstepping his master's regulations regarding slave punishment. "White overseer want to hold his job. . . . Nigger obersheer don't care too much. He know he going to stay on plantation anyhow."[12]

What is one to conclude from such accounts of driver brutality "above and beyond the call of duty"? A researcher could take these narratives at face value and forward the opinion that slavery so corroded the moral sensibilities of the leadership element within the slave community that they became the unfeeling sadists of legend. Certainly, it would be a simple task to attach any number and variety of psychologically derived theories of deviant personality behavior to such an historical interpretation.

More fruitful, however, would be an attempt to understand why such stories of driver cruelty were told to and recorded by the oral-history operatives of the depression era. When one considers that a majority of those who have interviewed the elderly ex-slaves were southern whites, a highly probable explanation gradually surfaces.

Afro-American interviewers were virtually excluded from the WPA collection projects in all of the southern states except Virginia, Louisiana, and Florida. Black participation was circumscribed by the fact that southern mores dictated the establishment of separate units for black and white workers, the cost of which was often prohibitive. State Writers' Project officials were extremely well attuned to local white public opinion in this regard. The director of the Alabama project called upon Tuskegee Institute faculty members to work, without pay, on the assembling of materials, but refused to hire a full-time black writer unless the WPA granted her additional funds. She felt that she could not replace any white employee with a Negro and would not hire a black researcher in a county that did not already have a white worker. In South Carolina, the state FWP director refused to hire blacks to conduct interviews even after white researchers experienced serious difficulty with the "gullah" dialect of the coastal regions. The director acted in this manner because she felt whites to be more "discriminating" in their reporting than Negroes would be if they were employed on the project.[13]

Even a cursory reading of the available narrative accounts and their scene-setting introductions reveals the patronizing, insensitive, condescending tone adopted by many of these "discriminating" interrogators. Few followed completely our modern-day "objective" interview procedures. More often the questions asked the ex-slaves were leading or insulting. After describing the "hiring out" process and noting that the $7 a month she had earned for "minding" a white family's children had always gone directly to her owners, Susan Hamlin of Charleston, was confronted with an abrupt and pointed series of questions from the FWP worker. "Don't you think that was fair?" the interviewer asked, "If you were fed and clothed by him, shouldn't he be paid for your work?" Responding in the only manner practicable at the time, the ex-slave replied, "course it been fair. I belong to him and he got to get something to take care of me." As C. Vann Woodward has noted, the white interviewer "regularly got what he asked for."[14]

Many southern whites involved in the collection of the oral accounts during the depression years were not yet liberated from the societal shackles of white supremacy doctrine and Jim Crow etiquette. They referred to the black respondents as "bucks," "darkeys," and "negresses."[15] Often their accounts of the former slaves' testimony were prefaced with remarks such as "Negroes make good house servants . . . ." or "Being a Negro, she naturally does not take life seriously . . . ."[16] On occasion, the whites became upset when the ex-slaves strayed from their expected roles. Arkansas writer Irene Robertson, who interviewed 286 former slaves for the FWP, described elderly Betty Krump as being "old, black, wealthy, and arrogant" because "she tells white people, the younger ones, to call her *Mrs.* Krump." Ms. Robertson was also surprised, upon first meeting ex-slave Molly Brown, to find that she had "unusually nice features for a woman of her race." In Lebanon, Ohio, FWP worker Miriam Logan discovered that neither of her respondents "had the kind of a story to tell that I was expecting to hear from what little I know about colored people." Disappointed in her attempt to have Celia Henderson and Samuel Sutton focus on "the songs and amusements of their youth," the interviewer was forced to admit "that most that they knew was work; did not sing or have a very good time."[17]

Confronted with interviewers such as these, it is not surprising that the ex-slaves were often less than completely candid in their responses. In the spring of 1937, eighty-seven-year-old Cornelia Andrews was questioned about her experiences under slavery and claimed that she had never been harshly beaten. Overhearing this denial of cruel treatment, Ms. Andrews's college-educated daughter came forward and ordered: "Open your shirt, mammy, and let the lady judge for herself." After her whip-scarred back was exposed, a true account of her beating by a white "pateroller" was immediately forthcoming. She then expanded her reminiscences to include stories of other slaves who had been brutalized.[18]

Although it is impossible to ascertain how many of the ex-slaves interviewed during the depression era were similarly reticent in exposing the more heinous cruelties inflicted by their former owners, some appreciation of the problem can be gained by making note of those accounts that describe informants who were either extremely hesitant or who adamantly refused to discuss "the dark side of slavery." When confronted by Afro-American interviewer Susie Byrd at a rest home in Petersburg, Virginia, in 1937, one such elderly respondent declared: "Lord chile, ef ya start me I kin tell ya a mess 'bout reb times, but I ain't tellin' white folks nuthin' 'cause I'm skeer'd to make enemies." As Charles S. Johnson's classic study of blacks in Macon County, Alabama, so graphically revealed, hard times in the agricultural South often meant an increased dependency upon "white friends" whose friendship was ever in danger of alienation through careless conversation.[19]

Martin Jackson, who had been born into slavery in Victoria County, Texas, in 1847 discussed this attitude with a FWP interviewer. He noted:

> Lots of old slaves closes the door before they tell the truth about their days of slavery. When the door is open, they tell how kind their masters was and how rosy it all was. You can't blame them for this, because they had plenty of early discipline, making them cautious about saying anything uncomplimentary about their masters.[20]

If the master class was to be largely absolved from initiating the recognized cruelties of slavery, any blame or condemnation could, and certainly did in many cases, fall upon two other immediately recognizable plantation authority symbols—the white overseer and the driver. Should the ex-slave narrator feel that an extensive critique of any white person would be unpolitic, the onus would then fall exclusively on the black foreman. To the extent that this interpretive maneuvering occurred, one can say that the narratives are tarnished—no more altered from a "factual" account than other forms of reminiscences and personal accounts, but nevertheless somewhat misleading. To the extent that historians can place the narratives in their historical context and can strive successfully to understand the social relationship that existed between interviewer and respondent, such inaccuracies can be mitigated.

Given the social factors involved in the interviewing situation, it is likely that the brutal drivers described in the narratives were neither as numerous, as depraved, or as motivated by perverse and selfish desires as an uncritical reader of the ex-slave accounts might be led to believe. Likewise, the southern slaveholders may need to be credited with a much larger share of the blame for the cruelties of slavery. They were guilty of more than simply employing drivers "more wicked than themselves." If the interviews with former slaves reveal exam-

ples of purposeful driver brutality, they also describe slave foremen
who, like the uncle of elderly Alabaman Patsy Larkin, gave whippings on the orders of his owner because "he could not help himself."
If some drivers carried out their unpleasant disciplinary duties with an
overabundance of vigor, others conspired against the very workings
of the chattel labor system.[21]

The narratives of the 1920s and 1930s describe black foremen who
were anything but unfeeling, pliant tools of the master class. Several
of the drivers exhibited this tendency by carrying through with the
form, but not the intent of their master's orders. Instructed to lash an
errant bondsman, Virginia driver Gabe—who "didn't like dat whippin' bus'ness"—would whip a wooden barn post while the intended
victim groaned and shrieked in mock agony. The subterfuge was so
well staged that on one occasion, after the supposedly chastened
bondsman "come runnin' out screamin' wid berry wine rubbed all
over his back," the master warned Gabe that if he didn't stop beating
the slaves so hard "he gonna git a lashin' hisself."[22]

Other drivers provided their black brothers with material and even
educational benefits. Ex-slave Thomas Goodwater told of a driver
who often killed cows and then allowed the slaves to skin them and
distribute the meat. Apparently neither the driver's master nor the
white plantation overseer ever uncovered this chicanery or figured out
the code by which the driver informed the other slaves of the availability of fresh beef. A Richmond County, Georgia, respondent asserted
that his former black overseer was the channel through which supplementary food could be obtained. Whenever the slaves felt their
rations to be inadequate they would tell the overseer and "he seed to it
that us got plenty." Eighty-seven-year-old Albert Carolina described
a black driver who whipped the slaves for infractions of plantation
rules, but nevertheless taught some of his fellow laborers to read.[23]

Field hands were appreciative of these dangerous-to-bestow favors
tendered by the "plantation elite." As ex-Tennessee bondsman Billy
Stamper noted, "Cullud folks don' min' bein' bossed by er cullud
man if he's smart an' good to 'em." In describing their feelings
toward their former overseers, the ex-slave narrators sometimes
characterized the black foremen in terms that are incompatible with
the bestial-driver stereotype. Richard Jones, who told an FWP interviewer of his introduction to field labor at the age of seventeen, noted

that the driver on his master's plantation "showed us how to do everything right" and apparently never overworked his charges. In describing the supervisory duties of "Uncle July Gist," Jones frankly asserted: "We liked him." In like manner, even though Charles Dortch's father Reuben, was a "boss" who never labored in the field, was never mistreated by the white overseer, and was a chattel who "seemed to have been more of a pet than a slave," there was no unfriendliness shown him by those more harshly treated. He never experienced "any trouble with the other slaves any more than he had with the white folks." According to his son, Dortch was "well liked."[24]

If some drivers possessed enough humanity to be favorably remembered some seventy years after slavery's demise, others were admired and even held in high esteem by the elderly ex-slaves. Charlie Snipes, who was responsible for pacing the hands on one southern plantation, was referred to by a Virginia narrator as the "bigges' cut-up in de quarters." His "prancin' an' singin' " was so infectious that sometimes the entire gang would take up the song—their "feet de de diddlin' an' steppin' high an' choppin' right in chune." Snipes's influence over the hands angered their white overseer and caused him to "yell an' cuss," but he couldn't "stop all dem slaves from feelin' good."[25]

David Goodman Gullins's father, black foreman John Mappin, was also something of a plantation celebrity. Described by his son as being "a good man" who "backed my mother in her efforts to bring us up right," Mappin came to be known as "Gullins" after his fellow slaves identified him with a circus character who had passed through the area. The foreman "was so much like the clown in his ways and sayings, that afterwards everyone started calling him Gullins." Apparently proud of his nickname, David's father retained it as his legally registered surname after the Civil War.[26]

Plantation life in general was not, of course, a very comical experience for the field hands or for the black foremen. Slave supervisory personnel often worked as hard as the laborers they directed. The South Carolina FWP narratives, for example, contain the account of elderly Louisa Davis whose father was foreman on master Jim Lemon's Little River plantation. Although he was "much trusted" by his owner, Louisa's "pappy" plowed and worked "just de same,

. . . maybe harder" than he had before winning his supervisory position. In like manner, foreman Elbert Cody's lot was not an easy one. Before he could begin his daily duties as plow gang foreman, he was obliged to assume the role of "feeder" by arising at least two hours before sunrise to help feed the "large number of horses and more than two hundred head of cattle" that had to be turned into the pastures or driven to the fields before the start of the regular working day. Where they experienced the long and arduous working day of the "common" slaves, the drivers were better able to resist the brutalizing tendencies of their position and to avoid becoming sadistically inclined "puppets" of the planter class.[27]

Some black supervisors were rewarded for their hard work. The narratives describe individual drivers who claimed they were "treated with every kindness" during slavery, were given better than average housing, were taught to "read and write and figger," and were allowed greater freedom of movement than the field hands.[28] Slave foremen who possessed a fair number of such privileges were often related to their owners by ties of kinship. The FWP interviewer of Charles Dortch noted that the ex-slave's grandfather, on his father's side, was either Dortch's first master or "someone closely connected with his master." His last master under slavery was the father of Charles' half-sister. Such relationships may account for Reuben Dortch's "boss" status as well as for the "good treatment" accorded the Dortch family during the days of slavery.[29]

Other drivers, less closely related to their owners, suffered from many of the same deprivations that constantly plagued the "less-favored" field hands. Relatively few masters believed that literacy would improve the managerial abilities of the black supervisory personnel. Consequently, drivers were seldom allowed access to the educational skills that could have transformed them into a true "slave elite." Those drivers who were determined to learn the art of reading and writing often had to gain their education through subterfuge, facing the same risks of discovery as ordinary slaves. Head man Caesar Oliver was said to have been a "smart slave" whose owner gave him the privilege of hiring himself out to do work as a stevedore. Nevertheless, Oliver was only occasionally able to find someone to "teach him 'A-B-C.' " His education was gained "only by night—And that couldn't be known."[30]

When slave foremen worked under the directorship of a white overseer, there was an even more remote possibility of gaining the type of information from the planters to which an "elite" should seemingly be privy. Joseph Higgerson, an ex-slave from Missouri, told of the division of labor supervision on the antebellum agricultural units with which he was familiar. The slave drivers reported to the overseer, who then carried this information on the progress of the crops and the productivity of the field hands to the plantation owner. Drivers "didn't ever get to go to the big house where the planter lived . . . the ovahseah reported to the Boss."[31]

Such a narrowed sphere of personal contact with the top decision-making elements of the plantation world could lead to a situation similar to the one that existed on a Clarke County, Mississippi, estate. There the resident driver "never was allowed to think up nothing for the slaves to do, but jest was told to make them work hard at what the master and his boys told them to do . . . he been taught he didn't know how to think, so he didn't try." If this particular foreman's mental processes were apparently somewhat stunted by the deprivations of the slave experience, he can at least be acquitted of the charge that drivers won the right to wide-ranging power and authority over their fellow slaves by working hand-in-glove with their owners.[32]

The ex-slave narratives of the 1920s and 1930s speak both of the physical and of the psychological distance that separated the "supervisory elite" from their white overlords. Several of the interviews describe how tellingly the black supervisor's humanity was tested by the adversities of plantation slavery. In one such account, "Aunt Janie" told of her father's supervisory duties on the estate of a "mean Massa" whose desire to speed up the field work was apparently much greater than his driver's desire to force the hands into an unwilling submission. Even though her father "didn' want ter drive de folks," the slaveholder "whip him an' make him." Greatly distressed over the role he was forced to play, the driver fell victim to the emotional strain that had resulted from this uneasy master-driver relationship. In recounting her life on the plantation, "Aunt Janie" recalled that her father would come home at the close of a work day, put his whip on the floor, and sit down in a chair and moan: "Nobody likes de driver." He then cried "till de tears drap in de fireplace" and was unable to "feel good ergain" until Janie's mother had fixed him some hoecake.

Such were the social and psychological pressures resulting from the demands of slave control that even Georgia ex-slave Ellen Claibourn's freedman grandfather, who had been "trusty and hon'able" as a slave, was moved to resign his first overseership after only one year because "he didn't wanter lose his religion trying to make slaves work."[33]

Given the stringent requirements of the job and the difficulty the driver experienced in attempting to meet the planter's demands while maintaining his own moral nature intact, it is understandable that the black foreman, like other bondsmen throughout the history of American Negro slavery, would occasionally react violently to the whites' attempts to transform him into a soul-less, dehumanized laborer. The slave narratives speak of this reaction and portray a foreman-overseer, foreman-master set of relationships that was often fraught with tension. In one of the accounts gathered in Virginia during the depression, ex-slave Nancy Williams recalled how her father had won a job as foreman because he could not tolerate the rule of his overseer. One day after the white man had cursed him for refusing to perform a task he deemed to be unsuited to his skills, the slave whipped out a knife and would have attacked his supervisor had it not been for the restraining arms of the other field hands. After hearing an account of the incident, the plantation owner dismissed the overseer and told Henrietta's father to "jes' take de plantation an' gwan run it." Such a man would not easily be transformed into a spineless, unwitting accomplice in the brutalization of his fellow blacks.[34]

Former bondsman Jefferson Franklin Henry also recounted a remarkable story of a "psychologically liberated" slave who was given a supervisory post following the firing of his white overseer. Black foreman Robert Scott's duties did not include the flogging of the other slaves because "Marse Robert done his own whippin'," but he did react decisively to the cruelties of such "correction." When master Robert Trammel attempted to whip Scott's wife, the foreman physically interposed himself between the two. Outraged at this display of "impudence," Trammel ran to get a gun from the "Big House." By the time the slaveholder returned to the scene of the attempted whipping, Scott had fled the plantation—not to reappear for several days. After he returned, on his own terms, "Marse Robert was so glad to git him back he never said a word to him 'bout leavin'."[35]

When one studies the lives of such slaves in the narrative accounts collected by the early oral-history projects of the 1920s and 1930s, it is not difficult to come to the conclusion that with the preservation of these records, modern-day researchers have indeed been granted a glimpse of slavery on the ex-slaves' "own terms." The distortions of time, age, interviewer predisposition, and editorial caprice, must, of course, be carefully weighed in determining the manner in which the materials may be best used by historians. But it also must be recognized that after viewing the driver from the perspective of the narratives, it is scarcely possible to maintain that the black supervisory personnel composed a universally brutal, perversely spoiled elite who readily subordinated the interests of fellow slaves to the "greater goal" of winning and maintaining favor with the whites. To have done so under the conditions to which they were subjected during slavery would have constituted a form of psychological and spiritual suicide, wholly incompatible with those narrative accounts that describe the drivers as very human men serving as extremely reluctant "tools" of the slaveholders.

THE BLACK AUTOBIOGRAPHIES

> This is no fiction, no exaggeration. If I have failed in anything, it has been in presenting to the reader too prominently the bright side of the picture.
>
> *Solomon Northup*

The transcribed interviews with former slaves that were collected during the 1920s and 1930s comprise a modern-day phase of an important literary tradition that extends back to the eighteenth century. The greatest vogue of this genre occurred during the era of the abolitionist crusade with the publication of several thousand autobiographical and semiautobiographical accounts of bondage written or narrated by blacks who had once been slaves. During the three decades of sectional controversy that preceded the Civil War, ex-slaves not only joined in the struggle for freedom, but also supplied the abolitionists with an extremely potent weapon in the form of their personal testimonies of "life in thralldom." Constituting the chief form of historical literature penned by Afro-Americans before the twentieth century, the black autobiographies remain invaluable for the light they shed on the various components of the southern plantation system.[1]

Scholars who have adjudged the autobiographies to be suitable for historical use have found that these controversial materials possess several important qualities that, after the application of appropriate tests for distortion and bias, eminently qualify them for use in the process of constructing a newer, more accurate picture of antebellum plantation life. Echoing the sentiments of Frederick Douglass, historians have gradually come to a full realization that planters and travelers could not "see things in the same light" as the chattels because, as "outsiders," they were incapable of viewing the world "from the same point from which the slave does." Armed with a healthy respect for this premise, as well as with a new perspective gained from the events of recent American social history, more and more students of plantation slavery have found themselves in agreement with ex-slave John Little, who told his antebellum interviewer: " 'Tisn't he who has stood and looked on, that can tell you what slavery is,—'tis he who has endured."[2]

Some supporters of the autobiographies have found the materials collected by the oral-history projects of the 1920s and 1930s to be lacking in comparison to the earlier black records. Margaret Jackson, for example, has studied both the testimony of black fugitives and the twentieth-century reminiscences contained in collections such as Benjamin Botkin's *Lay My Burden Down* and has concluded that the former group possessed "a higher degree of reliability." Unlike the more recent volumes she characterized as being tainted with "a promiscuous intermingling" of favorable and unfavorable views of the slave system, the antebellum accounts were not affected by the distortion of passing decades or the sheltering influence of youthfulness under slavery. Instead, the black autobiographies were in substantial agreement—and left "no room to doubt"—that the "lot of the Negro slave was a hard one."[3]

Other researchers have found the two black narrative sources to be complimentary. Although black women penned less than 12 percent of the antebellum accounts, about half of the depression era testimony was collected from female respondents. Even though the autobiographies contain considerably more information about slavery in the upper than in the lower South, the oral histories make up for this imbalance. If the reminiscences of the elderly slaves offer the advantage of a certain rural "earthiness," the nineteenth-century narratives give the reader a more lengthy and in-depth portrait of slave life. Certainly, the two forms of slave testimony, when combined, offer the reader a striking display of the variety of human personality types extant within the slave community.[4]

Although it would be pleasing to say that with the recognition of these black narratives historians have finally discovered the elusive documentary thread that will lead to a thorough and fully accurate characterization of the slave driver, such a statement would be both presumptuous and foolhardy given the literary history of the narratives themselves. Indeed, much of the antebellum controversy over the authenticity of the autobiographies was brought about by two "questionable" publications that claimed to describe the lives of drivers.

The first of these accounts, Charles Ball's *Slavery in the United States*, was the first book-length slave narrative published by the abolitionists. Following its appearance in 1836, skeptics became concerned that neither Ball nor a "Mr. Fisher" to whom the fugitive slave had allegedly dictated his story readily appeared in public to answer questions relating to the dramatic events described in the text. Not even the claim of necessary caution due to Ball's fugitive status could quiet murmurings that more than the true names of the families who had owned him had been fictionalized. Certainly, the situation was not improved by the discovery that another account published in 1836, *The Slave; or, Memoirs of Archy Moore*, was actually a work of fiction produced by white historian Richard Hildreth.[5]

Ball's account described the life of a young bondsman who was encouraged to believe that upon good behavior he would eventually rise to become personal waiter and then overseer for his owner. Even though these important posts appeared to the youth as "the highest points of honour and greatness in the whole world," he soon discovered how decisively a chattel's hopes could be frustrated by the death of "Old Master." Carried by the vicissitudes of estate division and sale from his Maryland birthplace to a harsher existence on the rice and cotton plantations of South Carolina and Georgia, Ball did eventually become foreman of a labor gang, but found the position to be both physically draining and psychologically disturbing. To meet the stringent requirements of his bedridden master, Ball was compelled to labor diligently and to cause his fellow slaves to "work hard too." Not infrequently he found it necessary to punish one of the field hands. At first, the black foreman felt "much repugnance" toward this aspect of his assigned duties, but with practice the whippings became "more familiar and less offensive." Although he hoped he would never become so hardened as to strip his charges naked before disciplining them or force the slaves to work without a sufficient allowance of food, Ball feared that "a few years of perseverance and experience" in the duties of the plantation foreman would turn him into "as inveterate a negro-driver as any in Georgia." In a sense "rescued" from this fate by an unexpected and arbitrary demotion to field hand status, Ball made up his mind to flee the Georgia cotton country even if his life "should be the forfeiture of the attempt." Although he eventually gained his freedom by outwitting and outrunning southern jailers and slave catchers, the ex-driver was forced to begin his new life in Pennsylvania without the companionship and support of his wife and children. His family remained in bondage somewhere in the lower South.[6]

Even though *Slavery in the United States* was less defamatory in its criticism of antebellum plantation life than were many later book-length accounts, Ball's narrative contained more than enough criticism of the plantation regime to anger countless southern sympathizers. If Ball could say, in all fairness, that the slaveholders were "neither more nor less than men, some of whom are good, and very many are bad," he was also willing to describe exactly how bad the worst of the whites could be. Ball thought that one white overseer with whom he had come into contact on a South Carolina cotton plantation was "a despot, more absolute, and more cruel than were any of those we read of in the Bible, who so grievously oppressed the children of Israel." To his Georgia master's shrewish wife, the former driver attributed a temper "as bad as that of a speckled viper, . . . her language, when she was enraged, was a mere vocabulary of profanity and virulence." Even this disagreeable woman's husband, whom Ball described as the best master he had served under during his years in bondage, was damned for neglecting to provide him with any clothing during a three-year period "except an old great coat, and a pair of boots."[7]

Beset by intense southern disagreement over this characterization of planter "gentility" and harmed by the stir over Hildreth's fictionalized biography, Ball's account was further discredited by the appearance of the American Anti-Slavery Society's *Narrative of James Williams. An American Slave, Who Was for Several Years a Driver on a Cotton Plantation in Alabama.* Williams was ostensibly a fugitive who had experienced the hardships of bondage in both the upper and lower South. His story was considered so great a contribution to the cause of freedom that it was committed to writing by poet John Greenleaf Whittier and published by the American Anti-Slavery Society (AASS) in 1838. Shortly thereafter, the tale began to attract considerable attention in those parts of the South where Williams claimed he had labored as a slave. In response to an *Alabama Beacon* article that asserted no such planter or plantation as Williams had mentioned was to be found anywhere in the state, the abolitionists launched an investigation of the narrative. After assembling considerable evidence from southern sources supportive of the *Beacon*'s charges, the Executive Committee of the New York branch of the AASS directed that the sale of the book be discontinued. Obviously embarrassed over the whole affair, ghostwriter Whittier told readers of the *Emancipator* that while the abolitionists were "still disposed to give credit in the main" to Williams's account, the cause of antislavery needed and would accept no "support of a doubtful character."[8]

It is unfortunate that Williams was not available for questioning during this heated controversy. Long before the furor erupted, he had been sent to England to guard against possible capture as a fugitive slave. Little is known about his overseas life. Had Williams been more willing or more able to defend the narrative, later historians might have been inclined to hazard the use of his account in reconstructing the life and times of the slave driver. As matters developed, however, students of black autobiography still consider the narrative to be "an outright fraud" and Williams to have been a free Negro "who culled stories from neighbors and invented others for a little ready cash."[9]

If Williams's story—which presented a graphic picture of a man who felt so "subdued and wretched" in the driver's office that he termed his existence "an earthly hell"—has been generally discredited, the account given by Ball has recently been given new life. After comparing the narrative with antebellum travel accounts, manuscript census returns, and histories of South Carolina, John Blassingame concluded that the work "may have been more reliable than the antebellum critics were willing to concede. This process of reevaluation is the same one that has moved historians to "rethink" the acceptability of other narratives as viable documentary sources germane to the writing of Afro-American history.[10]

Like the black testimony of the depression years, this "new" biographical "tool" of the historians is composed, in part, of accounts of bondage that describe tragic instances of driver-instigated cruelty. The narrative of Thomas H. Jones told how a "brutal" North

Carolina driver named Abraham wrenched the unwilling young Jones from his mother and acted as an unnecessarily "cruel guide" during the nine-year-old slave's journey to a new home on a distant plantation.[11] Both Monroe F. Jamison and William Grimes recalled members of the supervisory elite who used their positions to "get even" with fellow slaves they disliked.[12] Lewis Clarke described a Kentucky driver who whipped his own wife to death for stealing a pig. Having experienced the "overlordship" of such men, Clarke told the readers of his narrative that the driver was usually the "hardest-hearted and most unprincipled" slave on the plantation.[13]

On the other hand, the black autobiographies also describe drivers who were eminently humane in their dealings with other bondsmen. Fugitive slave Christopher Nichols, who was living in St. Catherines, Canada West, when his account was recorded by Benjamin Drew in 1855, recalled a foreman whose consideration for the weakened physical condition of a female slave was cancelled out only by his master's determined insistence that the sick woman be compelled to complete her assigned work. Edward Hicks of Chatham told Drew of an incident in which a head man's unwillingness to help the overseer catch and punish an unruly young field hand resulted in the black supervisor being stripped and flogged in front of his gang. Sam Aleckson's account of slavery on the Pine Top plantation near Charleston included a striking portrait of "Daddy Joe," a driver who delighted in relating black folktales to his children and in making his "sonorous" hymn-singing voice heard throughout the quarters. It is probable that those slaves who were fortunate enough to labor under drivers of this stamp would agree with former bondsman William Carney that "times were somewhat better" on plantations that had switched from white overseer to black foreman rule.[14]

Even though historians are faced with two apparently contradictory types of autobiographical testimony, it is not necessary for them to throw up their hands and conclude, simplistically, that some drivers were "good" and some were "bad." To do so would not only be a reversion to the romantic stereotyping of antebellum fiction, but would also give evidence of a gross misunderstanding of human personality. All men seem to have both good and bad "sides." All must face the very real social pressure of having their personal quotient of amiability interpreted variously by each individual with whom they come into daily contact. Moreover, it must be recognized that there were certain distinct forces operating upon the narrators of the antebellum accounts that may help to explain the seeming dichotomy between the two types of testimony.

Narrators such as Thomas Jones who described "brutal" drivers encountered during the days of their youth might have interpreted "brutality" in a much different manner had the particular incident described occurred later in life. In Jones's case, what the ex-slave remembered of his "cruel guide" may have been so inextricably tied to the fact of his separation from his mother as to be of little use in obtaining a wholly accurate characterization of driver Abraham. The stories of Jamison and Grimes that told of black foremen who were unfair to slaves with whom they were "on the outs" could just as easily be interpreted as instances of parents trying to protect their offspring against the harsher aspects of the plantation system. Even Lewis Clarke's account of driver cruelty can be seen in a different light when certain modifying phrases contained in his narrative are taken into consideration. The Kentucky driver did not simply take it upon himself to become both judge and jury in the matter of his wife's thievery. The account states that he was *"compelled"* to whip her "so severely that she never recovered." Likewise, just before Clarke penned his statement about the selection of unprincipled slaves as foremen, he noted that a black plantation supervisor had to be "very strict and severe, or else he will be turned out." The element of compulsion must be recognized before judgment is passed on the driver.[15]

Although it is possible that such factors, as well as the more commonly recognized one of abolitionist influence over the published version of the slaves' account, may have moved narrators to portray certain drivers in an unnecessarily unfavorable light, other forces undoubtedly compelled writers of black autobiography to speak of their former drivers in overly roseate terms. The mere fact that a fairly large percentage of those slaves whose stories of bondage were preserved had at one time actually occupied the position of head man, foreman, driver, or overseer, should be enough reason to treat the driver-narrators' words with a good deal of circumspection. Few people care to expose themselves before a nationwide reading audience as a brutalizer of their fellow man because, by doing so, they become separated from the very human community they seek to address. Moreover, it is doubtful that the black narrators would have generated much sympathetic support for the cause of abolition had the accounts characterized the fugitives as possessing personality flaws usually found only among escaped "prisoners" of a different type.

Although occasionally flawed and variously skewed—as are the other interpretive sources pertinent to the study of antebellum plantation life—the black autobiographies do possess the advantage of providing a contemporary, firsthand account of what it was like to be a slave. Not only are the narratives useful in recapturing the essence of the physical and cultural characteristics of the slave community, but they also become especially important to any examination of the slave's personality development. There is generally so much of what John Blassingame has termed "ego involvement" in the autobiographies that they are invaluable for the study of black self-concepts. Since these works focus on the mental life of the authors, describing their fears, joys, pains, dreams, insecurities, and frustrations, they provide modern scholars with numerous insights into both the varieties of black personality and the nature of interpersonal relations during slavery. By examining the accounts left us by antebellum slave drivers, it is hoped that some additional insights may be gained into the nature of the driver's office, the pressures operating upon him, and the degree to which he circumvented those pressures and preserved his humanity intact.[16]

The accounts left by the driver-narrators give a graphic description of the punishments dealt out by the supervisory elite, but even more so than in the case of the wife-whipping driver in Lewis Clarke's narrative, they leave the reader with the distinct impression that such acts brought the black foremen little "pride of place," were meted out only after a good deal of pressure had been applied by their owners, and were thus likely to be performed with the least amount of force acceptable to the slaveholder.

Henry Bibb told of how he was purchased by a Louisiana master because the cotton planter believed him to be "competent to do the same business" as had previously been performed by a white overseer. Encouraging Bibb to enter enthusiastically into his first whipping of a misbehaving house servant, the slaveholder promised him an easy existence if he would "do it up right." The slave remonstrated

3. **Henry Bibb**. Originally purchased to perform the duties of an overseer, Henry Bibb defends his family from a wolf pack during their attempted escape from bondage. From Henry Bibb, *Narrative of the Life and Adventures of Henry Bibb, An American Slave* (Westport, Conn.: Negro Universities Press, 1969 [New York: privately published, 1849]).

that he had never done such a thing and hoped he would not be compelled to whip the young woman. Angered by this reluctance, the planter said that if Bibb "knew not how to flog a slave, he would set me an example by which I might be governed." Bibb then stood by and watched his master lay some 200 stripes on the girl's back. Upon the completion of the flogging, Bibb was forced to wash the woman's back with salt brine. This whole scene was so revolting to the black overseer's feelings that he could "not refrain from shedding tears" over the cruelty in which he had just participated.[17]

William Wells Brown was also a reluctant performer of the tasks assigned to the slave elite. Hired out to speculator and "soul-driver" James Walker, he was made superintendent of the gangs of slaves being taken to the New Orleans market. During the steamer journey from St. Louis down the Mississippi, it was the superintendent's duty to prepare the older slaves for sale by shaving off their whiskers and plucking out or blackening grey hairs. After their arrival at the New Orleans slave pen, Brown was responsible for setting his charges to dancing and singing to make them appear "cheerful and happy" for their prospective buyers. In his autobiography, Brown lamented that he often had been compelled to "set them to dancing when their cheeks were wet with tears." As for his service with Walker, the slave wrote: "I had served him one year, and it was the longest year I ever lived." Upon the expiration of his term of hire, he was sent home to his owner "glad enough to leave the service of one who was tearing the husband from the wife, the child from the mother, and the sister from the brother."[18]

Brown and several other driver-narrators described the men for whom they labored in terms incompatible with any historical interpretation that portrays the black supervisors as willing and companionable "cohorts in crime." Speculator James Walker was described by Brown as being "tall, lean, and lank, with high cheek-bones, face much pitted with the small-pox, gray eyes with red eyebrows, and sandy whiskers." Certainly, "a more repulsive-looking person" could scarcely be found in a "community of bad-looking men" than this slave trader whose very countenance seemed to betray his innermost personality. In like manner, Henry Bibb considered Louisiana cotton planter and Baptist deacon Francis Whitfield to be "one of the basest hypocrites that I ever saw." According to the slave, the deacon looked like a saint, talked like the best of slaveholding Christians, but "acted at home like the devil." Other black foremen referred to their owners as "cowards," "unconscionable sinners," "hasty and high-tempered," "mean," "sneaky-looking," and "disagreeable."[19]

Undoubtedly, many such uncomplimentary comments were elic-ited by the narrators' unfavorable memories of the treatment they received at the hands of the whites. In his account of black bondage in Missouri, foreman Henry Clay Bruce not only claimed a commonal-ity of existence with the field hands, but also noted that the had received even more "scolding" from his master than the others because he was "held responsible for everything." Head man Isaac Williams was even more unfortunate in his choice of masters. Even though he "tried hard" to avoid getting into trouble, it seemed that at least once a year his owner would "get up with me for a whipping in some way." On one occasion, as punishment for stealing corn to make bread for the plantation Christmas celebration, Williams was tied to a tree, lashed with a carriage whip until the slaveholder "wore the lash off," and then bludgeoned so badly that he was incapacitated for three weeks. North Carolina foreman Gilbert Dickey experienced a similar chastisement for his initial refusal to mend a pair of shoes for his mistress. After the woman "flew into a passion" over his inso-lence, Dickey repaired the shoes, but later received "thirty blows" from her husband. He was also threatened with having his throat slit for behaving in this unacceptable manner. Such was the nature of the "favors" tendered to the "slave elite"![20]

It is not surprising to find that when treated in this manner, the drivers often rebelled—and in so doing evidenced the continued possession of an important degree of "control" over their own lives. Outraged at his whipping, Dickey told the whites that he had "no place appointed to die or to be buried" and "cared not when it happened." Thus, he vowed never to be whipped again and promised death to the first man who attempted to lay the lash on his back. Isaac Williams was similarly enraged by his brutal treatment and, when he had the opportunity, fought back against his tormentors. After being falsely accused of illegally slaughtering some of the plantation live-stock, the head man resisted his master's attempts to bind him, battled the slaves who were sent to subdue him, broke down the door of his smoke house "prison," and fled to the woods. Like Dickey, Wil-

liams made good his "power play" and returned to the plantation nine
days later with the guarantee that he would not be punished for his
brash behavior.[21]

Other driver-narrators rebelled against the slave system and sought
to win a more complete freedom by fleeing the South completely. The
publication of the narratives of fugitive drivers attests to the fact that
black foremen did not wait patiently for the boon of private manumission or government-sponsored emancipation to be offered them. The
autobiographical accounts of fugitive drivers tell of the compelling
forces that moved black supervisors to exchange their positions as
members of the "slave elite" for that of "common freedman."

A few drivers seem to have been taken in by self-pride or planter
rhetoric and sought to flee from the plantation South only after they
had come to the realization that any substantive "privileges" of office
were, in actuality, almost wholly nonexistent. One such slave, Lewis
Jones, arrived at this stage of awareness after years of faithful service
as foreman on a farm owned by a drunken master. After slaveholder
Thomas Sydan's death, his crippled wife was Jones's special charge.
In addition to his regular supervisory duties, the foreman was Nancy
Sydan's "main support"—making sure that she did not fall when
walking with the aid of crutches, lifting her into the seat of the
carriage, and even carrying her to the sick room when necessary.
Since it was well known throughout the neighborhood that Jones had
been "the making of the family," it is understandable that the loyal
slave would hope to be manumitted upon his mistress's death. When
the foreman went to his young masters to ask about the possibility of
gaining his freedom, he was greatly disappointed. The crippled
woman's sons only laughed at him and said that no such thought had
entered their minds. Finding that despite his lifelong service to the
Sydans he "hadn't anything to hope for from them," Jones and his
wife escaped to the North.[22]

Other drivers fled the plantation South after experiencing unexpected cruelties of a more physical nature. Even though Kentucky
foreman Joseph Sanford was "respected by everybody—could be
trusted, no matter what," he found that his master's decision to place
a white overseer in charge of the hands could lead to a significant
diminution of that respect. Found to be in violation of the new
overseer's rule about the slaves making certain that things were

"correct on the place" before going off to attend Sunday church services, the black foreman was whipped for the first time in twenty years. To Sanford, the actual beating did not hurt as much as "the scandal of it." He felt the flogging to be an "unsufferable" act of disrespect for such an old and faithful servant. His pride already in tatters, Sanford fled across the Ohio River to freedom when his master deprived the field hands of an accustomed holiday and promised more whippings if the pace of work did not pick up rapidly.[23]

Anticipated punishment of a different sort was the motivating factor behind the escape of black overseer Archer Alexander from his Louisiana "home" in early 1863. Influenced by "religious motives" to be so faithful and trustworthy that he "couldn't do no other than what was right," Alexander was nevertheless charged with aiding the Union war cause. It seems that he had learned that a party of Confederate sympathizers had partially sawed through the timbers of a bridge over which several companies of northern troops were soon to pass. Fearing for the lives of the Union soldiers, the black overseer crept away from the plantation one night and informed a local "Union man" of the impending disaster. This intelligence was conveyed to the approaching troops in time to have the bridge repaired. When charged with being an informer, Alexander was confined to his cabin lest he be shot by the outraged citizenry of the neighborhood. According to William G. Eliot, the minister to whom the slave later dictated his story, Alexander "saw plainly what was coming." Aware of his predicament, he asked "the good lord what this pore forsaken nigger should do" and received the answer: "Go for your freedom, ef you dies for it!" After numerous trials, the black overseer escaped from his tormenters, experienced the "manliness of freedom," and was "happy in it." As Eliot noted, the case of Archer Alexander proved that over even the "best" of slaves "the sword of uncertainty always hung, suspended by an invisible hair."[24]

Several drivers who later published accounts of their lives needed no such planter-initiated goads to action. Although they, too, experienced many of the pressures of the slave experience, their efforts to relieve those pressures were spurred on more by internal resources than by external stimuli. Solomon Northup, a free black man from New York who was kidnapped and sold into slavery in 1841, described such personal strengths in his narrative. From his varied experiences as free citizen, field hand, and driver, Northup came to the conclusion that although writers of fiction might portray slaves as being blissfully ignorant of their true state of existence, those who had learned the "secret thoughts" of the bondsmen knew that "ninety-nine out of every hundred are intelligent enough to understand their situation, and to cherish in their bosoms the love of freedom." As for himself, the ex-driver noted that there was "not a day" during his twelve years of enforced servitude in which he did not consider "the prospect of escape."[25]

Self-examination was the key to Peter Still's freedom from both the mental and the physical chains of bondage. At the age of twenty-one, the Alabama bondsman began to think seriously of "establishing a character for life." Having witnessed the "moral degradation" that prevailed among some of his fellows and having heard the "vulgar and blasphemous oath, the obscene jest, and the harsh tone of angry passion" that came from the lips of supposed white gentlemen, Still sought to "shun the insidious advances of every vice." Along with this commitment to noble purposes came an ardent desire for freedom. In reviewing the events of his life, he had discovered a good deal of past moral failings, but had found nothing "in feeling, thought, or act" that would prove him unfit for the possession of liberty. Although the "curse of slavery" had embittered his heart, the black foreman resolved, "with every power of his soul aroused," to "struggle to escape it" and to win back his "human birthright." He did this through self-purchase after spending some forty-nine years in slavery.[26]

Head man J.W. Loguen, known as "Jarm" while a slave in Tennessee, was also successful in preserving his personal integrity intact until he had accumulated the monetary wherewithal to make an escape feasible. While continuing to participate in the "ceremony of servile bows and counterfeit smiles" that had endeared him to his owners, Jarm planned for his freedom by quizzing a young white acquaintance about the distance from Tennessee to Illinois, the physical obstacles to be encountered during such a journey, and the condition of the Afro-American population in the free states. In his capacity as head man, Jarm was instrumental in putting the farm in "better order than it had ever been." Although Jarm's owner considered his labors to be evidence of trustworthiness and loyalty, the slave saw his work on the

4. **Solomon Northup**. Unwilling to inflict further punishment, driver Solomon Northup throws down his whip and is threatened with a severe flogging by the outraged slaveholder. From Solomon Northup, *Twelve Years a Slave: Narrative of Solomon Northrup* (New York: Dover Publications, Inc., 1970 [Buffalo: Derby, Orton and Mulligan, 1853]).

5. **Peter Still**. Following his "self-purchase," foreman Peter Still bids farewell to his wife, Vina. In parting, Still declared: "I will come back whether I find my people or not — I will come back . . ." From Kate E. R. Pickard, *The Kidnapped and the Ransomed. Being the Personal Recollections of Peter Still and His Wife "Vina," after Forty Years of Slavery* (Westport, Conn.: Negro Universities Press, 1968 [Syracuse: William T. Hamilton, 1856]).

plantation as a "school of agricultural education." As a free man he hoped to build a smooth-running farming operation "with his own strength and mind." Having acquired the necessary capital to pay for his trip North by illegally retailing whiskey while his master was away from home, Loguen made good his escape to Canada. In all of these plans and activities it seems that the black supervisor possessed a certain important advantage over the slaveholder. As was noted in the narrative, Loguen was able to "read his master's mind and motives like a book," while *he* was to his master "a sealed book." One endowed with such qualities of patience and calculated self-control might, for a season, make a good plantation manager, but it is unlikely that he would ever make a "good slave."[27]

Of all of the autobiographical accounts of slaves who had served as drivers, the narrative of Josiah Henson contains the most intriguing description of the complex, contemplative, and inner-directed nature of those fugitives drawn from the "slave elite." Born in Charles County, Maryland, in 1789, Henson both witnessed and experienced many of the perverse cruelties of the "peculiar institution," but was rescued from self-destructive bitterness by an early conversion to Christianity. Mixing Christian compassion for his dissipated master with a strict adherence to the Protestant work ethic as a mode of self-expression, Henson seemed to become a willing ally in the slaveholder's plan to maintain a profitable existence through the exploitation of black labor. On one occasion he participated in a scheme whereby the slaveholder sought to evade the impending judgment of a lawsuit by moving his human property from Maryland to Kentucky. As superintendent of farming operations and head market man, Henson personally conducted eighteen of his owner's slaves to their new homestead. His pride aroused by the great responsibility under which he labored, Henson led his charges along the Ohio shores without succumbing to the temptation to flee the land of slavery. Even when the party was told by black residents of Cincinnati that they were fools to continue their journey and surrender themselves once again to the overlordship of the planters, Henson resolutely forged onward. He greatly coveted the "immense admiration and respect" with which his master would regard the successful completion of his assigned task and felt that by shunning the voice of freedom he was honorably fulfilling the "duties of a slave to his master as appointed over him in the Lord."[28]

6. **J. W. Loguen**. While a head man in Tennessee, J. W. Loguen was considered by his owner to be devoted to the whites' agricultural interests. But, according to his narrative account, Loguen's true feelings and personality remained "a sealed book" to the slaveholder. From Jermain W. Loguen, *The Rev. J. W. Loguen, as a Slave and as a Freeman. A Narrative of Real Life* (Westport, Conn.: Negro Universities Press, 1968 [Syracuse: Daily Journal, 1859]).

During his three-year stay on the Kentucky estate of his owner's brother, Henson remained loyal to the whites' interests, exercised "general management" of the plantation, and garnered some of the personal freedoms that sometimes served as a reward for faithful service. In the spring of 1828, however, word was received from his Maryland master that all of the slaves taken to Kentucky—with the exception of Henson and his family—were to be sold. Even though he was exempted from a personal share in this "dreadful calamity," the black overseer could not help but see the deep agony experienced by his fellow chattels when this news reached the quarters. His thoughts rushed back to his own experience with a forced separation from loved ones at the age of five. As he contemplated these matters and listened to the "groans and outcries" of his afflicted companions, Henson's "eyes were opened" and he blamed himself for preventing his charges from escaping to the North while at Cincinnati. From that hour, he "saw through, hated, and cursed" the whole system of slavery. He realized for the first time that while he had been faithful to his master's interests he had been guilty of grossly neglecting "the welfare of the slaves." Determined not to be fooled again, Henson vowed to "pray, toil, dissemble, plot like a fox, and fight like a tiger" to gain "freedom, self-assertion, and deliverance" from the cruel caprices and fortunes of those "dissolute tyrants" who had formerly controlled his destiny.[29]

Planning his moves carefully and still hoping to obtain his freedom through an "honorable" self-purchase agreement, Henson found that the slaveholders were much less honorable than he. Realizing that their selfish and deceptive plans for him would be a "fatal blight" to his hopes for the establishment of a new life in the North, the mild-mannered slave became "more and more agitated with an almost uncontrollable fury." Controlling his rage and channeling it into a constructive "sharpening" of his wits, the black overseer and his family escaped from bondage during the fall of 1830. As he crossed into Canada from Buffalo, the once supremely loyal Christian servant threw himself on Canadian soil and "rolled in the sand, seized handfuls of it and kissed them, and danced around," until, in the eyes of several who were present, he seemed a madman. In response to a bystander who dismissed Henson's antics as the ravings of a "crazy fellow," the bondsman replied, "Oh, no, master! don't you know?

I'm free!'' Josiah Henson not only freed himself from the physical bondage of slavery after over forty years of servitude, but he also presented to the world a compelling example of a member of the slave supervisory elite who had, after considerable struggle with the behavioral ''cues'' of his environment, succeeded in triumphing over the psychologically corrosive forces inherent in the driver's job.[30]

In penning or dictating stories of their experiences under the ''peculiar institution'' the driver-narrators committed a collective act of rebellion against the coercions of slavery. As authors, the ex-slaves were self-consciously fighting for Afro-American rights and battling against the notion of black inferiority. Demanding freedom from the enslavement of mind and soul, as well as body, the black autobiographies furthered the abolitionists' program by proving to those who would hear that slaves were indeed capable of behaving like intelligent, rational human beings. But, more than this, since the choice of autobiography presupposes a belief in the primacy of the self, the narrative accounts affirmed the ex-slaves' personal belief in their own self-worth. Along with the evidence of the depression era narratives, the writings of antebellum travelers, and even certain of the materials left by the planters, the black autobiographies can be used to draw an untraditional, but convincing portrait of the intelligence, integrity, compassion, and endurance possessed by many of those who formed the ranks of the ''slave elite.''[31]

conclusion

> . . . there is not one book and only a few scattered articles
> on life in the slave quarters: we must rely mainly on such
> primary and undigested sources as slave narratives and
> plantation memoirs. A good student might readily be able
> to answer questions about the economics of the planta-
> tion, the life of the planters, the politics of slavery expan-
> sionism, or a host of other matters, but he is not likely to
> know much about the daily life and thoughts of slaves,
> about the relationship of field to house slaves, or about the
> relations between slave driver or foreman and other
> slaves. To make matters worse, he may well think he
> knows a good deal, for the literature abounds in un-
> documented assertions and plausible legends.[1]

Since Eugene Genovese used these words to sum up the state of the
discipline in late 1970, the study of the black American slave experience has undergone an important maturation-modernization process.
The appearance of scholarly volumes on the bondsman's social,
cultural, and family life has allowed Afro-American slave historiography to shed its previously all-too-monochromatic character.
Evidencing dissatisfaction with older emphases and interpretations,
historians have begun to examine both the great diversity of slave (that
is, human) personality types and the rich, resilient texture of group
life within the quarters. Increasingly, in both academic and popular
opinion, the antebellum slave community is being seen as the home of
a considerable number of skilled, self-directed, and often militant
men and women who were far more concerned with defining the
nature and quality of their own lives than they were with making
certain that whites were suitably pampered.

Despite these enlightening developments, the black drivers of the agricultural South have retained a composite historical character quite similar to that ascribed to Harriet Beecher Stowe's "barbarous, gutteral, half-brute" creations, Sambo and Quimbo. In their accounts of slave life, historians have described this important "plantation elite" with varying degrees of prejudice and understanding, but the most pervasive and certainly the most vivid image put forward has been that of a mean, perquisite-seeking class of men whose racial loyalties were grossly distorted by wiser and even more manipulative planters. Encouraged to feel superior to the field hands by grants of material goods and privileges, the drivers were said to have identified with the master class so completely that they became "instruments of superbrutality" toward other blacks. Thus, the unfortunate driver became the most detestable, degraded, and dehumanized member of the slave community.

Obviously, historians did not posit these images of driver perversity without having some type of documentary evidence to support their position. Much of this supporting data was gleaned from the writings and reminiscences of southern planters and from books penned by northern or foreign travelers. More recently, additional evidence has come from depression-era oral-history accounts of black life under slavery and from the newly respectable, underused antebellum slave narratives. All four categories of source material are subject to misuse and misinterpretation—a fallibility that has served to distort severely the historical characterization of the "driver elite." By recognizing and attempting to overcome these hazards, it is possible to use all four types of data to reconstruct a history of black drivers that is more compatible with modern understandings of slave life and culture.

Supported by various kinds of documentation, this study has shown that drivers were called upon to perform a number of diversified tasks. From the time they roused the hands in the morning until they made the nightly "cabin check," black supervisors were engaged in a multitude of job-related activities that were far too complex to have been performed by "half-brutes." Moreover, even as they measured and assigned the daily tasks, paced their "gang," monitored the condition of the plows, and served as their master's agents in transactions with merchants and tradesmen, the drivers entered into the life of the quarters in ways that revealed where their sociocultural roots lay. Throughout the history of slavery, drivers could be found in roles quite different from that of "Whipper." By performing the duties of husband, father, plantation preacher, or "corn general," they could assume new "identities" that gave free reign to their own personalities and interests.

Even though individual drivers possessed differing skills and were given varying amounts and types of "authority," they had one major quality in common—each was the "human property" of a white master. As such, the slave supervisors experienced most of the deprivations felt by their field hand brothers. Drivers did not escape exploitation. They could be demoted, sold, or whipped. Their families lived under a constant threat of separation or brutalization. The minor "perquisites of office" obtained by the drivers could in no way compensate for the day-to-day experience of living as chattel slaves in a professedly liberty-loving republic.

Acting upon a realistic appraisal of the social factors that bound them to their less "privileged" kinsmen, drivers cooperated with other blacks both in ameliorating the lot of the chattels and in rebelling against their common plight. The driver who faked "brutal whippings," covertly slaughtered livestock to supplement the diet of his fellows, engaged in pitched battles with white overseers, or joined the ranks of the fugitives could not be considered a mere "tool" of white economic interests. Numerous examples of drivers who in various ways sought to preserve their integrity—thereby refusing to be turned into psychologically devastated brutes—lend credence to the idea that insensitive, dehumanized slave supervisors were neither as numerous, as depraved, or as motivated by selfish and perverse desires as most historical accounts have led us to believe.

Certainly, during the era of slavery there were drivers who could be termed "men of their masters"—slaves who were deeply hated within the quarters for the alacrity and apparent devotion with which they did the whites' bidding. To be sure, there were drivers who seemed to fit the general description of "the men between"—individuals who were buffeted, perplexed, and sometimes made indecisive or ineffective by the tensions and conflicting loyalties of their position. But to an extent greater than historians have recognized, the black agricultural labor supervisors of the antebellum South were men who belonged to themselves, to their families, and to the larger slave community. By recognizing this fact, one can assert more readily that no matter what place they occupied in the planters' "pyramid of authority," black Americans under slavery refused to be crushed by the burdens they bore.

appendix

This appendix contains background information on the primary sources used in the writing of chapters 4, 5, and 6. Unlike the often-discussed documents and reminiscences left by the planters and their kin, the accounts of travelers, twentieth-century narrators, and antebellum autobiographers contain important insights and telling biases that are neither readily ascertained nor easily explained. For this reason, the brief essays that follow are designed to make these materials more understandable both in terms of their overall character and in regard to the ways in which they were created, collected, and preserved.

THE TRAVELERS' ACCOUNTS

During the first century and a half of American history, hundreds of travelers visited the southern portion of what is now the United States. At least one hundred fifty accounts penned by the visitors appeared in book or pamphlet form and even larger numbers were published in newspapers and periodicals of the day. The early travel books were usually written in narrative form and varied in length from four to over two-thousand pages. Fascinated with the land and peoples of the New World, visitors to the colonial American South concentrated upon topics related to natural history and Native American life. Few travelers seemed to be deeply interested in current agricultural practices, white servitude, or Afro-American slavery.[1]

By the last quarter of the eighteenth century, the number of travelers journeying through the South had multiplied dramatically. Botanists, geologists, and ornithologists were joined by religious itinerants, land hunters, and political philosophers who came to the

United States to see the new experiment in democracy at work. During the immediate postrevolutionary period and continuing into the first three decades of the nineteenth century, there emerged from the travel literature an increased awareness of the sectional peculiarities of the South. Especially noticed by northerners and British visitors who had followed the parliamentary debates over the abolition of slavery in England's overseas possessions was the growing southern reliance upon black slave labor in the production of staple crops such as tobacco, rice, cotton, and sugar.[2]

During the second and third decades of the nineteenth century, pleasure-seeking tourists from England and the Continent began to visit the South in noticeably large numbers. Some who later penned accounts of their experiences did so with no other aim than to produce a record of the unusual things they witnessed in the frontier society. Others, however, wrote to answer specific questions often asked by Europeans unfamiliar with American life or to set forth the "real" state of affairs in America. Although individual travel accounts tended to reflect the special occupational or intellectual interests of their authors, similarities did exist within the genre. Whether they were clergymen, scientists, sportsmen, promoters, journalists, or actors, the antebellum travelers shared a common middle to upper-class background and an almost overwhelming desire to visit either a slave plantation or a slave auction before their tour was completed. Their curiosity aroused by the American debate over slavery, visitors of all sorts journeyed to the South to see the masters and the slaves at home.[3]

The number of travelers visiting the South increased once again during the 1840s and 1850s as steamships replaced the Atlantic sailing packet and railroads quickened the pace of travel from northern cities southward. More than 110 visitors wrote books about their experiences during the 1836-45 period and another 150 travelers recorded and published their impressions of the South between 1846 and 1852. Slavery was a focal point of these observations not only because there was a substantial market for travel books of this nature in Great Britain, but also because Americans themselves had become caught up in the national struggle over the continued existence of the "peculiar institution." Triumphantly listing the "errors" of their predecessors, each traveler-interpreter formulated a personal estimation of black bondage. Whether influenced by hoped-for pecuniary rewards or by the prevailing sectional strife, travelers of this era could not be credited with having won the battle for functional objectivity in reporting what they saw in the slave South.[4]

Attempting to estimate the average length of time spent by travelers in the South is virtually impossible because of the incomplete nature of many of the visitors' recorded itineraries. Nevertheless, it appears that one to two months was about the usual time taken by a substantial number during the era of improved transportation. Even though considerable space may be devoted to descriptions of plantation life, some travelers' itineraries are so well concealed from the reader that one is not wholly convinced that the author of the account ever actually set foot on southern soil.[5]

Those travelers who actually did tour the South followed a single route often enough for it to be characterized as a sort of American "Grand Tour." The route led from Washington to New Orleans by way of Richmond, Norfolk, Fayetteville, Camden, Columbia, Augusta, Milledgeville, and Columbus. At Montgomery the trip continued by steamer to Mobile and then to New Orleans. The return journey was by water up the Mississippi and Ohio rivers to Louisville or Cincinnati and then overland to the East. The route was not infrequently transposed.[6]

During their travels, most visitors to the South took notes while they were making their observations. Some, however, waited until they had returned to familiar surroundings and thus wrote their accounts largely from memory. A significant number of the accounts were published as components of personal memoirs and autobiographies, rather than in separate volumes dealing solely with the author's journeyings. Many were not even sent to press by the traveler, but were transformed from manuscript into printed form by later editors. Travel narratives that appeared in contemporary magazines rather than as books were, on the whole, less likely to contain large amounts of extraneous matter dealing with the author's travels to other parts of the world.[7]

Historians who have used these accounts of the travelers' meanderings in formulating their interpretations of the slave South have done so with the realization that the views of outsiders often provide a much-needed check upon native opinions and prejudices. Often,

things too commonplace—or too unpleasant—for resident southerners to mention were noticed, investigated, and thereby exposed by the
travelers. Interestingly enough, the antebellum visitors were almost
as adept at exhibiting their own prejudices and preconceptions as they
were at exposing the often harsh mechanisms of plantation life. By
investigating the "mind-set" of the travelers as well as the physical
and social circumstances surrounding them as they viewed the plantations, one can better understand and interpret their comments regarding the character of the slave foremen.[8]

The first factor to consider in attempting to understand the travelers' world is the average southern visitor's total unfamiliarity with
people of color. Whether from the northern states or from overseas,
most travelers had little prior experience in mentally "sorting out"
the numerous visual images that buffeted them as they entered the
region of plantation slavery. Although some came prepared for the
experience of being "a stranger in a strange land" and therefore
steeled themselves to the "difficulty of forming a correct judgment,
even with close observation," other outsiders seemed to be over-
whelmed by their new experiences.[9]

Forced by a frail physique to vacation in the South during the fall
and winter of 1843-44, Henry B. Whipple found himself in surroundings far removed from those of his Jefferson County, New York,
birthplace. As he viewed the rice plantations stretched alongside the
Savannah River, Whipple wrote that all was new, all was strange, and
that he felt like "a being suddenly transfer'd to a stranger land."
After passing several dozen small boats rowed by slaves who were
"singing merrily 'Lucy Long' or 'Jim Crow,' " he noted that his
initial observation of the bondsmen had given him "the strangest
sensations I ever experienced." Like a "curious Yankee who sees a
great curiosity for the first time," Whipple longed to "touch & examine" the slaves to see if they were "men made of flesh and blood
like myself."[10]

Another traveler who sought out the medicinal values of the southern climate, Scottsman William Thomson, also experienced the "culture shock" of viewing blacks for the first time. After attending
Sunday services at a Baptist church in Beaufort, South Carolina,
during the fall of 1840, Thomson noted that the black portion of the
congregation, which was seated in the gallery of the church, had "a

very strange appearance to me.'' Having only recently arrived in the
United States, he found it "a novel sight" to see so many blacks
congregated in one place. "They appeared all very much alike," he
wrote, "as much so as a flock of sheep does to a stranger."[11]

Unfamiliarity with dark-skinned peoples, when combined with
preconceptions of Negroes gained through printed accounts or casual
conversations with equally uninformed acquaintances, could easily
lead to the stereotyping of black personality. Indeed, some foreign
travelers visiting the United States for the first time carried with them
the ability to make incredible generalizations about Americans.
England's James Stirling, for example, described a peculiarly American physiognomy in which the features even of the young were
"furrowed with lines of anxious thought and determined will."
Evidencing his ability to "read upon the nation's brow the extent of its
enterprise and the intensity of its desires," Stirling boldly declared
that "every American looks as if his eye were glaring into the far West
and the far Future." In like manner, J. S. Buckingham could attribute
the great uniformity of "stature, shape, feature, and expression" he
found among the whites of the United States to the "general equality
of their lot."[12]

Even though Buckingham characterized white American males as
having small heads, long features, and "slightly stooping" shoulders
and practically libeled white American womanhood by his description
of their "grave" expressions and "imperfect development of bust,"
his generalizations and stereotyping did no serious damage to the
white American ego. The preconceptions about blacks and slavery
that were carried to the slave South by antebellum travelers were much
more volatile. Although certain travelers, such as Boston's Nehemiah
Adams, could at least claim to have prepared themselves "to receive
dispassionately" the impressions that were soon to be made upon
their minds, others such as actress Fanny Kemble bluntly stated that
they were going to the South "prejudiced against slavery."[13]

The travelers' prejudices and their proclivity toward stereotyping
worked in various ways to distort the accounts of what they saw while
touring the plantation South. On an 1827-28 tour of North America,
Basil Hall's party was invited to spend a night at the country seat of a
South Carolina rice planter. In the absence of his master, head driver
Solomon welcomed the Halls to the plantation and supervised the

details of their visit. Evidencing great surprise at the capacity of "a race whom we have generally found so stupid," Mrs. Hall was pleased to find that the black servants "understand their business perfectly." In finding the establishment to be "under the most excellent management," the Halls also paid tribute to driver Solomon. Proving himself to be a most intelligent and agreeable guide—"more so, indeed, than it had ever occurred to us any slave-driver could possibly be"—Solomon served as a living contradiction to the mental image of the "stern, tyrannical" foreman the Halls had brought with them to the South. Still, Solomon was not deemed to be capable of acting like a well-mannered, intelligent human being without some sort of outside stimulus. As the Halls bid farewell to the plantation, Solomon and the other chief servants cheerfully shook hands and bowed to the departing guests. Mrs. Hall accounted for this cordial behavior in a way that gave the slaves little credit for their polite, mannerly deportment. "I believe we treated them with more civility and kindness than they are used to," she wrote, "and this gained their goodwill, I think much more than the dollars and half dollars that we gave them." White paternalism rather than self-developed black capability and achievement served as the Halls' explanation for what they saw on the South Carolina rice plantation. One can only wonder how much such an explanation helped others to rid themselves of inaccurate preconceptions about "stupid" slaves and "tyrannical" drivers.[14]

Various travelers faced similar problems in attempting to interpret what they witnessed during their tours. Visitors holding to antislavery tenets were often prone to blame the sins of the world upon the "peculiar institution." A key claim that degraded blacks while it ostensibly slammed the slave system was that made by Alexander Mackay when he voiced his belief that "servitude cannot long co-exist with intelligence." Slavery, according to many travelers, not only destroyed the chattel's self-respect, but it also witheld all encouragement from the laborer to improve his faculties, capacities, and skills. Touring South Carolina by rail in late 1859, John S.C. Abbott voiced a common opinion when he wrote that black plantation laborers were "as ignorant and helpless as children." Oppression had "burned out their eyes and cut the sinews of all their energies." Certainly, the plantation Negro represented "the lowest phase of humanity in the United States."[15]

Alongside this image of slave ignorance stood a stereotype of black indolence, filthiness, thievery, and general moral debasement. The much-traveled Frederick Law Olmsted gave his readers a graphic description of the formidable effects that slavery had on the development of black character. Having had no early training toward industry or self-direction, the generality of slave youth possessed an inbred tendency toward "indolent, careless, incogitant habits." Once in the fields, no systematic attempt was made to rescue them from their bad habits and they came permanently to possess personal traits that stood "at variance with industry, precision, forethought, and providence." To Olmsted, the great mass of laborers he viewed during his excursions appeared "very dull, idiotic, and brutelike." It required great mental effort for him to appreciate that the black plow hands were his "brethren" since they seemed to be little more advanced on the scale of humanity "than the beasts they drive."[16]

When portrayed as "brutes" by the travelers, slave laborers quite naturally took on certain characteristics of a lower order of creation. William Thomson informed the readers of his travel account that slaves were endowed with a peculiarly "nasty smell, commonly called *negro funk*." Margaret Hall vigorously seconded this opinion of slave uncleanliness by noting that even though the "nasty, black creatures" whom she had seen serving as house servants were "dressed in livery," they still appeared to be "so dirty." Finding it disagreeable to have "so many of those creatures going about," Mrs. Hall was relieved only by word from one of her southern acquaintances that she was not yet suffering the full impact of "negro funk." When summer arrived, the black servants would be "offensive beyond what can be described." Indeed, one of her friends in Charleston gave substance to this claim by telling Mrs. Hall that she could identify each one of her house slaves as they came up the stairs "without seeing them, merely by the smell."[17]

In addition to the images of slave ignorance, indolence, and uncleanliness that seemed to fill many travelers' minds, there was a vivid portrait drawn in numerous travel accounts of a peculiarly Afro-American type of moral debasement. William Thomson credited the slave community with so little internal police control of public morals that he accounted for the locks on slave cabin doors by offhandedly noting that "they steal like rats." Similarly, among the "detestible qualities" that Fanny Kemble found among the slaves of St.

Simon's Island was their inability to "know the difference between truth and falsehood."[18]

Other plantation visitors commented upon the bondsmen's supposed "vicious nature" and "slavish character." Charles Sealsfield, for example, believed that a "malignant and cruel disposition" characterized the black race. "Whether it be inborn, or the result of slavery," he would "leave to others to decide." Kemble believed the slaves to be not only tyrannical in their relationship with one another, but also "diabolically cruel to animals too." Both Kemble and the French traveler Alexis de Tocqueville accounted for such traits by blaming them on conditions prevailing in the plantation world. Certainly anyone "plunged in this abyss of wretchedness" for any length of time could come to possess "the thoughts and ambitions of a slave."[19]

Whether they felt the bondsman to be a vicious brute due to social conditioning or inherent meanness, travelers seemed much more interested in describing the result of such skewed personality development than they were in attempting to pin down definite causal factors. To de Tocqueville, the "product" of the plantation "abyss" was a being who admired his owners more than he hated them—a servant who found his "joy and pride in a servile imitation of his oppressors." When this sentiment was applied to the occupational structure, as it was in the account of E. S. Abdy's 1833-34 tour of the South, readers had little choice but to conclude, along with Abdy, that blacks made "more severe overseers than the whites."[20]

THE TWENTIETH-CENTURY NARRATIVES

During the late 1920s and the decade of the 1930s, several attempts were made to secure and preserve the testimony of the rapidly dwindling number of black Americans who had experienced personally the burdens of slavery. John B. Cade, historian and Extension Service director at Southern University in Scotlandville, Louisiana, initiated one of the first such projects in 1929 as an experimental component of his United States history course. While covering the topic of slavery, Cade conceived the idea of "securing views of the institution from living ex-slaves and ex-slave owners." Even though he was fully aware that the elderly blacks would be prone to "weave a good story for attentive listeners," he gave the innovative interviewing assignment to his class and eventually collected eighty-two interviews from thirty-six participating students. Certain of these materials were then used as the basis for an article that Cade penned for the *Journal of Negro History*. Stimulated by the success of the Louisiana study, Cade conducted a similar project at Prairie View State College from 1933 to 1938 that resulted in the recording of more than four hundred ex-slave interviews.[21]

A separate and independent project was also begun in 1929 at Fisk University in Nashville, Tennessee. As a part of sociologist Charles S. Johnson's Social Science Institute community study of the Fisk campus environs, a large number of former slaves were interviewed by Ophelia Settle of the Institute's research staff. Recognizing the value of preserving these firsthand accounts of plantation life, Johnson was instrumental in expanding the program so Settle could continue her interviews with ex-slaves throughout rural Tennessee and Kentucky. Thirty-seven of the one hundred narratives obtained were reproduced in the Institute's "Unwritten History of Slavery" in 1945. Along with the conversion experiences and autobiographies of ex-slaves gathered during the years 1927-29 by Fisk graduate student Andrew P. Watson and published in 1945 under the title "God Struck Me Dead," the Settle narratives made Fisk the early center of efforts to record the oral testimony of the aged survivors of the slave era.[22]

The first attempt to involve the federal government in the collection of ex-slave remembrances was made by Lawrence D. Reddick, of Kentucky State Industrial College in 1934. Reddick's studies under Charles Johnson, his participation in the Fisk Social Science Institute project, and his awareness of the plight of unemployed blacks during the depression years moved him to propose a plan whereby black college graduates would conduct interviews with ex-slaves in the six states of the Ohio River Valley. Aside from the intrinsic historical value of such an undertaking, the project would provide employment for a segment of the black population that had been, as Reddick noted, "left out generally in the program of recovery." Supported in his efforts by Johnson and Carter G. Woodson of the Association for the Study of Negro Life and History (ASNLH), Reddick was pleased to find the Federal Emergency Relief Administration (FERA) favorably disposed toward projects that would remove white-collar workers from the relief rolls and employ them in useful tasks. Although an expanded version of his proposal never advanced beyond the planning stage, some two hundred and fifty interviews from the pilot study were collected in Indiana and Kentucky during 1934 and 1935.[23]

In May 1935 President Roosevelt issued an executive order establishing the Works Progress Administration (WPA). Under the WPA, the relief functions for which its FERA predecessor had been created were broadened and better coordinated. Several arts projects designed to aid the growing number of white-collar unemployed were approved and rushed into operation under the auspices of the WPA's Federal Writers' Project. Although preliminary plans for the Writers' Project did not include the collection of ex-slave reminiscences, oral-history projects sponsored by state components of the FWP in Georgia, Florida, and South Carolina during 1936 convinced the national office that such an undertaking would be worthwhile. In April 1937 instructions were sent from the Washington office to eighteen southern and border states directing FWP workers to begin interviewing ex-slaves. The total number of people interviewed during the 1937-39 project is not known, but seventeen states eventually turned in some twenty-two hundred narratives to the national office. Upon the termination of the FWP in 1939, the responsibility for the final disposition of the transcribed interviews was assumed by the Writers' Unit of the newly created Library of Congress Project. The chief editor of the Writers' Unit, folklorist Benjamin A. Botkin, directed the processing of materials. Following the arrangement of the manuscripts and accompanying photographs by states, seventeen bound volumes of FWP narratives were placed in the Rare Book Room of the Library of Congress in 1941. Four years later, Botkin published excerpts from this Slave Narrative Collection in his book *Lay My Burden Down*. Botkin's compilation of material from the depression-era interviews captured the flavor of the ex-slave interviews and apparently long satisfied the needs of American historians, but nevertheless contained only a small sample of the vast ten thousand-page, 3.5 million-word Collection.[24]

The use of this ex-slave testimony in constructing historical accounts of the antebellum period has been long urged, but seldom heeded. Perhaps evidencing his concern that the oral-history materials he had worked so hard to collect and preserve would go unused, Lawrence Reddick criticized the narrow scope and "traditional" treatment of existing slave studies at a fall 1936 gathering of the ASNLH. The black historian felt it to be a "waste of time" for scholars to continue to base their research upon plantation records, planter journals, and the "usually superficial impressions of travelers" when there was "not yet a picture of the institution as seen through the eyes of the bondsman himself." Despite his urgings, it seemed that only a few scholars, such as sociologist E. Franklin Frazier, were willing to use the materials compiled by Fisk's oral history projects.[25]

The call for increased use of nontraditional source materials in the writing of black American history continued to be heard in the decades following the completion of the Cade, Fisk, and FWP projects. In his 1944 critique of the "plantation legend," Richard Hofstadter recommended that future histories of slavery be "written in large part from the standpoint of the slave." During 1950 John Hope Franklin lamented that most of the available writings about blacks were based upon what some outside and frequently partial observer had said or thought about blacks. To make matters worse, source materials provided by outsiders were often subjected to little rigorous "critical examination" while those originating from within the Afro-American community were "not even considered by researchers." In a 1952 journal article, Kenneth Stampp supported the thrust of these comments by asserting that for "proper balance and perspective" to be achieved, the institution of slavery had to be viewed "through the eyes of the Negro as well as through the eyes of the white master." Some estimation of the degree to which these suggestions were heeded during the 1940s and 1950s may be gained by noting that during the heyday of the "New Left" historians, demands for the writing of American history "from the bottom up" contained the same call for an increased use of slave testimony.[26]

Why have historians been so hesitant to make use of the FWP and other narrative materials? To some degree, unavailability and relative inaccessibility may have discouraged extensive use of the interviews. John Cade's Louisiana interviews were destroyed after the publication of his "Out of the Mouths of Ex-Slaves" article in 1935, his 1932 M.A. thesis of the same title has vanished from the Prairie View

College library, and the bulk of his 1933-38 interviews remain housed in the Southern University Archives.[27] Many of the narratives collected by Settle and Reddick were in private possession and materials contributed by state components of the FWP, but not included in the Slave Narrative Collection, were housed in the WPA storage collection in the Library of Congress or in state depositories. Much of the FWP data became widely available only with the appearance of George Rawick's Greenwood Press reprint editions in 1972 and 1978.[28]

A more important hindrance to the widespread use of the ex-slave testimony has been the seemingly "flawed" nature of the materials. Recognizing that over two-thirds of the respondents in the FWP project had reached the age of eighty when interviewed and 15 percent were over ninety-three, historians have been extremely cautious in their acceptance of the interviews as believable accounts of antebellum plantation life. Scholars accustomed to acting in a circumspect manner when dealing with personal reminiscences feared the black narrators displayed so many lapses of memory and included in their accounts so much exaggeration, self-flattery, and contradictory testimony, as well as obvious errors of historical fact, that their views of slavery were more than slightly tainted. In addition, historians recognized the secondhand nature of much of the descriptive material contained in the interviews—a consequence of the youth of the respondents under slavery.[29]

Like certain of the traveler accounts and planter reminiscences, some of the recorded talks with former bondsmen were "toned down" or "spiced up" according to editorial preference. Even when the ex-slave's views were purportedly transcribed in his own words, the interview may have been "doctored." A most interesting case of the alteration of narrative materials appears in the records of Talbot County, Georgia, interviewer J. Ralph Jones. During 1936 and 1937, Jones conducted five interviews that were returned to the Georgia office of the WPA. Three of the five transcribed by the state office are almost identical to the copies Jones retained. The other two were significantly reduced in length and seriously distorted. Jones' recorded conversations with ex-slaves Rias Body and Washington Allen were edited to delete references to runaways, cruel punishments, blacks serving in the Union Army, and Afro-Americans voting during Reconstruction. About half of the seventeen hundred-word section excluded from the WPA typescript of the Allen interview referred to slave traders, the religious life of the slaves, the songs they sang, and the tricks they played on the patrollers. Moreover, the transcript gave the impression that Allen spoke in dialect, using such words as "de," "dis," "chilluns," "fokes," and "fetched." In his records, however, Jones noted that Allen used "excellent English."[30]

Despite these hindrances, historians' respect for and use of black oral history has increased significantly in recent years. Today, it would be considered an absurdity to pen a new account of antebellum slave life without considering carefully the testimony of ex-bondsmen. When used in a circumspect manner, these records offer the researcher an invaluable, irreplaceable "window on the past."

THE BLACK AUTOBIOGRAPHIES

Popular literary interest in the life of black slaves seems to have emerged during the latter part of the seventeenth century with the appearance in 1688 of Mrs. Aphra Behn's *Oroonoko*, the story of an idealized African slave martyr, but it was not until 1760 and the publication of *A Narrative of the Uncommon Sufferings and Surprising Deliverance of Briton Hammon, a Negro Man* that black biography could be separated from fictional accounts of "noble" servants suffering from the "tyranny of color." Although such tales of adventure continued to appear in various formats throughout the eighteenth century, the slave narratives did not become especially numerous until they had become inextricably associated with the cause of organized antislavery.[31]

Eagerly sought out for publication by abolitionist editors who realized the role they could play as effective counterpropaganda to that disseminated by the pro-slavery South, the autobiographical accounts came to enjoy immense popularity in the pre-Civil War decades. Popular narratives, such as those of William Wells Brown, Josiah Henson, Solomon Northup, and Moses Roper, went through numerous editions and were sold at antislavery meetings, lectures, and church gatherings as well as at book shops on both sides of the

Atlantic. The autobiographies, whether in bound, pamphlet, or periodical form, became so numerous that one critic writing in the early 1850s expressed his belief that the "whole literary atmosphere has become tainted" with "those literary nigritudes—those little tadpoles of the press . . . which run to editions of hundreds of thousands."[32]

As an integral part of the northern abolitionists' propaganda machine, the black autobiographies received a good deal of criticism during the antebellum years. These harsh barbs have tellingly affected the willingness of modern-day scholars to use the accounts in the construction of interpretive studies of plantation slavery. Because the narratives were often taken down by white abolitionists and then rewritten by them to conform to the literary standards of the time, historians such as Ulrich Phillips and Clement Eaton have concluded that "as a class their authenticity is doubtful." Certainly, some abolitionist editors seemed to proceed far beyond the reasonable goal of helping the slaves with the mechanics of grammar and composition. In some narratives, it is obvious that the sparse details supplied by the fugitive have been "fleshed out" to heighten reader interest and involvement. Other accounts contain literary devices that were almost certainly beyond the ken of unlettered slaves or attribute to the slaves extremely complicated historical, religious, and philosophical arguments designed to show that southern bondage violated divine law and the natural rights of man. Indeed, some accounts were so romanticized that they were stylistically closer to the popular Indian-escape literature of frontier America than they were to traditional biographies.[33]

In addition to being charged with possessing this disconcerting list of "flaws," black autobiographies have been said to be "nonrepresentative" in several respects. One common objection to the narratives is the claim that most of the writers were atypical slaves— that only the more abused and discontented blacks fled the South and that only the most perceptive and gifted of these recorded their experiences for posterity. Indeed, the percentage of fugitives among the narrators was significantly higher than the percentage of blacks who escaped from bondage. John Blassingame has calculated that although less than 5 percent of the bondsmen successfully followed the North Star to freedom, fugitives wrote about 35 percent of all narratives with the remainder being written by slaves who purchased their freedom, were manumitted, or were freed after the Civil War began.[34]

Another objection, one that probably troubled the slaveholders even more than it has modern critics, stems from the fact that the black autobiographies tended to focus intently upon the cruelties of the plantation labor system. In many accounts there was a preoccupation, amounting at times almost to an obsession, with the whips, paddles, chains, and spiked collars used to control the slaves. The intended effect of such a description of southern life was to convince the northern reader that his unreflecting passivity in regard to the slavery question actually constituted nothing less than an outright, immoral complicity in the maintenance of a cruel and inhumane institution. For those southern planters who fancied themselves as agents of "uplift" to uncivilized Africans, the horrors described in such accounts seemed to libel and to wholly misrepresent the nature of southern society.[35]

A third "nonrepresentative" characteristic of the black autobiographies can be said to apply to similarly patterned accounts penned in other eras. As with most firsthand, participatory recollections, the abolitionist-sponsored narratives were subject to the elements of unreliability natural to the autobiographical format. Since few men are willing to reveal to strangers the *whole* truth about themselves, it is very easy for such writings to exaggerate both the intensity of the tribulations experienced by the author and the strength and responsiveness of his internal resources in attempting to surmount the stated difficulties. Thus, the black autobiographies may be nonrepresentative in the picture they draw of the author's "real" personality.[36]

Aware of such objections to the black narratives, antebellum editors strove mightily to convince the northern reading public of the validity of the slaves' stories. Many book-length accounts included prefaces written by "authoritative" sources or compilations of letters attesting both to the high moral character of the author and the truthfulness of what he had written. Should such printed affirmations of truth fail to convince the skeptical reader, the abolitionists were prepared to resort to more graphic displays. On one occasion, to prove that it was feasible for Henry "Box" Brown to have escaped from bondage by being nailed inside of a crate and shipped via Adams

Express Company lines from Richmond to Philadephia, British supporters reenacted the entire episode. After a box was built to the
specifications given in his narrative, Brown was confined inside and
driven from Bradford to Leeds. Upon his arrival, the fugitive slave,
still in his box, but now accompanied by waving banners and a blaring
band, became the main focus of attention as the procession made its
way through the main streets of the city. After a two and three-quarter
hour confinement, Brown reappeared to the cheers of his captivated
audience.[37]

Although they have usually failed to match the abolitionists'
creativity, modern-day supporters of the narratives have also presented compelling arguments designed to convince skeptics of the
veracity of the Afro-Americans' testimony. To the charge that the
accounts contained an overabundance of abolitionist propagandizing,
scholars such as John Blassingame and Charles H. Nichols have
responded with convincing character studies that portray the editors of
the narratives as "an impressive group of people noted for their
integrity." Most of those for whom sufficient biographical data is
available were engaged in professions and businesses where they had
an opportunity to acquire a good deal of experience in applying rules
of evidence and in separating truth from fiction. Many of these
lawyers, teachers, ministers, and physicians actually had little or no
connection with professional abolitionism and took great pains to
present the stories in a manner that would not be criticized. The
editors were apparently rewarded for their circumspection because
relatively few of the narratives were challenged by antebellum
southerners.[38]

Modern supporters of the slaves' testimony also point to the fact
that the published accounts edited by whites are not the only sources
of early black autobiography. Many of the fugitives had received
enough education to write their own stories of life in bondage. Indeed,
some accounts penned by the slaves were so lacking in style, so
ungrammatical, and so straightforward that they could only have been
written by relatively unschooled men. Other surviving narratives
come not from book publishers, but rather from contemporary journals, court proceedings, and church records. By comparing the different types of testimony, interested scholars have found sufficient
correspondence to convince them of the general truthfulness of the
autobiographical accounts.[39]

As for the "nonrepresentative" nature of the antebellum recollections, supporters admit that the most compelling accounts in the narrative record have been composed largely by "exceptional" slaves, but claim that to doubt the relevancy of stories written by such bondsmen is "a specious argument in its inception." The great slave narrative, like all great autobiography, must of necessity be the work of the unusually perceptive viewer. Such gifted individuals possess the capacity to interpret historical events with extraordinary insight and clarity. To exclude these "exceptional" accounts would be to eliminate all powerful autobiographies as distortions of the events they pretend to describe. Moreover, as Marion Starling has noted in her study of the black narratives, it is very possible that the slave authors were not fewer proportionately than the percentile relationship between authors and nonauthors in the nonslave world of their day.[40]

notes

INTRODUCTION

1. Suzanne Keller, *Beyond the Ruling Class: Strategic Elites in Modern Society* (New York, 1963), p. 25; T. B. Bottomore, *Elites and Society* (New York, 1964), pp. 1-17.

2. Harold D. Lasswell, Daniel Lerner, and C. Easton Rothwell, *The Comparative Study of Elites* (Stanford, Calif., 1952), pp. 6-7; Vilfredo Pareto, *The Rise and Fall of the Elites: An Application of Theoretical Sociology* (Totowa, N.J., 1968), pp. 60-63, 86-87; Rupert Wilkinson, "Elites and Effectiveness," in *Governing Elites: Studies in Training and Selection,* ed. by Rupert Wilkinson (New York, 1969), pp. 217-221.

3. For example, see LeRoi Jones, *Blues People: Negro Music in White America* (New York, 1963), pp. 121-125; Walter Rodney, *West Africa and the Atlantic Slave-Trade* (Nairobi: East African Publishing House, 1967), pp. 7-14; Jesse Lemisch, "New Left Elitism: A Rejoinder," *Radical America,* I (September-October, 1967), 43-53.

4. James V. Downton, Jr., *Rebel Leadership: Commitment and Charisma in the Revolutionary Process* (New York, 1973), p. 23; Amitai Etzioni, "Dual Leadership in Complex Organizations," *American Sociological Review,* XXX (October, 1965); E. P. Hollander, *Leaders, Groups, and Influence* (New York, 1964), p.6; Burleigh B. Gardner and William F. Whyte, "The Man in the Middle: Position and Problems of the Foreman," *Applied Anthropology,* IV (Spring, 1945), 1-28.

5. For additional perspectives on the inappropriateness of "definitive" labels as they apply to interpretations of slavery, see Kenneth M. Stampp, "Introduction: A Humanistic Perspective," in *Reckoning with Slavery: A Critical Study in the Quantitative History of American Negro Slavery,* ed. by Paul A. David, Herbert G. Gutman, Richard Sutch, Peter Temin, Gavin Wright (New York, 1976), pp. 1-3; Eugene D. Genovese, *Roll, Jordan, Roll: The World the Slaves Made* (New York, 1974), p.676. For a random sampling of scholarly reviews that seem to seek definitive solutions to historical conundrums, see *Journal of American History,* LXIII (June,

1976), pp. 98-99, 154, 161, 184; *Journal of American History*, LXIII (September, 1976), pp. 430, 450.

6. Harriet Beecher Stowe, *Uncle Tom's Cabin* (New York, 1962 [Boston, 1852]), pp. 353-354. Mrs. Stowe defended her work by noting: "That the representations of . . . the features of life generally, as described on Legree's plantation, are not wild and fabulous drafts on the imagination, or exaggerated pictures of exceptional cases, there is the most abundant testimony before the world, and has been for a long number of years." Harriet Beecher Stowe, *A Key to Uncle Tom's Cabin: Presenting the Original Facts and Documents Upon which the Story Is Founded* (Boston, 1853), p. 43.

7. Stowe, *Uncle Tom's Cabin*, pp. 353-354, 356, 363, 366, 383, 401-402, 421-422. For other less well-known, but somewhat more "well-rounded," antebellum fictional treatments of slave drivers, see William Gilmore Simms, "The Snake of the Cabin," in *The Wigwam and the Cabin (Life in America)* (Ridgewood, N.J., 1968 [New York, 1845]), pp. 180-189; William Gilmore Simms, "Caloya; or, the Loves of the Driver," in *The Wigwam and the Cabin, or Tales of the South* (Charleston, 1852), pp. 127-195; Richard Hildreth, *The White Slave; or, Memoirs of a Fugitive* (Boston, 1852), pp. 189-192. For an appraisal of the drivers as "stock figures for villainy" in antebellum fiction, see Francis Pendleton Gaines, *The Southern Plantation: A Study in the Development and the Accuracy of a Tradition* (New York, 1925), pp. 147-148. For a recent "plantation novel" that exhibits the continuing influence of Mrs. Stowe's work, see George McNeill, *The Plantation* (New York, 1975), p. 68.

CHAPTER 1
WHO WERE THE SLAVE DRIVERS?

1. *Webster's New Collegiate Dictionary* (Springfield, Mass., 1973), p. 1091; *Webster's Third New International Dictionary of the English Language* (Springfield, Mass., 1963), p. 2139; Harold Wentworth and Stuart Berg Flexner, eds., *Dictionary of American Slang* (New York, 1975), p. 485.

2. John Hebron Moore, *Agriculture in Ante-Bellum Mississippi* (New York, 1958), p. 66; D. E. Huger Smith, "A Plantation Boyhood," in *A Carolina Rice Plantation of the Fifties*, ed. by Alice R. Huger Smith (New York, 1936), p. 66; J. C. Furnas, *Goodbye to Uncle Tom* (New York, 1956), p. 127; V. Alton Moody, "Slavery on Louisiana Sugar Plantations," *Louisiana Historical Quarterly*, VII (April, 1924), 211. In 1937 the great-grandson of rice planter Nathaniel Heyward wrote that the term *slave driver*

may have originated in colonial South Carolina as a result of the necessarily close supervision given newly arrived, non-English-speaking slaves by a ''domesticated Negro'' supervisor: ''When this Negro put them to work in the field, he was required to follow them foot to foot, so as to direct them how to use the few implements given them. . . . His walking behind them naturally suggested the idea that he was driving them, and hence the term came into general use. . . .'' Duncan Clinch Heyward, *Seed from Madagascar* (Chapel Hill, 1937), pp. 157-158.

3. These terms will be used interchangeably throughout the study—with *driver, foreman,* and *slave* or *black supervisor* being the most frequently appearing appellations. In contemporary accounts, drivers were sometimes referred to as *overseers.* Although such men did become either formally designated or de facto overseers when no white overseer was employed on the estate, to avoid confusion the term *overseer* will generally refer to a white or free black supervisor. When *overseer* is used to describe a slave supervisor, either the context or appropriate modifiers will make the individual's actual status readily apparent.

4. See, for example, Orland Kay Armstrong, *Old Massa's People: The Old Slaves Tell Their Story* (Indianapolis, 1931), p. 150; Bell Irvin Wiley, *Southern Negroes, 1861-1865* (New Haven, 1938), pp. 49-51; Mrs. Nicholas Ware Eppes, *The Negro of the Old South: A Bit of Period History* (Chicago, 1925), pp. 111-112; Federal Writers' Project, *Slave Narratives, A Folk History of Slavery in the United States from Interviews with Former Slaves:* Oklahoma narratives, XIII (Washington, D.C., 1941), p. 124, reprinted in *The American Slave: A Composite Autobiography,* ed. by George P. Rawick, VII (Westport, 1972), p. 124. Future references to the Slave Narrative Collection will be limited to citations from the more readily accessible Rawick edition.

5. See, for example, Rawick, *American Slave,* VI, pp. 62-63; Rawick, *American Slave,* XVI, p. 88; Rawick, *American Slave,* II, Pt. 1, p. 10.

6. Rawick, *American Slave,* XIII, Pt. 3, p. 269; Rawick, *American Slave,* IX, Pt. 3, p. 285; Rawick, *American Slave,* XIII, Pt. 4, pp. 177, 298; Rawick, *American Slave,* XII, Pt. 2, p. 13.

7. John Thompson, *The Life of John Thompson, A Fugitive Slave* (Worcester, 1856), p. 20; Kate E. R. Pickard, *The Kidnapped and the Ransomed. Being the Personal Recollections of Peter Still and His Wife "Vina," after Forty Years of Slavery* (Syracuse, 1856), pp. 35-36, 184-185; Jacob Stroyer, *My Life in the South* (Salem, 1898), pp. 23-24; Rawick, *American Slave,* XVII, p. 97; John Brown, *Slave Life in Georgia: A Narrative of the Life, Sufferings, and Escape of John Brown, A Fugitive Slave,* ed. by F. N. Boney (Savannah, 1972 [London, 1855]), pp. 37-38; Louis

Hughes, *Thirty Years a Slave* (Milwaukee, 1897), pp. 45-46.

8. In 1806 the Territorial Assembly of Louisiana made the presence of a white or free black overseer mandatory on every plantation. By 1850 at least twenty-five free blacks—twenty-two of whom were listed as mulattoes in the census of that year—were employed as overseers on Louisiana plantations. H. E. Sterkx, *The Free Negro in Ante-Bellum Louisiana* (Rutherford, N.J., 1972), p. 216; Annie Lee West Stahl, "The Free Negro in Ante-Bellum Louisiana," *Louisiana Historical Quarterly*, XXV (April, 1942), 391. For examples of free blacks employed as plantation labor supervisors in other regions, see Charles S. Sydnor, *Slavery in Mississippi* (Baton Rouge, 1966 [New York, 1933]), p. 220; William Jay, *Inquiry into the Character and Tendency of the American Colonization and American Anti-Slavery Societies* (New York, 1840 [1835]), p. 22; Marina Wikramanayake, *A World in Shadow: The Free Black in Antebellum South Carolina* (Columbia, 1973), p. 95; John Hope Franklin, *The Free Negro in North Carolina, 1790-1860* (Chapel Hill, 1943), pp. 147-148; Luther Porter Jackson, *Free Negro Labor and Property Holding in Virginia, 1830-1860* (New York, 1942), pp. 84-86; W. M. Mitchell, *The Under-Ground Railroad* (London, 1860), pp. iii-vi; Rawick, *American Slave*, XVII, pp. 300-301; Isaac Mason, *Life of Isaac Mason as a Slave* (Worcester, 1893), pp. 9-10.

9. For seventeenth-century examples of blacks employed as labor supervisors, see Helen Tunnicliff Catterall, ed., *Judicial Cases Concerning American Slavery and the Negro*, I (Washington, D.C., 1926), p. 78; *Maryland Gazette* (Annapolis), January 14-21, 1728-1729; Russell R. Menard, "The Maryland Slave Population, 1658 to 1730: A Demographic Profile of Blacks in Four Counties," *William and Mary Quarterly*, XXXII (January, 1975), 36.

10. Menard, "Maryland," pp. 36-37, 49-51.

11. Ulrich Bonnell Phillips, *American Negro Slavery* (Baton Rouge, 1969 [New York, 1918]), p. 247; Frederick Law Olmsted, *A Journey in the Seaboard Slave States with Remarks on Their Economy* (New York, 1859 [1856]), pp. 436-437; *Boston Recorder*, July 8, 1817; Kenneth M. Stampp, *The Peculiar Institution: Slavery in the Ante-Bellum South* (New York, 1956), p. 54; Heyward, *Seed*, pp. 105, 180; Rawick, *American Slave*, XVII, pp. 96-97; P. C. Weston, "Management of a Southern Plantation," *De Bow's Review*, XXII (January, 1857), 40; James Herbert Stone, "Black Leadership in the Old South: The Slave Drivers of the Rice Kingdom" (Ph.D. dissertation, Florida State University, 1976), pp. 18-24, 160-161.

12. William Kauffman Scarborough, *The Overseer: Plantation Management in the Old South* (Baton Rouge, 1966), p. 81; John B. Cade, "Out of the Mouths of Ex-Slaves," *Journal of Negro History*, XX (July, 1935), 314; Sydnor, *Slavery in Mississippi*, p. 73; Rawick, *American Slave*, IV, Pt. 2, p.

72; Julia Floyd Smith, *Slavery and Plantation Growth in Antebellum Florida, 1821-1860* (Gainesville, 1973), p. 71; Solomon Northup, *Twelve Years a Slave*, ed. by Sue Eakin and Joseph Logsdon (Baton Rouge, 1968 [Buffalo, 1853]), p. 159; Charles Ball, *Slavery in the United States: A Narrative of the Life and Adventures of Charles Ball* (New York, 1970 [1837]), pp. 147-148.

13. A study of industrial slave foremen, whether located in rural or urban areas of the South, is beyond the scope of this work. For an introduction to these industrial and craft operatives who supervised the slave sawyers, mill hands, tanners, and carpenters of the Old South, see Robert S. Starobin, *Industrial Slavery in the Old South* (New York, 1970), pp. 91-92, 105-109, 164,169-173; Olmsted, *Seaboard States*, pp. 102-103; Abigail Curlee, "A Study of Texas Slave Plantations, 1822 to 1865" (Ph. D. dissertation, University of Texas, Austin, 1932), p. 113; John Witherspoon DuBose, "Recollections of the Plantation," *Alabama Historical Quarterly*, I (Spring, 1930), 69; Edward T. Tayloe to B. O. Tayloe, August 20, 1833, Tayloe Papers, University of Virginia Library, Charlottesville; Rawick, *American Slave*, XII, Pt. 1, pp. 189-190; Rawick, *American Slave*, VII, pp. 266-268.

14. Scarborough, *Overseer*, pp. 13, 178-179; Stampp, *Peculiar Institution*, p. 40; Edwin Adams Davis, ed., *Plantation Life in the Florida Parishes of Louisiana, 1836-1846, as Reflected in the Diary of Bennet H. Barrow* (New York, 1943), p. 410; Rawick, *American Slave*, V, Pt. 3, p. 270. For slave-oriented perspectives on the various positions and status levels within the slave community, see Rawick, *American Slave*, III, Pt. 4, pp. 147-148; John W. Blassingame, "Status and Social Structure in the Slave Community: Evidence from New Sources," in *Perspectives and Irony in American Slavery*, ed. by Harry P. Owens (Jackson, Miss., 1976), pp. 137-151.

15. Robert William Fogel and Stanley L. Engerman, *Time on the Cross*, Vol. I: *The Economics of American Negro Slavery* (Boston, 1974), p.141. For examples of females performing driver-related tasks, see Arthur P. and Marion J. Ford, *Life in the Confederate Army and some Experiences and Sketches of Southern Life* (New York, 1905), pp. 129-136; Charles L. Perdue, Jr., Thomas E. Barden, and Robert K. Phillips, eds., *Weevils in the Wheat: Interviews with Virginia Ex-Slaves* (Charlottesville, 1976), p. 117; M. F. Jamison, *Autobiography and Work of Bishop M. F. Jamison, D.D.* (Nashville, 1912), pp. 22-23. For an interesting statement by a former slave manager regarding the relative laboring abilities of men and women, see Charles Nordhoff, *The Freedmen of South-Carolina* (New York, 1863), pp. 4-5, 8.

16. Louis Hughes, *Thirty Years a Slave* (Milwaukee, 1897), pp. 22-23;

Andrew Phelps McCormick, *Scotch-Irish in Ireland and in America* (n. p., 1897), p. 151; William H. Holcombe, "Sketches of Plantation-Life," *Knickerbocker*, LVII (June, 1861), 632; Rawick, *American Slave*, V, Pt. 4, pp. 113-114; John Witherspoon DuBose, "Autobiographical Sketches: Recollections of the Plantation—The Canebrake Negro, 1850-1865," p. 4, J. W. DuBose Papers, Alabama Dept. of Archives and History, Montgomery.

17. Eugene D. Genovese, *Roll, Jordan, Roll: The World the Slaves Made* (New York, 1974), p. 489; Benjamin Drew, ed., *A North-Side View of Slavery, the Refugee: or the Narratives of Fugitive Slaves in Canada* (Reading, Mass., 1969 [Boston, 1856]), p. 97; Curlee, "Slave Plantations," p. 113.

18. Weymouth T. Jordan, *Hugh Davis and His Alabama Plantation* (University, Ala., 1948), pp. 62-65, 69-71; J. D. B. De Bow, *The Industrial Resources, Statistics, Etc. of the United States*, II (New York, 1854), pp. 336-337; H. M. Henry, *The Police Control of the Slave in South Carolina* (Emory, Va., 1914), pp. 26-27; Zaphaniah Kingsley, *A Treatise on the Patriarchal, or Cooperative System of Society as it Exists . . . Under the Name of Slavery* (Freeport, N. Y., 1970 [n.p., 1829]), p. 15; Harriet Martineau, *Retrospect of Western Travel*, I (London, 1838), pp. 250-251; J. H. Bernard, "The Importance of Grass Crops—Unsuccessful Experiments," *Farmers' Register*, V (July 1, 1837), 172-173; Foby, "Management of Servants," *Southern Cultivator*, XI (August, 1853), 226-228; Thomas Spalding, "On the Culture, Harvesting and Threshing of Rice, and on the Rust in Cotton," *Southern Agriculturist*, VIII (April, 1835), 169-174; Edmund Ruffin, "Incidents of My Life," MSS, II, pp. 227-228, Edmund Ruffin Papers, Southern Historical Collection, University of North Carolina, Chapel Hill.

19. William Allen, *Life and Work of John McDonogh* (Baltimore, 1886), p. 50; Lane Carter Kendall, "John McDonogh—Slave Owner," *Louisiana Historical Quarterly*, XVI (January, 1933), 130-131; M. Boyd Coyner, Jr., "John Hartwell Cocke of Bremo: Agriculture and Slavery in the Ante-Bellum South" (Ph.D. dissertation, University of Virginia, 1961), pp. 376-384; Walter L. Fleming, "Jefferson Davis, the Negroes and the Negro Problem," *Sewanee Review*, XVI (October, 1908), 408-410.

20. "Overseers," *American Cotton Planter*, II (1854), 150; Holcombe, "Plantation-Life," p. 627; "On the Causes of the Long-Continued Decline, and Great Depression of Agriculture in Virginia," *Farmers' Register*, IV (April 1, 1837), 727.

21. John Mercer Langston, *From the Virginia Plantation to the National Capitol* (Hartford, 1894), p. 12; Henry, *Police Control*, pp. 18-19; Henry Bibb, *Narrative of the Life and Adventures of Henry Bibb, An American*

Slave (New York, 1849), p. 83; Helen Tunnicliff Catterall, ed., *Judicial Cases Concerning American Slavery and the Negro*, II (Washington, D.C., 1926), p. 359; William Edwards Clement, *Plantation Life on the Mississippi* (New Orleans, 1952), p. 179.

22. The perplexities of determining a "conventional ratio" of drivers to slaves have been increased by the various definitions of *driver*—officially appointed or otherwise—given by those historians who have broached the subject as well as by the differing crops and methods of crop production that prevailed throughout the Old South. For a historiographical perspective on this question, see Phillips, *American Negro Slavery*, p. 228; Ralph Betts Flanders, *Plantation Slavery in Georgia* (Chapel Hill, 1933), p. 143; Genovese, *Roll*, p. 366; and the sources cited in chapter 2, notes 31 and 32, this book.

23. J. Carlyle Sitterson, *Sugar Country: The Cane Sugar Industry in the South, 1753-1950* (Lexington, 1953), p. 63; Frederick Law Olmsted, *A Journey in the Back Country* (New York, 1860), p. 47; "Carter Papers," *Virginia Magazine*, VII (July, 1899), 64-68; Fisk University, *Unwritten History of Slavery: Autobiographical Accounts of Negro Ex-Slaves* (Westport, 1974 [Nashville, Tenn., 1945]), p. 55.

24. William S. Pettigrew to his sister, ca. 1860, Pettigrew Papers, Southern Historical Collection, University of North Carolina, Chapel Hill; Robert F. W. Allston to Benjamin Allston, August 29, 1860, in *The South Carolina Rice Plantation as Revealed in the Papers of Robert F. W. Allston*, ed. by J. H. Easterby (Chicago, 1945), pp. 164-165; Perdue, Barden, and Phillips, *Weevils*, p. 110; Armstrong, *Massa's People*, p. 211; William Green, *Narrative of Events in the Life of William Green* (Springfield, Mass., 1853), pp. 6-7; William Webb, *History of William Webb* (Detroit, 1873), pp. 9-10.

25. Drew, *North-Side View*, p. 190. For examples of other tall, muscular drivers, see Sarah Bradford, *Harriet Tubman: The Moses of Her People* (New York, 1961 [1886]), p. 39; Rawick, *American Slave*, XIII, Pt. 3, p. 187; Rawick, *American Slave*, VII, p. 77; Olmsted, *Back Country*, pp. 81-82; Bernard Robb, *Welcum Hinges* (New York, 1960 [1942]), pp. 59-60.

26. Harry Smith, *Fifty Years of Slavery in the United States of America* (Grand Rapids, 1891), pp. 34, 39; Northup, *Twelve Years*, p. 244; James Battle Avirett, *The Old Plantation: How We Lived in Great House and Cabin Before the War* (New York, 1901), p. 62.

27. William S. Pettigrew to his sister, ca. 1860, Pettigrew Papers. See also Joe Gray Taylor, *Negro Slavery in Louisiana* (Baton Rouge, 1963), p. 80; Genovese, *Roll*, pp. 369-370.

28. Rawick, *American Slave*, VI, p. 117; Rawick, *American Slave*, XV, Pt. 2, p. 301. See also *Virginia Gazette* (Williamsburg), March 23, 1769;

Heyward, *Seed*, p. 113; Ulrich B. Phillips, ed., *Plantation and Frontier Documents: 1649-1863*, I (Cleveland, 1909), p. 139.

29. Smith, "Plantation Boyhood," p. 65. See also Rawick, *American Slave*, XVI, p. 52.

30. Rawick, *American Slave*, VIII, Pt. 2, p. 1; Kemp Plummer Battle, *Memories of an Old-Time Tar Heel*, ed. by William James Battle (Chapel Hill, 1945), p. 126; Perdue, Barden, and Phillips, *Weevils*, p. 317; Work Projects Administration, Savannah Unit, Georgia Writers' Project, *Drums and Shadows: Survival Studies Among the Georgia Coastal Negroes* (Athens, 1940), p. 166; Rawick, *American Slave*, IX, Pt. 3, p. 139.

31. See Rawick, *American Slave*, XIII, Pt. 3, pp. 112-113; Rawick, *American Slave*, X, Pt. 5, p. 339.

32. Sam Aleckson, *Before the War, and After the Union: An Autobiography* (Boston, 1929), p. 61.

33. E. E. McCollam Diary, November 1, 1846, Dept. of Archives, Louisiana State University, Baton Rouge; Elisha Cain to Mary Telfair, December 14, 1840 in Phillips, *Plantation and Frontier Documents*, I, p. 335.

34. Avery Craven, *Edmund Ruffin, Southerner: A Study in Secession* (New York, 1932), p. 19; John Thompson, *The Life of John Thompson, A Fugitive Slave* (Worcester, 1856), pp. 46-48. See also William Proctor Gould Diary, January 2, 1855, Alabama Dept. of Archives and History, Montgomery; Thomas R. Harrison to John Hartwell Cocke, July 10, 1828, J. H. Cocke Papers, University of Virginia Library, Charlottesville; Davis, *Diary of Bennet H. Barrow*, pp. 86, 90, 99, 100, 154; Rawick, *American Slave*, XIV, p. 303; William Parker, "The Freedman's Story," *Atlantic Monthly*, XVII (February, 1866), 154.

35. Rawick, *American Slave*, V, Pt. 4, p. 129. See also Rawick, *American Slave*, VIII, Pt. 1, p. 30.

36. Rawick, American Slave, XIII, Pt. 3, p. 229; Rawick, *American Slave*, XVII, p. 235; Rawick, *American Slave*, XIII, Pt. 4, p. 195; Heyward, *Seed*, p. 179; Manual of Rules, James Henry Hammond Papers, Library of Congress.

37. Smith, "Plantation Boyhood," p. 64; William Thomson, *A Tradesman's Travels in the United States and Canada, in the Years 1840, 41, & 42* (Edinburgh, 1842), pp. 190-191; Charles Lyell, *A Second Visit to the United States of North America*, I (London, 1850), p. 358; Sydnor, *Slavery in Mississippi*, p. 74; Olmsted, *Seaboard States*, p. 439. Georgia planter W. W. Hazzard expressed an interesting reason for entrusting his driver with extensive disciplinary powers. He wrote: "I rarely punish myself, but make my driver, virtually an, executive officer, to inflict punish-

ments; that I may remove from the mind of the servant who commits a fault, the unfavourable impression, too apt to be indulged in, that it is for the pleasure of punishing, rather than for the purpose of enforcing obedience and establishing good order that punishments are inflicted.'' W. W. Hazzard, "On the General Management of a Plantation," *Southern Agriculturist*, IV (July, 1831), 350.

38. Olmsted, *Seaboard States*, p. 431.

39. Sydnor, *Slavery in Mississippi*, p. 74; Hazzard, "General Management," p. 352; Pickard, *Peter Still*, p. 155; Smith, *Fifty Years*, pp. 40-41; John Brown, *Slave Life in Georgia: A Narrative of the Life, Sufferings, and Escape of John Brown, a Fugitive Slave*, ed. by F. N. Boney (Savannah, 1972 [London, 1855]), p. 109; Linda Brent, *Incidents in the Life of a Slave Girl*, ed. by L. Maria Child (New York, 1973 [Boston, 1861]), p. 95; Rawick, *American Slave*, III, Pt. 4, pp. 116-117.

40. William S. Pettigrew to Moses, August 30, 1856, September 16, 1856, and July 6, 1857; Moses to William S. Pettigrew, September 6, 1856, Pettigrew Papers, Southern Historical Collection, University of North Carolina, Chapel Hill. See also John Nevitt Diary, July 21, 1827; August 10, 1827; December 14, 1827; January 14, 1828, John Nevitt Plantation Papers, Southern Historical Collection, University of North Carolina, Chapel Hill.

41. Rawick, *American Slave*, VI, p. 434; Rawick, *American Slave*, II, Pt. 1, p. 158; Edward A. Pollard, *Black Diamonds Gathered in the Darkey Homes of the South* (New York, 1860), pp. 79-80; James Benson Sellers, *Slavery in Alabama* (University, Ala., 1950), pp. 248-249; Wendell Holmes Stephenson, "A Quarter-Century of a Mississippi Plantation: Eli J. Capell of 'Pleasant Hill,' " *Mississippi Valley Historical Review*, XXIII (December, 1936), 357.

42. Rawick, *American Slave*, XII, Pt. 1, pp. 80, 83; Rawick, *American Slave*, XVII, pp. 156, 199; Rawick, *American Slave*, XIII, Pt. 3, p. 270. See also Rawick, *American Slave*, VII, p. 303.

43. Rawick, *American Slave*, XII, Pt. 1, pp. 80-81; Rawick, *American Slave*, XVII, p. 156. See also Hallie Q. Brown, ed., *Homespun Heroines and other Women of Distinction* (Xenia, Ohio, 1926), p. 104; Rawick, *American Slave*, XV, Pt. 2, pp. 301-303.

44. Ulrich Bonnell Phillips and James David Glunt, eds., *Florida Plantation Records from the Papers of George Noble Jones* (St. Louis, 1927), p. 47; Heyward, *Seed*, pp. 101-102; Rawick, *American Slave*, XVI, pp. 51-52; Rawick, *American Slave*, VI, p. 154. See also Northup, *Twelve Years*, p. 128.

45. An example of such privileges was given in the FWP narrative of former Louisiana slave Fred Brown. In describing plantation marriage prac-

tices, Brown noted: "Sometimes de overlooker don' let dem git married. I 'splains it dis way. He am used to father de chillun. . . . De overlooker, he am portly man. Dem dat him picks he overlooks, and not 'low dem to marry or to go round with other nigger men. If dey do, its whippin' 'sho'. De massa raises some fine, portly chillen, and dey sol' some, after dey's half-grown, for $500 and sometimes more." Rawick, *American Slave*, IV, Pt. 1, p. 158. See also Frances Anne Kemble, *Journal of a Residence on a Georgian Plantation in 1838-1839*, ed. by John A. Scott (New York, 1961 [1863]), pp. 269-270; Rawick, *American Slave*, XVII, p. 168; Rawick, *American Slave*, VII, p. 13; Henry S. Foote, *Casket of Reminiscences* (Washington, D.C., 1874), pp. 201-205.

46. Perdue, Barden, and Phillips, *Weevils*, p. 26.

47. Basil Hall, *Travels in North America, in the Years 1827 and 1828*, III (Edinburgh, 1829), pp. 144-145. See also Norman B. Wood, *The White Side of a Black Subject: A Vindication of the Afro-American Race* (Chicago, 1897), pp. 303-304. The prices received for drivers at such auctions varied greatly. Selling price was dependent more upon the age, health, and assumed usefulness and productivity of the slave as well as upon market factors such as supply-demand and year sold than it was upon the mere fact that the bondsman in question had once served as a driver. Foremen were not inevitably the most valuable slaves to appear in plantation inventories and estate appraisals. The family described by Hall was "knocked down" for $1,450. For estimates of the cash value of individual drivers, see Bennett Harrison Wall, "Ebenezer Pettigrew, An Economic Study of an Ante-Bellum Planter" (Ph.D. dissertation, University of North Carolina, Chapel Hill, 1946), p. 135; Davis, *Diary of Bennet H. Barrow*, pp. 394-396; List and Inventory of the Negro[e]s on the Plantation of Messrs. Bruce, Seddon, & Wilkins St. James [Parish, La.], Nov. 22nd, 1849 in James Coles Bruce Family Papers, University of Virginia Library, Charlottesville; Work Projects Administration, Savannah Unit, Georgia Writers' Project, "Drakies Plantation," *Georgia Historical Quarterly*, XXIV (September, 1940), 224; Phillips and Glunt, *Florida Plantation Records*, pp. 534-535; James Habersham to William Knox, July 8, 1772 in Phillips, *Plantation and Frontier Documents*, I, p. 319.

48. Jermain W. Loguen, *The Rev. J. W. Loguen, as a Slave and as a Freeman. A Narrative of Real Life* (Syracuse, 1859), pp. 258-259; William G. Eliot, *The Story of Archer Alexander, from Slavery to Freedom, March 30, 1863* (Boston, 1885), pp. 41-42, 75-82. See also James L. Smith, *Autobiography of James L. Smith* (Norwich, 1881), p. 4.

49. Perdue, Barden, and Phillips, *Weevils*, p. 26. See also Rawick, *American Slave*, XIV, Pt. 1, p. 356; Rawick, *American Slave*, IX, Pt. 3, p.

120; Peter Randolph, *From Slave Cabin to the Pulpit*: The Autobiography of Rev. Peter Randolph (Boston, 1893), pp. 15-16.

50. Rawick, *American Slave*, IV, Pt. 1, pp. 1-2.

51. Randolph, *Autobiography*, pp. 15-16. See also Kemble, *Journal*, pp. 317-318; Francis B. Leigh, *Ten Years on a Georgia Plantation Since the War* (London, 1883), pp. 183-185.

52. Sitterson, *Sugar Country*, p. 90; Hazzard, "General Management," pp. 351-352; Mary Howard Schoolcraft, *Letters on the Condition of the African Race in the United States*, in *Plantation Life: The Narratives of Mrs. Henry Rowe Schoolcraft* (New York, 1969 [Philadelphia, 1852]), p. 12. For examples of "connubial incompatibility" between individual drivers and their wives, see Ebenezer Pettigrew to Mary S. Bryan, June 9, 1837, Bryan MSS, North Carolina Dept. of Archives and History, Raleigh; Charles S. Sydnor, *A Gentleman of the Old Natchez Region: Benjamin L. C. Wailes* (Durham, 1938), p. 107. For examples of particularly sly and rebellious slaves within the drivers' households, see Davis, *Diary of Bennet H. Barrow*, p. 164; Rawick, *American Slave*, VII, p. 129; Rawick, *American Slave*, XVII, p. 97.

53. Perdue, Barden, and Phillips, *Weevils*, p. 317.

54. See Genovese, *Roll*, pp. 199, 258.

55. Victoria V. Clayton, *White and Black Under the Old Regime* (Milwaukee, 1899), pp. 23-24. For examples of other driver-preachers, see Rawick, *American Slave*, IV, Pt. 1, p. 274; Charles Emery Stevens, *Anthony Burns: A History* (Boston, 1856), p. 165; Josiah Henson, *An Autobiography of the Rev. Josiah Henson ("Uncle Tom") from 1789 to 1881* (Reading, Mass., 1969 [London, 1881], pp. 26, 139-140; Drew, *North-Side View*, p. 91; Olmsted, *Seaboard States*, p. 451.

56. Mary Boykin Chesnut, *A Diary from Dixie*, ed. by Ben Ames Williams (Boston, 1949 [New York, 1905]), pp. 148-149. For examples of other drivers who were prayer leaders and devout communicants, see Charles C. Jones, *The Religious Instruction of the Negroes in the United States* (Savannah, 1842), p. 57; J. H. Cocke Journal, December 20, 1852, J. H. Cocke Papers, University of Virginia Library, Charlottesville; G. Lewis, *Impressions of America and the American Churches* (Edinburgh, 1845), p. 128; Benjamin Allston to Robert F. W. Allston, March 31, 1861 in Easterby, *Papers of Robert F. W. Allston*, p. 173.

57. For a case study of the alienating effects that white Christian hypocrisy—in both the South and the North—had upon one bondsman's religious beliefs, see William L. Van Deburg, "Frederick Douglass: Maryland Slave to Religious Liberal," *Maryland Historical Magazine*, LXIX (Spring, 1974), 27-43.

58. William Still, *The Underground Rail Road* (Philadelphia, 1871), p. 420.

59. Mary Stevenson, ed., *The Diary of Clarissa Adger Bowen, Ashtabula Plantation, 1865* (Pendleton, S.C., 1973), p. 48; John B. Adger, *My Life and Times, 1810-1899* (Richmond, Va., 1899), pp. 346-348. For a story about another driver who had the ability to argue "with an obstinancy worthy of Gibbon or Voltaire" that the Bible "contradicted itself in many places," see Holcombe, "Plantation-Life," p. 622.

60. E. Merton Coulter, *Thomas Spalding of Sapelo* (University, La., 1940), pp. 83-84; Caroline Couper Lovell, *The Golden Isles of Georgia* (Boston, 1932), pp. 103-104; Work Projects Administration, *Drums and Shadows*, p. 161. For stories of other Islamic drivers, see Lyell, *Second Visit*, I, p. 359; David Brown, *The Planter: or, Thirteen Years in the South. By a Northern Man* (Philadelphia, 1853), pp. 126-127. For Harris's rendering of the Bu Allah traditions, see *The Story of Aaron (So Named) The Son of Ben Ali* (Boston, 1896) and *Aaron in the Wildwoods* (Boston, 1897). For an account of the hardships faced by one Islamic slave because of his religious beliefs, see Philip D. Curtin, ed., *Africa Remembered: Narratives by West Africans from the Era of the Slave Trade* (Madison, 1968), p. 41. See also Terry Alford, *Prince Among Slaves* (New York, 1977).

61. Loguen, *Narrative*, p. 265.

62. Perdue, Barden, and Phillips, *Weevils*, p. 279; Page Thacker, *Plantation Reminiscences* (Owensboro, Ky., 1878), p. 46; Charles Lanman, *Haw-Ho-Noo; or Records of a Tourist* (Philadelphia, 1850), p. 142; Mary Ross Banks, *Bright Days in the Old Plantation Time* (Boston, 1882), pp. 121-123.

63. Garnett Andrews, *Reminiscences of an Old Georgia Lawyer* (Atlanta, 1870), pp. 10-11. For other descriptions of corn generals and driver-generals at work, see Rawick, *American Slave*, XIII, Pt. 4, pp. 81, 119-120; Rawick, *American Slave*, VI, pp. 199-200.

64. Banks, *Bright Days*, pp. 126-127; Rawick, *American Slave*, XIII, Pt. 4, pp. 144-145; Wall, "Ebenezer Pettigrew," p. 109; Avirett, *Old Plantation*, p. 146.

65. Rawick, *American Slave*, V, Pt. 3, p. 214; Rawick, *American Slave*, XIII, Pt. 4, p. 120; Genovese, *Roll*, pp. 315-319.

66. For accounts of drivers who remained on the job throughout the Civil War, see Rawick, *American Slave*, XI, pp. 324-327; Rawick, *American Slave*, VIII, Pt. 2, pp. 300-301; Rawick, *American Slave*, VI, p. 224; Rawick, *American Slave*, III, Pt. 4, p. 46.

67. Rawick, *American Slave*, VII, pp. 251-253. For stories of other runaways and black Union troops drawn from the ranks of the drivers, see H.

C. Bruce, *The New Man: Twenty-Nine Years a Slave, Twenty-Nine Years a Free Man* (York, Pa., 1895), pp. 104, 107-109; William Wells Brown, *The Black Man, His Antecedents, His Genius, and His Achievements* (New York, 1863), pp. 291-297; D. E. Huger Smith to Mrs. William Mason Smith, July 24, 1863, in *Mason Smith Family Letters, 1860-1868,* ed. by Daniel E. Huger Smith, Alice R. Huger Smith, and Arney R. Childs (Columbia, S.C., 1950), p. 56; Eleanor P. and Charles B. Cross, eds., *Glencoe Diary: The War-Time Journal of Elizabeth Curtis Wallace* (Chesapeake, Va., 1968), p. 27; Rawick, *American Slave,* XI, p. 30.

68. G. P. Whittington, ed., "Concerning the Loyalty of Slaves in North Louisiana in 1863: Letters from John H. Ransdell to Governor Thomas O. Moore, dated 1863," *Louisiana Historical Quarterly,* XIV (October, 1931), 491-492, 495. See also Genovese, *Roll,* pp. 98-99; W. Sweet to Adele Petigru Allston, August 31, 1864; Jesse Belflowers to Adele Petigru Allston, October 19, 1864, in Easterby, *Papers of Robert F. W. Allston,* pp. 298, 310; Chesnut, *Diary,* pp. 244-245.

69. Rawick, *American Slave,* VIII, Pt. 2, pp. 346-348, 350.

70. Rawick, *American Slave,* IV, Pt. 2, pp. 77-78; Rawick, *American Slave,* VII, pp. 227-228. See also Rawick, *American Slave,* XIV, pp. 60-61.

71. Rawick, *American Slave,* VII, pp. 289, 292-293; Rawick, *American Slave,* II, Pt. 1, pp. 118-119, 122. See also Rawick, *American Slave,* VII, pp. 300-301; Rawick, *American Slave,* X, Pt. 6, p. 49.

72. Rawick, *American Slave,* IX, Pt. 3, p. 56; Rawick, *American Slave,* VIII, Pt. 2, p. 348. For other examples of the type of provisions made by slaveholders for the employment of their former drivers, see Rawick, *American Slave,* VI, pp. 211-212; Rawick, *American Slave,* VIII, Pt. 2, pp. 300-301; Rawick, *American Slave,* XIII, Pt. 3, p. 114; Rawick, *American Slave,* VII, p. 130; Rawick, *American Slave,* IV, Pt. 2, p. 244; Stephenson, "Eli J. Capell," pp. 373-374.

73. Benjamin Allston to Ellen Allston, January 12, 1868, in Easterby, *Papers of Robert F. W. Allston,* pp. 239-240.

74. Rawick, *American Slave,* XII, Pt. 1, p. 79. See also Rawick, *American Slave,* XV, Pt. 2, p. 36; Clayton, *White and Black,* pp. 168-169.

75. Rawick, *American Slave,* X, Pt. 6, p. 49; Adger, *Life and Times,* pp. 348-349; Stevenson, *Diary of Clarissa Adger Bowen,* p. 93; Bruce, *New Man,* p. 112; Rawick, *American Slave,* VI, p. 427; Rawick, *American Slave,* XVII, p. 201.

76. Bruce, *New Man,* p. 155; Rawick, *American Slave,* III, Pt. 3, pp. 45-46; Vernon Lane Wharton, *The Negro in Mississippi, 1865-1890* (New York, 1965 [Chapel Hill, 1947]), pp. 42, 145; Rawick, *American Slave,* XI, p. 54.

77. Rawick, *American Slave*, VI, pp. 117-118.

78. Walter L. Fleming, *Civil War and Reconstruction in Alabama* (New York, 1905), p. 210.

79. Bruce, *New Man*, pp. 99-100.

CHAPTER 2
THE HISTORIANS

1. J. C. Furnas, *Goodbye to Uncle Tom* (New York, 1956), p. 4.

2. Ulrich Bonnell Phillips, *Life and Labor in the Old South* (Boston, 1963 [1929]), pp. 196, 199-200. For Phillips's opinion of the quality of white labor see Phillips, *American Negro Slavery: A Survey of the Supply, Employment and Control of Negro Labor as Determined by the Plantation Regime* (New York, 1918), p. 395; Phillips, *Life and Labor*, pp. 182-183.

3. Phillips, *Life and Labor*, pp. 196, 207, 305; Phillips, *American Negro Slavery*, pp. 281, 339.

4. Phillips, *Life and Labor*, p. 327; Phillips, *American Negro Slavery*, p. 339.

5. Phillips, *Life and Labor*, p. 383, preface p. 2.

6. For a study of the racism and nativism evidenced by historians of the Phillips era, see I. A. Newby, *Jim Crow's Defense: Anti-Negro Thought in America, 1900-1930* (Baton Rouge, 1965), pp. 52-82.

7. Carter G. Woodson, review of Phillips, *American Negro Slavery*, *Mississippi Valley Historical Review*, V (March, 1919), 480-482.

8. I. A. Newby, "Historians and Negroes," *Journal of Negro History*, LIV (January, 1969), 37-39. The number of accounts slighting the driver's responsibilities, capabilities, and simple presence are legion. For a particularly interesting example of this type of treatment, see Caleb Perry Patterson, *The Negro in Tennessee, 1790-1865* (Austin, 1922), pp. 69-70.

9. Albert Bushnell Hart, *Slavery and Abolition, 1831-1841* (New York, 1906), p. 120; Charles Sackett Sydnor, *Slavery in Mississippi* (New York, 1933), pp. 74-75; V. Alton Moody, "Slavery on Louisiana Sugar Plantations," *Louisiana Historical Quarterly* VII (April, 1924), p. 211; Carl Bridenbaugh, *Myths & Realities: Societies of the Colonial South* (New York, 1968 [Baton Rouge, 1952]), p. 63; William Dosite Postell, *The Health of Slaves on Southern Plantations* (Baton Rouge, 1951), pp. 25-26.

10. Kenneth M. Stampp, *The Peculiar Institution: Slavery in the Ante-Bellum South* (New York, 1956), p. vii.

11. Phillips, *American Negro Slavery*, p. 307; Stampp, *Peculiar Institution*, pp. 34, 146, 151, 335; Kenneth M. Stampp, "The Daily Life of the

Southern Slave," in *Key Issues in the Afro-American Experience,* I, ed. by Nathan I. Huggins, Martin Kilson, and Daniel M. Fox (New York, 1971), p. 121.

12. Elkins's "Sambo" and that of *Uncle Tom's Cabin* fame were, as Ann Lane has pointed out, slaves of differing characteristics, but both could be said to have suffered grievously from those elements within the plantation system that tended to cause a skewing and degradation of human personality. See Ann J. Lane, Introduction to *The Debate Over Slavery: Stanley Elkins and His Critics,* ed. by Ann J. Lane (Urbana, 1971), p. 16; Stanley M. Elkins, *Slavery: A Problem in American Institutional and Intellectual Life* (Chicago, 1968 [1959]), pp. 82-86.

13. John A. Garraty, ed., "Stanley M. Elkins: Slavery," in *Interpreting American History: Conversations with Historians,* I (New York, 1970), p. 198; Elkins, *Slavery,* p. 104.

14. See Earl E. Thorpe, "Chattel Slavery & Concentration Camps," *Negro History Bulletin,* XXV (May, 1962), 175; Lane, *Debate,* p. 17.

15. Bruno Bettelheim, *The Informed Heart: Autonomy in a Mass Age* (New York, 1960), pp. 123, 169, 171, 179-187, 235; Bruno Bettelheim, "Individual and Mass Behavior in Extreme Situations," *Journal of Abnormal and Social Psychology,* XXXVIII (October, 1943), 417.

16. Elkins, *Slavery,* pp. 112-113.

17. Elie A. Cohen, *Human Behavior in the Concentration Camp* (New York, 1953), pp. 199-203; Erving Goffman, *Asylums: Essays on the Social Situation of Mental Patients and Other Inmates* (Garden City, 1961), pp. 64-65; Terrence Des Pres, *The Survivor: An Anatomy of Life in the Death Camps* (New York, 1976), pp. vi, 56, 94, 108, 116-118, 151-155, 199, 202.

18. Elkins, *Slavery,* pp. 137-139.

19. Stampp, *Peculiar Institution,* see especially chapters 3 and 10.

20. In recent years, Stampp and Elkins have been subjected to a good deal of criticism for their limited use of the slave narrative materials. See William W. Nichols, "Slave Narratives: Dismissed Evidence in the Writing of Southern History," *Phylon,* XXXII (Winter, 1971), 403-409; Robert William Fogel and Stanley L. Engerman, *Time on the Cross, Vol. II: Evidence and Methods–A Supplement* (Boston, 1974), pp. 225-235.

21. John W. Blassingame, *The Slave Community: Plantation Life in the Antebellum South* (New York, 1972), pp. vii-viii, 153, 161, 210, 213, 216.

22. J. Carlyle Sitterson, "The William J. Minor Plantations: A Study in Ante-Bellum Absentee Ownership," *Journal of Southern History,* IX (February, 1943), 65. A decade later, Sitterson could still write that "it would be interesting to know more about the drivers—their ages, type of Negro, methods used to get work from the slaves, and the attitude of the other

Negroes toward them— but unfortunately the plantation journals say almost nothing about them." J. Carlyle Sitterson, *Sugar Country: The Cane Sugar Industry in the South, 1753-1950* (Lexington, 1953), p. 64.

23. Eugene D. Genovese, "The Legacy of Slavery and the Roots of Black Nationalism," *Studies on the Left,* VI (November-December, 1966), 9; Eugene D. Genovese, "American Slaves and Their History," *New York Review of Books,* XV (December 3, 1970), 34.

24. Eugene D. Genovese, *Roll, Jordan, Roll: The World the Slaves Made* (New York, 1974), pp. xvi-xvii, 6-7, 146-147, 658-659.

25. Genovese, *Roll,* pp. 366, 378-380, 382-384, 386-387, 493. In an earlier study of the antebellum ex-slave autobiographies, Gilbert Osofsky also recognized the powerful positive influence that drivers could have by serving as "models of behavior and authority" for the younger slaves. See Gilbert Osofsky, ed., *Puttin' On Ole Massa: The Slave Narratives of Henry Bibb, William Wells Brown, and Solomon Northup* (New York, 1969), pp. 38-39.

26. See Randall M. Miller, "The Man in the Middle: The Black Slave Driver," paper presented at the Organization of American Historians' meeting, April 9, 1976, St. Louis, Missouri; William L. Van Deburg, "The Slave Drivers of Arkansas: A New View from the Narratives," *Arkansas Historical Quarterly,* XXXV (Autumn, 1976), 231-245.

27. Genovese, *Roll,* pp. 3, 387. For other recent interpretations that have stressed the ambiguous nature of the driver's role, see Earl E. Thorpe, *The Old South: A Psychohistory* (Durham, 1972), pp. 134-136; Leslie Howard Owens, *This Species of Property: Slave Life and Culture in the Old South* (New York, 1976), p. 122; James Herbert Stone, "Black Leadership in the Old South: The Slave Drivers of the Rice Kingdom" (Ph.D. dissertation, Florida State University, 1976), pp. 173, 187-188, 228-229; Nathan Irvin Huggins, *Black Odyssey: The Afro-American Ordeal in Slavery* (New York, 1977), pp. 137, 156, 158.

28. Stanley Feldstein, *Once a Slave: The Slaves' View of Slavery* (New York, 1971), pp. 13, 118-121; John T. Kneebone, "Sambo and the Slave Narratives: A Note on Sources," *Essays in History,* XIX (1975), 18.

29. George P. Rawick, *From Sundown to Sunup: The Making of the Black Community* (Westport, 1972), pp. 3, 59-60, 95-96.

30. Robert S. Starobin, "Privileged Bondsmen and the Process of Accommodation: The Role of Houseservants and Drivers as Seen in Their Own Letters," *Journal of Social History,* V (Fall, 1971), 50, 52, 58. For an instructive shift in Starobin's interpretation of the drivers, see his *Blacks in Bondage: Letters of American Slaves* (New York, 1974), pp. 11-13. Both the advantages and disadvantages of using these sources for the study of the black foremen will be seen in chapter 3. For the views of another well-known

historian whose opinion of the driver changed over the years, compare Clement Eaton's account in *A History of the Old South* (New York, 1949), p. 259 with that in his *The Mind of the Old South* (Baton Rouge, 1967), pp. vii, 184-187, 198-199.

31. Robert William Fogel and Stanley L. Engerman, *Time on the Cross*, I, *The Economics of American Negro Slavery* (Boston, 1974), pp. 40, 147, 149, 192, 196, 209-215, 231; Fogel and Engerman, *Time on the Cross*, II, pp. 39-40, 151-152. For an earlier study that stressed the superior quality of black labor, see C. L. R. James, "The Atlantic Slave Trade and Slavery: Some Interpretations of Their Significance in the Development of the United States and the Western World," in *Amistad 1*, ed. by John A. Williams and Charles F. Harris (New York, 1970), pp. 149-154.

32. Fogel and Engerman, *Time on the Cross*, I, pp. 4, 8; Richard Sutch, "The Treatment Received by American Slaves: A Critical Review of the Evidence Presented in *Time on the Cross*," *Explorations in Economic History*, XII (October, 1975), 349-352; Paul A. David and Peter Temin, "Slavery: The Progressive Institution?" *Journal of Economic History*, XXXIV (September, 1974), 767; Herbert Gutman and Richard Sutch, "Sambo Makes Good, or Were Slaves Imbued with the Protestant Work Ethic," in *Reckoning with Slavery: A Critical Study in the Quantitative History of American Negro Slavery* (New York, 1976), 80-87; Peter Kolchin, "Toward a Reinterpretation of Slavery," *Journal of Social History*, IX (Fall, 1975), 104, 112; Herbert G. Gutman, *Slavery and the Numbers Game: A Critique of Time on the Cross* (Urbana, 1975), 9, 48, 65-69.

33. Gutman, *Numbers Game*, pp. 28, 166-169; Sutch, "Treatment," p. 346. See also Sterling Plumpp, review of *Time on the Cross*, *Black Books Bulletin*, III (Spring, 1975), 54-58.

34. Gutman, *Numbers Game*, p. 169; Fogel and Engerman, *Time on the Cross*, I, p. 223. For a study that posits the existence of a black work ethic that was "at once a defense against an enforced system of economic exploitation and an autonomous assertion of values generally associated with preindustrial peoples" see Genovese, *Roll*, pp. 285-294, 309-324.

CHAPTER 3
THE PLANTERS

1. W. J. Cash, *The Mind of the South* (New York, 1960 [1941]), pp. 129-131. See also Paul H. Buck, *The Road to Reunion, 1865-1900* (Boston, 1937), pp. 209-213.

2. James Battle Avirett, *The Old Plantation: How We Lived in Great House and Cabin Before the War* (New York, 1901), pp. 7-8, 14, 200. See

also Victoria Clayton, *White and Black Under the Old Regime* (Milwaukee, 1899), pp. 131, 195; Isaac DuBose Seabrook, *Before and After or the Relations of the Races at the South*, ed. by John Hammond Moore (Baton Rouge, 1967), p. 60; J. G. Clinkscales, *On the Old Plantation: Reminiscences of His Childhood* (Spartanburg, S.C., 1916), p. 5.

3. Basil W. Duke, *Reminiscences of General Basil W. Duke, C.S.A.* (Freeport, N.Y., 1969 [New York, 1911]), pp. 225-229. See also Norman B. Wood, *The White Side of a Black Subject: A Vindication of the Afro-American Race* (Chicago, 1897), pp. 290-291; John Witherspoon DuBose, "Autobiographical Sketches: Recollections of the Plantation—The Canebrake Negro, 1850-1865," J. W. DuBose Papers, Alabama Dept. of Archives and History, Montgomery, pp. 1-12; Samuel H. Chester, *Pioneer Days in Arkansas* (Richmond, 1927), pp. 38, 46.

4. Susan Dabney Smedes, *Memorials of a Southern Planter* (Baltimore, 1888 [1887]), pp. 3, 190; Andrew Phelps McCormick, *Scotch-Irish in Ireland and in America* (n.p., 1897), p. 150; Duncan Clinch Heyward, *Seed from Madagascar* (Chapel Hill, 1937), pp. 209-210. See also Margaret Devereux, *Plantation Sketches* (Cambridge, 1906), pp. ix, 1; Walter F. Peterson, ed., "Slavery in the 1850s: The Recollections of an Alabama Unionist" [Wade Hampton Richardson], *Alabama Historical Quarterly*, XXX (Fall and Winter, 1968), 219-220; Kemp Plummer Battle, *Memories of an Old-Time Tar Heel*, ed. by William James Battle (Chapel Hill, 1945), pp. 125, 185. An interesting statement as to the "excellent" memory of the postbellum writers may be found in Julia E. Harn, "Old Canoochee-Ogeechee Chronicles," *Georgia Historical Quarterly*, XV (December, 1931), 346.

5. Bernard Robb, *Welcum Hinges* (New York, 1960 [1942]), p. 20; Devereux, *Plantation Sketches*, p. 27; Belle Kearney, *A Slaveholder's Daughter* (New York, 1969 [1900]), pp. 64-65. See also Smedes, *Memorials*, p. 80; Clayton, *White and Black*, p. 131; Page Thacker, *Plantation Reminiscences* (Owensboro, Ky., 1878), p. 69.

6. Anna Hardeman Meade, *When I Was a Little Girl: The Year's Round on the Old Plantation* (Los Angeles, 1916), pp. 20-24. See also Avirett, *Old Plantation*, pp. 91-95.

7. Clinkscales, *Old Plantation*, pp. 21-22, 29-30. See also Battle, *Tar Heel*, pp. 126-129.

8. John B. Adger, *My Life and Times, 1810-1899* (Richmond, 1899), p. 347; Arney R. Childs, ed., *Rice Planter and Sportsman: The Recollections of J. Motte Alston, 1821-1909* (Columbia, 1953), pp. 108-109. See also R.Q. Mallard, *Plantation Life Before Emancipation* (Richmond, 1892), p. 235.

9. Seabrook, *Before and After*, p. 60; Avirett, *Old Plantation*, p. 62.

10. Avirett, *Old Plantation*, pp. 62, 117; Julia E. Harn, "Old Canoochee-Ogeechee Chronicles: Life Among the Negroes," *Georgia Historical Quarterly*, XVI (June, 1932), 146. Some slaveholders were said to have gone to their graves trusting in the faithfulness of their drivers. Only a few weeks before his death in 1865, planter Joseph McCormick was said to have remarked that he had owned black foreman Prince Monroe for over twenty years and "if he has ever deceived me or told me a falsehood, I did not detect it or suspect it." McCormick, *Scotch-Irish*, p. 148.

11. Varina Jefferson Davis, *Jefferson Davis, Ex-President of the Confederate States of America: A Memoir by His Wife*, I (New York, 1890), pp. 176-177, 180. For an interesting survey of the lack of critical evaluation evidenced by historians who have used Mrs. Davis's portrait of Pemberton, see Eron Rowland, *Varina Howell, Wife of Jefferson Davis*, I (New York, 1927), pp. 215, 274-275; Walter L. Fleming, "Jefferson Davis, the Negroes and the Negro Problem," *Sewanee Review*, XVI (October, 1908), 408-411; Dennis Murphree, "Hurricane and Brierfield: The Davis Plantations," *Journal of Mississippi History*, IX (April, 1947), 102.

12. F. G. Ruffin, "Overseers," *Southern Planter*, XVI (May, 1856), 148; "An Overseer," "On the Conduct and Management of Overseers, Drivers, and Slaves," *Farmers' Register*, IV (June, 1836), 114.

13. Foby, "Management of Servants," *Southern Cultivator*, XI (August, 1853), 226; Manual of Rules, James Henry Hammond Papers, Library of Congress. See also W. W. Hazzard, "On the General Management of a Plantation," *Southern Agriculturist*, IV (July, 1831), 351-352.

14. R. King, Jr., "On the Management of the Butler Estate, and the Cultivation of the Sugar Cane," *Southern Agriculturist*, I (December, 1828), 527; "An Overseer," "Conduct and Management," p. 115.

15. J. H. Bernard, "The Importance of Grass Crops—Unsuccessful Experiments," *Farmers' Register*, V (July 1, 1837), 172; Manual of Rules, James Henry Hammond Papers, Library of Congress; "An Overseer," "Conduct and Management," p. 115. See also Heyward, *Seed*, pp. 104, 181; Clayton, *White and Black*, p. 23; Samuel H. Chester, *Pioneer Days in Arkansas* (Richmond, 1927), pp. 38-40.

16. John D. Legare, "Account of an Agricultural Excursion made into the South of Georgia in the winter of 1832," *Southern Agriculturist*, VI (March-November, 1833), reprinted in Eugene L. Schwaab, ed., *Travels in the Old South: Selected from Periodicals of the Times*, I (Lexington, 1973), pp. 257-260. See also "An Overseer," "Conduct and Management," p. 115; J. Carlyle Sitterson, "The William J. Minor Plantations: A Study in Ante-Bellum Absentee Ownership," *Journal of Southern History*, IX (February, 1943), 65.

17. William S. Pettigrew to Moses and Henry, September 20, 1858,

October 9, 1858; William S. Pettigrew to Moses, June 12, 1857, October 8, 1858, Pettigrew Papers, Southern Historical Collection, University of North Carolina, Chapel Hill. See also William S. Pettigrew to Moses, July 12, 1856, August 30, 1856; William S. Pettigrew to Moses and Henry, December 18, 1857, Pettigrew Papers. For recent compilations of such slave-master correspondence, see John W. Blassingame, ed., *Slave Testimony: Two Centuries of Letters, Speeches, Interviews, and Autobiographies* (Baton Rouge, 1977), and Randall M. Miller, ed., *"Dear Master": Letters of a Slave Family* (Ithaca, 1978).

18. William S. Pettigrew to Moses, June 24, 1856, Pettigrew Papers. See also William S. Pettigrew to Moses and Henry, September 21, 1857, Pettigrew Papers; C. C. Jones to Cato, January 28, 1851, Charles Colcock Jones Papers, Special Collections, Tulane University, New Orleans.

19. William S. Pettigrew to Moses, June 24, 1856, July 12, 1856, Pettigrew Papers. See also William S. Pettigrew to Moses and Henry, September 29, 1857, Pettigrew Papers. For the more stringent types of punishment meted out to errant slaves by Pettigrew, see William S. Pettigrew to Moses and Henry, December 18, 1857, Pettigrew Papers.

20. Moses to William S. Pettigrew, August 9, 1856; Henry to William S. Pettigrew, August 9, 1856, Pettigrew Papers. See also Henry to William S. Pettigrew, August 2, 1856, Pettigrew Papers; Harford to Charles Tait, November 6, 1826, Tait Family Papers, Alabama State Department of Archives and History, Montgomery; Cato to C. C. Jones, September 3, 1852; Andrew to C. C. Jones, September 10, 1852, Jones Papers; Isaac Stephens to William Elliott, October 22, 1849, Elliott-Gonzales Papers, Southern Historical Collection, University of North Carolina, Chapel Hill.

21. Henry to William S. Pettigrew, September 12, 1857, Pettigrew Papers. See also Henry to William S. Pettigrew, July 5, 1856, December 19, 1857, February 27, 1858; Moses to William S. Pettigrew, July 5, 1856, Pettigrew Papers. For the views of other historians on the degree of accommodation evidenced in the letters, see Robert S. Starobin, "Privileged Bondsmen and the Process of Accommodation: The Role of Houseservants and Drivers as Seen in Their Own Letters," *Journal of Social History,* V (Fall, 1971), 51-52, 58, 63; Eugene D. Genovese, *Roll, Jordan Roll: The World the Slaves Made* (New York, 1974), p. 377.

22. Henry to William S. Pettigrew, August 20, 1856, October 10, 1857; Moses to William S. Pettigrew, February 6, 1858, Pettigrew Papers. See also Cato to C. C. Jones, March 3, 1851, Jones Papers; Jacob to William Elliott, July 31, 1862, Elliott-Gonzales Papers. For examples of Henry and other foremen serving as health-care advocates and paramedical aides to the

slave community, see Henry to William S. Pettigrew, August 20, 1856, January 30, 1858, March 20, 1858, Pettigrew Papers; William Dosite Postell, *The Health of Slaves on Southern Plantations* (Baton Rouge, 1951), p. 65; George P. Rawick, ed., *The American Slave: A Composite Autobiography*, XII, (Westport, 1972), Pt. 1, p. 49; Frances Anne Kemble, *Journal of a Residence on a Georgian Plantation in 1838-1839* (New York, 1863), p. 208.

23. For examples of the slaveholders' lack of trust in their drivers as seen in antebellum newspapers and agricultural periodicals, see James C. Darby, "On Planting and Managing a Rice Crop," *Southern Agriculturist*, II (June, 1829), 248-249; "A City Rustic," "On Overseers," *Charleston Mercury*, October 2, 1829; Hazzard, "General Management," p. 352; P. C. Weston, "Management of a Southern Plantation," *DeBow's Review*, XXII (January, 1857), 42.

24. Robert F. W. Allston to Joseph Allston, January 13, 1859 in J. H. Easterby, ed., *The South Carolina Rice Plantation as Revealed in the Papers of Robert F. W. Allston* (Chicago, 1945), p. 151.

25. Paul Leland Haworth, *George Washington: Farmer* (Indianapolis, 1915), pp. 62, 192-193; Ulrich Bonnell Phillips, *Life and Labor in the Old South* (Boston, 1929), p. 250; George Washington to William Pearce, December 18, 1793, in *The Writings of George Washington from the Original Manuscript Sources, 1745-1799*, XXXIII, ed. by John C. Fitzpatrick (Washington, D.C., 1940), p. 194; George Washington to William Pearce, July 5, 1795, in Fitzpatrick, *Writings of George Washington*, XXXIV, pp. 230-231.

26. Jack P. Greene, ed., *The Diary of Colonel Landon Carter of Sabine Hall, 1752-1778*, I (Charlottesville, 1965), pp. 299, 301, 358. See also Greene, *Diary of Colonel Landon Carter*, I, p. 583; Charles Pettigrew to Ebenezer Pettigrew, October 25, 1804, Pettigrew Papers; Moore Rawls to Lewis Thompson, December 24, 1857, Lewis Thompson Papers, Southern Historical Collection, University of North Carolina, Chapel Hill; Priscilla M. Bond Diary, December 22, 1861, Dept. of Archives, Louisiana State University, Baton Rouge.

27. Boyd Smith to David Weeks, August 20, 1834, David F. Weeks Collection, Department of Archives and Manuscripts, Louisiana State University, Baton Rouge; J. C. Carnothan to William P. Gould, May 26, 1847, in Charles S. Davis, *The Cotton Kingdom in Alabama* (Montgomery, 1939), p. 59; Greene, *Diary of Colonel Landon Carter*, I, pp. 429-430, 451, 465-466; Jack P. Greene, ed., *The Diary of Colonel Landon Carter of Sabine Hall, 1752-1778*, II (Charlottesville, 1965), p. 741; Franklin L. Riley, ed.,

"Diary of a Mississippi Planter, January 1, 1840, to April, 1863,"
Publications of the Mississippi Historical Society, X (Oxford, 1909), pp.
421-422, 468.

28. See especially R. Elam Tanner to J. H. Cocke, September 25, 1846, J.
H. Cocke Papers, University of Virginia Library, Charlottesville; S. S.
Woodley to William S. Pettigrew, January 7, 1855, Pettigrew Papers;
Coyner, "John Hartwell Cocke," pp. 121, 339, 395-396; Edwin Adams
Davis, ed., *Plantation Life in the Florida Parishes of Louisiana, 1836-1846,
as Reflected in the Diary of Bennet H. Barrow* (New York, 1943), p. 181;
Ulrich Bonnell Phillips and James David Glunt, eds., *Florida Plantation
Records from the Papers of George Noble Jones* (St. Louis, 1927), p. 395;
George Washington to Joh. Thompson, July 2, 1766, in *The Writings of
George Washington*, II, ed. by Worthington Chauncey Ford (New York,
1889), pp. 211-212. For an intriguing story of a driver whose "rascality"
included complicity in a double murder plot directed at two white overseers,
see A. K. Farrar to H. W. Drake, September 5, 1857, Alexander K. Farrar
Papers, Dept. of Archives, Louisiana State University, Baton Rouge.

29. M. Boyd Coyner, Jr., "John Hartwell Cocke of Bremo: Agriculture
and Slavery in the Ante-Bellum South" (Ph.D. dissertation, University of
Virginia, 1961), pp. 336-338. Cocke also gave cash bonuses and premiums
to encourage temperance.

30. Robert Elam Tanner to J. H. Cocke, April 25, 1840, J. H.
Cocke Papers; J. H. Cocke to Louisa Cocke, January 15, 1840, J. H.
Cocke Papers; Diary of John Hartwell Cocke, January 26, 1848,
J. H. Cocke Papers. In his use of black foremen as managers, Cocke
eventually fell afoul of an Alabama law that required the presence of the
owner or his white agent on any farm containing more than six slaves. See
R. D. Powell to J. H. Cocke, October 19, 1860, J. H. Cocke Papers. For an
account of another planter who was beset by "partying" slaves, led by
members of the slave elite, see Doctrine W. Davenport to Ebenezer Pettigrew, February 21, 1836, Pettigrew MSS, North Carolina Dept. of Archives
and History, Raleigh.

31. Greene, *Diary of Colonel Landon Carter*, II, p. 601. See also Haller
Nutt to Alonzo Snyder, December 15, 1844, Alonzo Snyder Papers, Dept. of
Achives, Louisiana State University, Baton Rouge.

32. John Evans to George Noble Jones, October 18, 1854, in Phillips and
Glunt, *Florida Plantation Records*, p. 110.

33. Joseph Allston to Robert F. W Allston, September 25, 1823 in Easterby, *Papers of Robert F. W. Allston*, p. 63.

34. J. H. Cocke Journal, January 20, 1850, January 1851; February 26,
1851, J. H. Cocke Papers.

35. Richard D. Powell to John Hartwell Cocke, August 14, 1857, J. H.

Cocke Papers. See also Rachael O'Connor to David Weeks, June 22, 1829, David F. Weeks Collection; Doctrine W. Davenport to Ebenezer Pettigrew, December 26, 1835, Pettigrew MSS, North Carolina Dept. of Archives and History, Raleigh.

36. John Berkley Grimball Diary, October 17, 1832, October 20, 1832; November 2, 1832; November 3, 1832, Southern Historical Collection, University of North Carolina, Chapel Hill.

CHAPTER 4
THE TRAVELERS

1. Alexander Mackay, *The Western World; or Travels in the United States in 1846-47*, II (London, 1849), p. 321.

2. Thomas L. Nichols, *Forty Years of American Life*, I (London, 1864), pp. 174-176. See also John S. C. Abbott, *South and North; or Impressions Received During a Trip to Cuba and the South* (New York, 1860), pp. 123-124; James Stirling, *Letters from the Slave States* (London, 1857), p. 264.

3. Mackay, *Western World*, I, pp. ix-x; Philo Tower, *Slavery Unmasked: Being a Truthful Narrative of a Three Years' Residence and Journeying in Eleven Southern States* (Rochester, 1856), pp. 208, 215-216; James Redpath, *The Roving Editor: or, Talks with Slaves in the Southern States* (New York, 1859), p. 181.

4. Lady Emmeline Stuart-Wortley, *Travels in the United States, etc. During 1849 and 1850* (New York, 1855), p. 117.

5. Frederick Law Olmsted, *A Journey in the Back Country* (New York, 1860), p. 51; Richard O. Curry and Joanna Dunlap Cowden, eds., *Slavery in America: Theodore Weld's American Slavery as It Is* (Itasca, Ill., 1972 [New York, 1839]), p. 136. See also C. G. Parsons, *An Inside View of Slavery; A Tour Among the Planters* (Savannah, 1974 [Boston, 1855]), p. 33. Slaveholders could, of course, seek to influence the opinions of visitors even before they reached the plantation. While traveling down the Mississippi on the steamer "Belle Key" in 1850, one traveler was told by a planter's wife that her husband "never was able to enjoy real peace of mind" because "the thought of his slaves, and the wish to do them justice, and to treat them well, disturbed him day and night; he was always afraid of not doing enough for them." Fredrika Bremer, *The Homes of the New World; Impressions of America*, II, trans. by Mary Howitt (New York, 1853), p. 185.

6. "An Englishman in South Carolina, December, 1860, and July, 1862," *Continental Monthly*, III (January, 1863), 114; Stuart-Wortley, *Travels*, pp. 119-120.

7. William Thomson, *A Tradesman's Travels, in the United States and Canada, in the Years 1840, 41, & 42* (Edinburgh, 1842), pp. 192-194.

8. Nehemiah Adams, *A South-Side View of Slavery; or, Three Months at the South, in 1854* (Boston, 1855), pp. 14, 18, 23, 62-63. See also David Brown, *The Planter: or, Thirteen Years in the South. By a Northern Man* (Philadelphia, 1853), pp. 49-50, 58-59, 68-69.

9. Herbert Anthony Kellar, ed., *Solon Robinson, Pioneer and Agriculturist*, II (Indianapolis, 1936), p. 295; Letter to the editor of the *National Intelligencer* reprinted in the *Boston Recorder*, July 8, 1817; Adams, *South-Side View*, p. 63. See also Thomson, *Tradesman's Travels*, pp. 190-191.

10. Curry and Cowden, *Slavery*, p. 135; Stirling, *Letters*, p. 289; Tower, *Slavery Unmasked*, pp. 414-415; Philo Tower told of conversing with a planter about an instance of cruelty he had witnessed. The slaveholder noted that had he been in his company, Tower would not have observed such a scene. "When I whip niggers," he said, "I take them out of sight and hearing." Tower, *Slavery Unmasked*, p. 209.

11. Olmsted, *Back Country*, pp. 381-382; "An Englishman in South Carolina, December, 1860, and July, 1862," *Continental Monthly*, II (December, 1862), 692.

12. Olmsted, *Back Country*, pp. 49, 382; Frances Anne Kemble, *Journal of a Residence on a Georgian Plantation in 1838-1839* (New York, 1863), p. 84; Adams, *South-Side View*, p. 97; Joseph Sturge, *A Visit to the United States in 1841* (Boston, 1842), p. 46.

13. Curry and Cowden, *Slavery*, p. 134; Tower, *Slavery Unmasked*, pp. 216, 413-414; Redpath, *Roving Editor*, pp. 119, 135, 157.

14. Louis Fitzgerald Tasistro, *Random Shots and Southern Breezes*, II (New York, 1842), p. 13.

15. Armstrong Archer, *A Compendium of Slavery, as It Exists in the Present Day in the United States of America* (London, 1844), p. 37. See also Curry and Cowden, *Slavery*, pp. 56-57, 63-64; Parsons, *Inside View*, pp. 18-21; Olmsted, *Back Country*, p. 81.

16. Bremer, *Homes*, I, p. 297. See also Arthur Singleton, *Letters from the South and West* (Boston, 1824), p. 78; Curry and Cowden, *Slavery*, p. 72.

17. S. A. O'Ferrall, *A Ramble of Six Thousand Miles through the United States of America* (London, 1832), p. 196.

18. Earl E. Thorpe, *The Old South: A Psychohistory* (Durham, 1972), p. 115. See also Stanley M. Elkins, *Slavery: A Problem in American Institutional and Intellectual Life* (Chicago, 1959, 1968, 1976), p. 3.

19. G. W. Featherstonhaugh, *Excursion Through the Slave States*, I (London, 1844), pp. 120-124, 169-170. See also "Sketches of the South

Santee,'' *American Monthly Magazine*, VIII (November, 1836), 431; Frederick Law Olmsted, *A Journey in the Seaboard Slave States, with Remarks on Their Economy* (New York, 1859), pp. 432-435; Howard Corning, ed., *Journal of John James Audubon Made During His Trip to New Orleans in 1820-1821* (Cambridge, 1929), pp. 109-110; Emily P. Burke, *Reminiscences of Georgia* (n.p., 1850), pp. 228-229; Charles Lyell, *A Second Visit to the United States of North America*, II (London, 1850), pp. 10-11.

20. Kemble, *Journal*, pp. 79-80, 160, 168, 176.

21. Ibid., pp. 57, 81, 113, 176.

22. Ibid., pp. 81, 176.

23. Ibid., pp. 176, 249-250, 276.

24. Ibid., pp. 80, 250. For Kemble's somewhat different opinion of the mulatto driver, Bran, see pages 201, 215-216, 298, 303, 317. For an account of a Mississippi driver who was killed attempting to protect his wife from a whipping, see Curry and Cowden, *Slavery*, pp. 49-50.

25. Redpath, *Roving Editor*, pp. v-vi, 2, 135.

26. Ibid., pp. 269-274, 282.

27. Ibid., pp. 274-279.

28. Ibid., pp. 280, 283. For an account of a driver who was executed for bludgeoning his master to death, see Thomson, *Tradesman's Travels*, pp. 186-188.

29. Parsons, *Inside View*, pp. ix, 3-4.

30. Ibid., pp. 170-171.

31. Ibid., p. 171.

32. Ibid., p. 171.

33. Ibid., pp. 172-174, 229. For an account of a driver who was ''broken'' for the crime of stealing peas, see Lester B. Shippee, ed., *Bishop Whipple's Southern Diary, 1843-1844* (Minneapolis, 1937), p. 40.

CHAPTER 5
THE TWENTIETH-CENTURY NARRATIVES

1. David Brion Davis, ''Slavery and the Post-World War II Historians, *Daedalus*, CIII (Spring, 1974), 3-7.

2. Ulrich Bonnell Phillips, *American Negro Slavery: A Survey of the Supply, Employment and Control of Negro Labor as Determined by the Plantation Regime* (New York, 1918), preface, pp. 1-2.

3. George M. Fredrickson and Christopher Lasch, ''Resistance to Slavery,'' *Civil War History*, XIII (December, 1967), 318-319; Bennett H. Wall,

"African Slavery," in *Writing Southern History: Essays in Historiography in Honor of Fletcher M. Green*, ed. by Arthur S. Link and Rembert W. Patrick (Baton Rouge, 1965), p. 177; Kenneth M. Stampp, "Rebels and Sambos: The Search for the Negro's Personality in Slavery," *Journal of Southern History*, XXXVII (August, 1971), 367-369.

4. Roscoe E. Lewis, "The Life of Mark Thrash," *Phylon*, XX (Winter, 1959), 389-403.

5. Kenneth M. Stampp, "The Historian and Southern Negro Slavery," *American Historical Review*, LVII (April, 1952), 613.

6. Howard Zinn, *The Politics of History* (Boston, 1970), p. 41.

7. Phillips, *American Negro Slavery*, preface, pp. 1-2.

8. C. Vann Woodward, "History from Slave Sources," *American Historical Review*, LXXIX (April, 1974), 475.

9. George P. Rawick, ed., *The American Slave: A Composite Autobiography*, IV (Westport, 1972, 1974, Pt. 2, pp. 41, 43-44. See also Rawick, *American Slave*, XII, Pt. 2, p. 238; Elizabeth Lomax, "Slaves," *Direction*, I (No. 3, 1938), 88-90; Lyle Saxon, Edward Dreyer, and Robert Tallant, *Gumbo Ya-Ya: A Collection of Louisiana Folk Tales* (Boston, 1945), p. 242; Orland Kay Armstrong, *Old Massa's People: The Old Slaves Tell Their Story* (Indianapolis, 1931), p. 218.

10. Rawick, *American Slave*, VI, pp. 66-68; J. Ralph Jones, "Portraits of Georgia Slaves," *Georgia Review*, XXI (Spring, 1967), 130; Armstrong, *Massa's People*, p. 218.

11. Rawick, *American Slave*, V, Pt. 3, pp. 209-210, 212.

12. Rawick, *American Slave*, II, Pt. 2, pp. 306, 309-310, 317. See also Rawick, *American Slave*, IV, Pt. 1, p. 205; Rawick, *American Slave*, III, Pt. 3, pp. 48-49; Rawick, *American Slave*, XIV, Pt. 1, pp. 312-313; Rawick, *American Slave*, XII, Pt. 2, p. 29; Rawick, *American Slave*, VI, pp. 1-3.

13. Norman R. Yetman, "The Background of the Slave Narrative Collection," *American Quarterly*, XIX (Fall, 1967), pp. 546-551; Allen Francis Kifer, "The Negro Under the New Deal, 1933-1941" (Ph.D. dissertation, University of Wisconsin, 1961), pp. 237-239. See also Jerre Mangione, *The Dream and the Deal: The Federal Writers' Project, 1935-1943* (Boston, 1972), pp. 257-259. C. Vann Woodward has noted that where black interviewers were used the "whole atmosphere" of the accounts changed: "The thick dialect diminishes and so do deference and evasiveness and tributes to planter benevolence. Candor and resentment surface more frequently." Woodward, "Slave Sources," p. 474. For an interesting firsthand account of a white interviewer's adaptation to the "racial etiquette" of the Mississippi Delta region, see William R. Ferris, Jr., "The Collection of Racial Lore: Approaches and Problems," *New York Folklore Quarterly*, XXVII (September, 1971), 261-279.

14. Rawick, *American Slave*, II, Pt. 2, pp. 226-227; Woodward, "Slave Sources," p. 474. The South Carolina narratives contain an account in which an ex-slave told her white interviewer: "'Oh, I been know your father en your grandfather en all of dem. Bless mercy, child, I don't want to tell you nothin' but what to please you. Lord, I glad to see your face. It look so lovin en pleasin, just so as I is always know you." Rawick, *American Slave*, II, Pt. 1, p. 288.

15. Rawick, *American Slave*, VII, p. 25; Rawick, *American Slave*, XII, Pt. 1, p. 17; Rawick, *American Slave*, XIII, Pt. 3, p. 154. For an enlightening commentary on the depreciatory treatment of Afro-Americans in the FWP's American Guide Series, see Monty Noam Penkower, *The Federal Writers' Project: A Study in Government Patronage of the Arts* (Urbana, 1977), pp. 140-143.

16. Rawick, *American Slave*, XVI, p. 73; Rawick, *American Slave*, XI, p. 8.

17. Rawick, *American Slave*, IX, Pt. 4, p. 219; Rawick, *American Slave*, VIII, Pt. 1, p. 303; Rawick, *American Slave*, XVI, p. 44. For an interview conducted by black workers that evidences a different approach to the question of the "beauty" of black facial characteristics, see Charles L. Perdue, Jr., Thomas E. Barden, and Robert K. Phillips, eds., *Weevils in the Wheat: Interviews with Virginia Ex-Slaves* (Charlottesville, 1976), p. 315.

18. Rawick, *American Slave*, XIV, pp. 29-30.

19. Perdue, Barden, and Phillips, *Weevils*, p. 205; Charles S. Johnson, *Shadow of the Plantation* (Chicago, 1934), pp. 27, 35-36, 98, 197. See also Rawick, *American Slave*, VI, p. 102; Rossa B. Cooley, *Homes of the Free* (New York, 1926), pp. 122-124; Gladys-Marie Fry, *Night Riders in Black Folk History* (Knoxville, 1975), pp. vii-viii.

20. Rawick, *American Slave*, IV, Pt. 2, p. 189. For accounts of respondents who were somewhat bolder than usual in their unfavorable descriptions of antebellum whites, see Rawick, *American Slave*, XIV, Pt. 1, pp. 360-362 and J. Ralph Jones, "Portraits of Georgia Slaves," *Georgia Review*, XXI (Summer, 1967), 273. For accounts of ex-slaves who reported cruelties, but shifted the blame to "faceless" whites rather than to their own former master or overseer, see Rawick, *American Slave*, VII, p. 4; Rawick, *American Slave*, III, Pt. 3, p. 113.

21. John B. Cade, "Out of the Mouths of Ex-Slaves," *Journal of Negro History*, XX (July, 1935), 317.

22. Work Projects Administration, Workers of the Writers' Program, State of Virginia, *The Negro in Virginia* (New York, 1940), p. 156. See also Saxon, Dreyer, and Tallant, *Gumbo Ya-Ya*, p. 234; Rawick, *American Slave*, XII, Pt. 1, pp. 189-190.

23. Rawick, *American Slave*, II, Pt. 2, p. 166; Rawick, *American Slave*,

XIII, Pt. 4, pp. 356-357; Rawick, *American Slave*, II, Pt. 1, pp. 197-198. Goodwater described the driver's code in the following manner: "He go 'round an' tell the slaves dey better go an' git some fish 'fore all go. Any time any one say e hab fish it was understood e mean cow-meat."

24. Armstrong, *Massa's People*, p. 217; Rawick, *American Slave*, III, Pt. 3, p. 65; Rawick, *American Slave*, VIII, Pt. 2, p. 170. See also Fisk University, *Unwritten History*, pp. 292-295.

25. Work Projects Administration, *Negro in Virginia*, pp. 65-66.

26. Rawick, *American Slave*, XII, Pt. 2, pp. 81-82.

27. Rawick, *American Slave*, II, Pt. 1, pp. 299-300; Rawick, *American Slave*, XII, Pt. 1, p. 196. See also Rawick, *American Slave*, VI, pp. 168-169; Rawick, *American Slave*, VII, p. 216; Armstrong, *Massa's People*, p. 42.

28. Rawick, *American Slave*, XV, pp. 210-211; Rawick, *American Slave*, III, Pt. 4, p. 148; Rawick, *American Slave*, VII, p. 67; Rawick, *American Slave*, XVI, pp. 18-19; Rawick, *American Slave*, XVII, pp. 96-97; Rawick, *American Slave*, II, Pt. 2, pp. 184-185. One particularly privileged driver was reported to have been allowed to "sot down, smoke cigars and drink whiskey" with his master after giving a troublesome fellow slave the prescribed "250 licks." Rawick, *American Slave*, V, Pt. 4, p. 38.

29. Rawick, *American Slave*, VIII, Pt. 2, pp. 170, 172. See also Fisk University, *Unwritten History*, pp. 292, 295.

30. Rawick, *American Slave*, III, Pt. 3, pp. 217-219. See also Eugene D. Genovese, *Roll, Jordan, Roll: The World the Slaves Made* (New York, 1974), p. 370; Rawick, *American Slave*, XVI, p. 59.

31. Rawick, *American Slave*, XI, p. 177.

32. Rawick, *American Slave*, VII, p. 216.

33. Armstrong, *Massa's People*, pp. 218-219; Rawick, *American Slave*, XII, Pt. 1, p. 185.

34. Perdue, Barden, and Phillips, *Weevils*, p. 317. See also Rawick, *American Slave*, II, Pt. 2, p. 237; Rawick, *American Slave*, VIII, Pt. 2, pp. 346-347.

35. Rawick, *American Slave*, XII, Pt. 2, pp. 184-185, 187. See also Rawick, *American Slave*, XI, pp. 27-30, 164, 177; Rawick, *American Slave*, XVI, p. 58; Rawick, *American Slave*, VII, p. 251.

CHAPTER 6
THE BLACK AUTOBIOGRAPHIES

1. Norman R. Yetman, "The Background of the Slave Narrative Collection," *American Quarterly*, XIX (Fall, 1967), 536; John W. Blassingame,

"Black Autobiographies as History and Literature," *Black Scholar*, V (December, 1973-January, 1974), 8; Charles H. Nichols, Jr., "Slave Narratives and the Plantation Legend," *Phylon*, X (3rd Quarter, 1949), 203; Benjamin Botkin, ed., *Lay My Burden Down: A Folk History of Slavery* (Chicago, 1945), p. ix. In her 1946 study of the black narratives, Marion Starling noted that some six thousand slave autobiographical or semiautobiographical accounts have been located. One-half of this total belongs to the period of slavery and the other half has resulted from more recent attempts to interview aged survivors. In addition to antebellum autobiographies and depression-era narratives, there exists a number of published accounts that were issued during the post-Civil War decades. These were often written by black ministers as fund-raising devices for themselves and their churches. See Marion Wilson Starling, "The Slave Narrative: Its Place in American Literary History" (Ph.D. dissertation, New York University, 1946), p. 454; George P. Rawick, *From Sundown to Sunup: The Making of the Black Community* (Westport, 1972), p. xv; John W. Blassingame, "Using the Testimony of Ex-Slaves: Approaches and Problems," *Journal of Southern History*, XLI (November, 1975), 480.

2. Frederick Douglass, *My Bondage and My Freedom* (New York, 1855), p. 339; Benjamin Drew, ed., *A North-Side View of Slavery, The Refugee: or the Narratives of Fugitive Slaves in Canada* (Boston, 1856), p. 142. In 1926 black historian Carter Woodson expressed this point of view when he wrote of the fugitives: "As bondmen, they were generally too illiterate to express themselves. Freed and brought North to be educated, however, they often bore intelligent testimony against the institution. In so doing, they have given a picture of the institution from a different point of view." Carter G. Woodson, *The Mind of the Negro as Reflected in Letters Written During the Crisis, 1800-1860* (Washington, D.C., 1926), p. 260.

3. Margaret Young Jackson, "An Investigation of Biographies and Autobiographies of American Slaves Published Between 1840 and 1860: Based Upon the Cornell Special Slavery Collection" (Ph.D. dissertation, Cornell University, 1954), pp. ii-iv, 121-122, 198.

4. Blassingame, "Testimony," pp. 480, 490; Julius Lester, *To Be a Slave* (New York, 1970 [1968]), p. 14.

5. Charles Harold Nichols, Jr., "A Study of the Slave Narrative" (Ph. D. dissertation, Brown University, 1948), p. 26; Starling, "Slave Narrative," pp. 141, 320-321; Charles Ball, *Slavery in the United States: A Narrative of the Life and Adventures of Charles Ball* (New York, 1837), p. 136.

6. Ball, *Slavery*, pp. 25, 348, 381-387.

7. Ibid., pp. 139-140, 268, 348, 350-351, 363.

8. Vernon Loggins, *The Negro Author: His Development in America*

(New York, 1931), pp. 100-101; Nichols, "Study," p. 7; Starling, "Slave Narrative," pp. 323-324, 330; *Emancipator*, August 30, 1838, September 20, 1838. Support for the withdrawal of the narrative was not unanimous within abolitionist circles. After the controversy died down, it was again listed for sale among the books sponsored by the AASS. See *Liberator*, June 14, 1839; Loggins, *Negro Author*, p. 103.

9. Loggins, *Negro Author*, pp. 101-102. See also Blassingame, "Testimony," p. 477; Gilbert Osofsky, ed., *Puttin' On Ole Massa: The Slave Narratives of Henry Bibb, William Wells Brown, and Solomon Northup* (New York, 1969), p. 12.

10. James Williams, *Narrative of James Williams, An American Slave; Who Was for Several Years a Driver on a Cotton Plantation in Alabama* (New York, 1838), pp. 42, 57; Ball, *Slavery*, pp. v-vi; Blassingame, "Testimony," pp. 477-478.

11. Thomas H. Jones, *The Experience of Thomas H. Jones, Who Was a Slave for Forty-Three Years* (Boston, 1862), pp. 8-10.

12. M. F. Jamison, *Autobiography and Work of Bishop M. F. Jamison, D.D.* (Nashville, 1912), pp. 25-27; William Grimes, *Life of William Grimes, the Runaway Slave, Brought Down to the Present Time* (New Haven, 1855), reprinted in *Five Black Lives*, ed. by Arna Bontemps (Middletown, Conn., 1971), pp. 65-67, 70.

13. Lewis and Milton Clarke, *Narrative of the Sufferings of Lewis and Milton Clarke....* (Boston, 1846), pp. 27, 122. See also Jacob Stroyer, *My Life in the South* (Salem, 1898), pp. 14-15; William H. Heard, *From Slavery to the Bishopric in the A.M.E. Church: An Autobiography* (Philadelphia, 1924), p. 26; Moses Roper, *A Narrative of the Adventures and Escape of Moses Roper, from American Slavery* (London, 1843), p. 23.

14. Drew, *North-Side View*, pp. 49, 184; Sam Aleckson, *Before the War, and After the Union: An Autobiography* (Boston, 1929), pp. 61-64; William Still, *The Underground Rail Road* (Philadelphia, 1871), p. 436.

15. For other examples of drivers who were compelled to inflict severe punishments, see Drew, *North-Side View*, p. 50; Moses Grandy, *Narrative of the Life of Moses Grandy, Late a Slave in the United States of America* (Boston, 1844), p. 17; Octavia V. Rogers Albert, *The House of Bondage or Charlotte Brooks and Other Slaves* (New York, 1890), p. 40. For an impassioned apologetic penned by the son of a Virginia driver, see Peter Randolph, *From Slave Cabin to the Pulpit: The Autobiography of Rev. Peter Randolph* (Boston, 1893), pp. 210-213.

16. John W. Blassingame, *The Slave Community: Plantation Life in the Antebellum South* (New York, 1972), pp. 227-228.

17. Henry Bibb, *Narrative of the Life and Adventures of Henry Bibb, An*

American Slave (New York, 1849), pp. 112-114. See also Harry Smith, *Fifty Years of Slavery in the United States of America* (Grand Rapids, 1891), pp. 126-127.

18. William Wells Brown, *Sketches of Places and People Abroad: The American Fugitive in Europe* (Boston, 1855), pp. 11-13, 16; William Wells Brown, *Narrative of William W. Brown, A Fugitive Slave* (Boston, 1847), pp. 39-40, 42-43, 46, 62-63; William Wells Brown, *The Black Man, His Antecedents, His Genius, and His Achievements* (New York, 1863), p. 19. See also Josephine Brown, *Biography of an American Bondman, by His Daughter* (Boston, 1856), pp. 25-28.

19. William Wells Brown, *My Southern Home: or, the South and Its People* (Boston, 1880), p. 108; Bibb, *Narrative*, pp. 108-110; Samuel Hall, *47 Years a Slave: A Brief Story of His Life Before and After Freedom Came to Him* (Washington, Ia., 1912); Drew, *North-Side View*, pp. 46, 176, 212; Still, *Underground Rail Road*, pp. 420, 481.

20. H. C. Bruce, *The New Man: Twenty-Nine Years a Slave, Twenty-Nine Years a Free Man* (York, Pa., 1895), pp. 86-87; Drew, *North-Side View*, pp. 38, 177.

21. Drew, *North-Side View*, pp. 38-39, 177. Although examples of fugitive slave drivers are fairly numerous, there is little evidence to show that drivers sought to engage in conspiracies or widespread insurrectionary activity aimed at overthrowing the slave system. Even though Nat Turner, leader of the Southampton County, Virginia, rebellion, often has been referred to as an overseer or foreman, no conclusive evidence for this claim has ever been forwarded. During his 1831 foray, Turner did meet with Aaron Harris, overlooker at the Newit Harris plantation, who attempted to dissuade the slaves from going on by arguing that they did not have a chance against the whites' powerful forces. For the various views on Turner's status, see William Sidney Drewry, *The Southampton Insurrection* (Washington, D.C., 1900), p. 28; Ulrich Bonnell Phillips, *American Negro Slavery: A Survey of the Supply, Employment and Control of Negro Labor as Determined by the Plantation Regime* (New York, 1918), p. 480; Herbert Aptheker, *Nat Turner's Slave Rebellion* (New York, 1968 [1966]), p. 36. For the role played by Aaron Harris, see Drewry, *Southampton Insurrection*, pp. 52-54; Stephen B. Oates, *The Fires of Jubilee: Nat Turner's Fierce Rebellion* (New York, 1976 [1975]), pp. 91-92. For evidence linking drivers to other conspiracies, see Herbert Aptheker, *American Negro Slave Revolts* (New York, 1963 [1943]), p. 211; Robert Mitchell to John Marshall, September 23, 1793, in *Calendar of Virginia State Papers and other Manuscripts, from August 11, 1792, to December 31, 1793*, VI, ed. by Sherwin McRae (Richmond, 1886), p. 547; John Oliver Killens, ed., *The Trial*

Record of Denmark Vesey (Boston, 1970), pp. 19-20. For three plausible explanations of the drivers' seeming inability to "decisively organize their people" for insurrectionary purposes, see Eugene D. Genovese, *Roll, Jordan, Roll: The World the Slaves Made* (New York, 1974), pp. 387, 659; William Kauffman Scarborough, ed., *The Diary of Edmund Ruffin*, Vol. I: *Toward Independence, October, 1856-April, 1861* (Baton Rouge, 1972), p. 391; Solomon Northup, *Twelve Years a Slave.* . . . (Buffalo, 1853), p. 190.

22. Still, *Underground Rail Road*, pp. 465-466. See also Still, *Underground Rail Road*, p. 301; James L. Smith, *Autobiography of James L. Smith* (Norwich, 1881), p. 134.

23. Drew, *North-Side View*, pp. 252-255. See also Drew, *North-Side View*, pp. 117-120, 212; Still, *Underground Rail Road*, pp. 272-273, 434.

24. William G. Eliot, *The Story of Archer Alexander, from Slavery to Freedom, March 30, 1863* (Boston, 1885), pp. 28, 41, 45-48, 84. See also Still, *Underground Rail Road*, p. 396.

25. Northup, *Twelve Years*, pp. 158, 183. Northup's narrative has been rated traditionally as one of the most reliable of the autobiographical accounts. Even Ulrich Phillips could write of the account: "Though the books of this class are generally of dubious value this one has a tone which engages confidence." Phillips, *American Negro Slavery*, p. 445.

26. Kate E. R. Pickard, *The Kidnapped and the Ransomed. Being the Personal Recollections of Peter Still and His Wife "Vina," after Forty Years of Slavery* (Syracuse, 1856), pp. 81-83. See also Robert Brent Toplin, "Peter Still Versus the Peculiar Institution," *Civil War History*, XIII (December, 1967), 340-349.

27. Jermain W. Loguen, *The Rev. J. W. Loguen, as a Slave and as a Freeman. A Narrative of Real Life* (Syracuse, 1859), pp. 226-227, 236-237, 257. See also Still, *Underground Rail Road*, pp. 403-406, 481.

28. Josiah Henson, *An Autobiography of the Rev. Josiah Henson ("Uncle Tom") from 1789 to 1881* (London, 1881), pp. 32-37. For an interesting literary history of the various editions of Henson's *Autobiography* and his connection with Harriet Beecher Stowe's "Uncle Tom," see Robin W. Winks, *The Blacks in Canada: A History* (New Haven, 1971), pp. 181-194.

29. Henson, *Autobiography*, pp. 17-18, 38, 40.

30. Henson, *Autobiography*, pp. 42-63, 69-70. For an account of Henson's participation in the Underground Railroad, see pages 79-87, 111-112. For an account of a black foreman who behaved in a similar manner upon crossing into Canada, see Sarah Bradford, *Harriet Tubman: The Moses of Her People* (New York, 1961 [1886]), pp. 48-53, and Ray Allen Billington, ed., *The Journal of Charlotte L. Forten: A Free Negro in the Slave Era* (New York, 1961 [1953]), p. 180.

31. Charles H. Nichols, "Who Read the Slave Narratives?" *Phylon*, XX (Summer, 1959), 152; Blassingame, "Black Autobiographies," pp. 2, 9; Starling, "Slave Narrative," pp. 52-53; Sidonie Smith, *Where I'm Bound: Patterns of Slavery and Freedom in Black American Autobiography* (Westport, 1974), p. 10; Stephen Butterfield, *Black Autobiography in America* (Amherst, 1974), p. 12.

CONCLUSION

1. Eugene D. Genovese, "American Slaves and Their History," *New York Review of Books*, XV (December 3, 1970), 34.

APPENDIX

1. Thomas D. Clark, ed., *Travels in the Old South*, Vol. I: *The Formative Years, 1527-1783* (Norman, Okla., 1956), pp. 33-36.

2. Thomas D. Clark, ed., *Travels in the Old South*, Vol. II: *The Expanding South, 1750-1825* (Norman, Okla., 1956), pp. ix-xii.

3. Jane Louise Mesick, *The English Traveller in America, 1785-1835* (New York, 1922), pp. 8-9, 12, 16; Max Berger, *The British Traveller in America*, 1836-1860 (New York, 1943), pp. 13-14, 17, 110, 114; Thomas D. Clark, ed., *Travels in the Old South*, Vol. III: *The Ante Bellum South, 1825-1860* (Norman, Okla., 1959), pp. xv-xvi.

4. Berger, *British Traveller*, pp. 14, 17-18, 22; Clark, *Travels*, III, pp. 103-104, 197, 339-340.

5. Clark, *Travels*, III, p. 198.

6. Ibid., p. 8.

7. Clark, *Travels*, I, p. xvii; Eugene L. Schwaab, ed., *Travels in the Old South: Selected from Periodicals of the Times*, I (Lexington, 1973), p. ix.

8. Berger, *British Traveller*, p. 6.

9. Nehemiah Adams, *A South-Side View of Slavery; or, Three Months at the South, in 1854* (Boston, 1855), p. 8; Charles Joseph Latrobe, *The Rambler in North America*, I (London, 1836), p. 306. For an account of an earlier generation of white adventurers who came into sudden contact with blacks, see Winthrop D. Jordan, *White Over Black: American Attitudes Toward the Negro, 1550-1812* (Chapel Hill, 1968), pp. 3-43.

10. Lester B. Shippee, ed., *Bishop Whipple's Southern Diary, 1843-1844* (Minneapolis, 1937), pp. xi-xii, 12-13.

11. William Thomson, *A Tradesman's Travels in the United States and*

Canada, in the Years 1840, 41, & 42 (Edinburgh, 1842), pp. 175-176.

12. James Stirling, *Letters from the Slave States* (London, 1857), p. 368; J. S. Buckingham, *The Slave States of America*, I (London, 1842), pp. 487-489.

13. Buckingham, *Slave States*, I, p. 489; Adams, *South-Side View*, p. 8; Frances Anne Kemble, *Journal of a Residence on A Georgian Plantation in 1838-1839* (New York, 1863), p. 11.

14. Basil Hall, *Travels in North America, in the Years 1827 and 1828* (Edinburgh, 1829), III, pp. 177-180, 184-185; Una Pope-Hennessy, ed., *The Aristocratic Journey: Being the Outspoken Letters of Mrs. Basil Hall Written During a Fourteen Months' Sojourn in America, 1827-1828* (New York, 1931), pp. 221-222.

15. Alexander Mackay, *The Western World; or Travels in the United States in 1846-47*, II (London, 1849), p. 130; Frederick Law Olmsted, *A Journey in the Seaboard Slave States, with Remarks on Their Economy* (New York, 1859), p. 711; John S. C. Abbott, *South and North; or Impressions Received During a Trip to Cuba and the South* (New York, 1860), pp. 168, 175.

16. Olmsted, *Seaboard*, pp. 18-19, 146, 469-470; Frederick Law Olmsted, *A Journey Through Texas: or, a Saddle-Trip on the Southwestern Frontier* (New York, 1859), pp. 21-22.

17. Thomson, *Tradesman's Travels*, p. 189; Pope-Hennessy, *Aristocratic Journey*, pp. 217-218.

18. Thomson, *Tradesman's Travels*, p. 189; Kemble, *Journal*, p. 305.

19. Charles Sealsfield, *The Americans as They Are; Described in a Tour through the Valley of the Mississippi* (London, 1828), pp. 176-177; Kemble, *Journal*, p. 305; Alexis de Tocqueville, *Democracy in America*, ed. by J. P. Mayer and Max Lerner, trans. by George Lawrence (New York, 1969 [Paris, 1835, 1840]), p. 317.

20. de Tocqueville, *Democracy*, p. 317; E. S. Abdy, *Journal of a Residence and Tour in the United States of North America, from April, 1833, to October, 1834*, II (London, 1835), pp. 215-216.

21. John B. Cade, "Out of the Mouths of Ex-Slaves," *Journal of Negro History*, XX (July, 1935), 295; Norman R. Yetman, "The Background of the Slave Narrative Collection," *American Quarterly*, XIX (Fall, 1967), 540; Charles L. Perdue, Jr., Thomas E. Barden, and Robert K. Phillips, eds., *Weevils In the Wheat: Interviews with Virginia Ex-Slaves* (Charlottesville, 1976), p. xii; Gladys-Marie Fry, *Night Riders in Black Folk History* (Knoxville, 1975), pp. 17-18.

22. Fisk University, *Unwritten History of Slavery: Autobiographical Accounts of Negro Ex-Slaves* (Westport, 1974 [Nashville, 1945]), p. iv; Fry,

Night Riders, pp. 18-19; Yetman, "Background," pp. 540-541; Perdue, Barden, and Phillips, *Weevils*, pp. xi-xii; Fisk University, *God Struck Me Dead: Religious Conversion Experiences and Autobiographies of Negro Ex-Slaves* (Westport, 1974 [Nashville, 1945]), p. iii.

23. Yetman, "Background," pp. 541-543; B. A. Botkin, "The Slave as His Own Interpreter," *Library of Congress Quarterly Journal of Current Acquisitions*, II (November, 1944), 37-38; Perdue, Barden, and Phillips, *Weevils*, p. xiii; William F. McDonald, *Federal Relief Administration and the Arts* (Columbus, 1969), pp. 720-721.

24. Botkin, "Interpreter," pp. 38, 40; Yetman, "Background," pp. 543-544, 548-550, 552-553; McDonald, *Federal Relief Administration*, p. 722; Perdue, Barden, and Phillips, *Weevils*, pp. xiv-xvii; Benjamin Botkin, ed., *Lay My Burden Down: A Folk History of Slavery* (Chicago, 1945), pp. vii-viii. Louisiana did not participate in the Writers' Project ex-slave study. Narratives were collected there after the termination of the Project. A book using some of this material was published in 1945 under the title, *Gumbo Ya-Ya*. Carbon typescripts of the original narratives were deposited in the Louisiana State Library, Baton Rouge.

25. L. D. Reddick, "A New Interpretation for Negro History," *Journal of Negro History*, XXII (January, 1937), 20; E. Franklin Frazier, "The Negro Slave Family," *Journal of Negro History*, XV (April, 1930), 204-205.

26. Richard Hofstadter, "U. B. Phillips and the Plantation Legend," *Journal of Negro History*, XXIX (April, 1944), 124; Kenneth M. Stampp, "The Historian and Southern Negro Slavery," *American Historical Review*, LVII (April, 1952), 618; John Hope Franklin, "New Perspectives in American Negro History," *Social Education*, XIV (May, 1950), 198-199; Howard Zinn, *The Politics of History* (Boston, 1970), p. 41.

27. Fry, *Night Riders*, p.17; Yetman, "Background," p. 540.

28. Yetman, "Background," pp. 541, 543, 553; Botkin, "Interpreter," p. 41.

29. Yetman, "Background," p. 535; C. Vann Woodward, "History from Slave Sources," *American Historical Review*, LXXIX (April, 1974), 472-473. A disclaimer of the liabilities of youthfulness under slavery can be found in the Virginia Writers' Project study, *The Negro in Virginia*, p. 27. For an evaluation of the differing qualities of reminiscences offered by each post-slavery generation of Afro-Americans, see Fry, *Night Riders*, p. 31.

30. Fry, *Night Riders*, pp. 22-23; J. Ralph Jones, "Portraits of Georgia Slaves," *Georgia Review*, XXI (Spring, 1967), 126; John W. Blassingame, "Using the Testimony of Ex-Slaves: Approaches and Problems," *Journal of Southern History*, XLI (November, 1975), 484-485.

31. Marion Wilson Starling, "The Slave Narrative: Its Place in American Literary History" (Ph.D. dissertation, New York University, 1946), pp. 1, 67, 428; Arna Bontemps, "The Slave Narrative: An American Genre," introduction to *Great Slave Narratives*, ed. by Arna Bontemps (Boston, 1969), p. xii. The first recorded black narrative appeared in 1703 in the transactions of the Colonial Society of Massachusetts under the caption *Adam Negro's Tryall*. The account dealt with a black indentured servant whose master sought to hold him beyond his seven-year period of service. For accounts of whites who claimed to have been held as slaves in colonial America, see Peter Williamson, *The Life and Curious Adventures of Peter Williamson, Who Was Carried Off from Aberdeen and Sold as a Slave* (London, 1759) and *Memoirs of an Unfortunate Young Nobleman, Returned from a Thirteen Years Slavery in America, Where He Had Been Sent by the Wicked Contrivance of His Cruel Uncle* (London, 1743).

32. Yetman, "Background," p. 536; Larry Gara, *The Liberty Line: The Legend of the Underground Railroad* (Lexington, 1961), p. 123; Stephen Butterfield, *Black Autobiography in America* (Amherst, 1974), p. 12; Starling, "Slave Narrative," p. 312; "Black Letters; or Uncle Tom-Foolery in Literature," *Graham's Magazine*, XLII (January, 1853), 214-215.

33. Julius Lester, *To Be a Slave* (New York, 1968), p. 14; Ulrich Bonnell Phillips, *Life and Labor in the Old South* (Boston, 1929), p. 219; Clement Eaton, *The Mind of the Old South* (Baton Rouge, 1967), p. 174; Blassingame, "Testimony," p. 478. John Blassingame has estimated that a little more than half of the fugitive slave narratives were written by abolitionists, but that often the stories told them by the slaves were not distorted. Instead they were simply written down as dictated by the fugitive or copied from court and church records. John W. Blassingame, *The Slave Community: Plantation Life in the Antebellum South* (New York, 1972), p. 232.

34. Charles H. Nichols, *Many Thousand Gone: The Ex-Slaves' Account of Their Bondage and Freedom* (Bloomington, 1969 [Leiden, 1963]), p. xii; Blassingame, "Testimony," p. 480.

35. Butterfield, *Black Autobiography*, pp. 35-36.

36. Starling, "Slave Narrative," p. 310; Blassingame, *Slave Community*, p. 228.

37. Margaret Young Jackson, "An Investigation of Biographies and Autobiographies of American Slaves Published Between 1840 and 1860: Based upon the Cornell Special Slavery Collection" (Ph.D. dissertation, Cornell University, 1954), pp. 328-329; *Liberator*, July 11, 1851.

38. Blassingame, "Testimony," pp. 474-477; William W. Nichols, "Slave Narratives: Dismissed Evidence in the Writing of Southern History," *Phylon*, XXXII (Winter, 1971), 161; Lester, *To Be a Slave*, p. 14.

39. Blassingame, *Slave Community*, p. 232; Starling, "Slave Narrative," p. 313; Blassingame, "Testimony," pp. 479-480. As an example of the "internal proofs" available to scholars, compare John Brown's description of life in Theophilus Freeman's New Orleans slave pen with that contained in Solomon Northup's narrative. John Brown, *Slave Life in Georgia: A Narrative of the Life, Sufferings, and Escape of John Brown, A Fugitive Slave* (London, 1855), p. 96; Solomon Northup, *Twelve Years a Slave. . . .* (Buffalo, 1853), pp. 51-60.

40. Gilbert Osofsky, ed., *Puttin' On Ole Massa: The Slave Narratives of Henry Bibb, William Wells Brown, and Solomon Northup* (New York, 1969), pp. 10-11; Starling, "Slave Narrative," p. 453.

selected bibliography

PRIMARY SOURCES, UNPUBLISHED

Alabama Department of Archives and History, Montgomery

J.W. DuBose Papers
William Proctor Gould Diary
Tait Family Papers

Duke University Library, Durham, North Carolina

John Ball, Sr., and John Ball, Jr., Papers
Francis Porteus Corbin Papers
Ebenezer Jackson Letterbooks
Louis Manigault Papers

Georgia Historical Society, Savannah

Pinckney Family Papers

University of Georgia Library, Athens

Charles Colcock Jones, Jr., Collection

Henry Huntington Library, San Moreno, California

Cabell Family Papers

Library of Congress, Washington, D.C.

James Henry Hammond Papers
George Teamoh Journal, Carter G. Woodson Collection of Negro
    Papers

Louisiana State University, Department of Archives, Baton Rouge

Priscilla M. Bond Papers
Thomas Butler and Family Papers
Alexander K. Farrar Papers
A. Ledoux and Company Record Book
E. E. McCollam Diary
William J. Minor and Family Papers
Alonzo Snyder Papers
Leonidas P. Spyker Diary
Lewis Stirling and Family Papers
David F. Weeks Collection

North Carolina Department of Archives and History, Raleigh

Bryan Manuscripts
Pettigrew Manuscripts

University of North Carolina, Southern Historical Collection, Chapel Hill

Archibald Hunter Arrington Papers
Arnold-Screven Family Papers
Everard Green Baker Diary and Plantation Notes
John Berkley Grimball Diary
John Houston Bills Diary
Elliott-Gonzales Family Papers
Heyward-Ferguson Papers
Kollock Plantation Books
Andrew McCollam Papers
Manigault Family Papers

John Nevitt Plantation Papers
Pettigrew Family Papers
Edmund Ruffin Papers
Josiah Smith, Jr., Lettercopy Book
Sparkman Family Papers
Lewis Thompson Papers
Henry Clay Warmoth Magnolia Plantation Journal
Benjamin C. Yancey Papers

South Carolina Historical Society, Charleston

Robert Francis Withers Allston Family Papers
Allston-Pringle-Hill Papers
Charles Izard Manigault Letterbook
Arthur Middleton Papers

South Carolina State Historical Commission, Columbia

Slavery Collection

University of South Carolina Library, Columbia

Ball Family Papers
Glover Family Papers
James Henry Hammond Plantation Book and Journal
Manigault Family Papers
Ezekiel Pickens Papers
Read-Lance Family Papers

University of Texas, Barker Texas History Center, Austin

Pugh Family Papers

Tulane University Library, New Orleans

Charles Colcock Jones Papers
Orange Grove Plantation Papers

University of Virginia, Alderman Library, Charlottesville

James Coles Bruce Family Papers
J. H. Cocke Papers
Harry M. Sherman Family Papers
Tayloe Papers

PRIMARY SOURCES, PUBLISHED

Abbot, John S. C. *South and North; or Impressions Received During a Trip to Cuba and the South.* New York: Abbey & Abbot, 1860.

Abdy, E. S. *Journal of a Residence and Tour in the United States of North America, from April, 1833, to October, 1834.* 3 vols. London: John Murray, 1835.

Acklen, Joseph A. S. "Rules in the Management of a Southern Estate." *DeBow's Review* XXI (December, 1856), 617-20.

Adams, Nehemiah. *A South-Side View of Slavery; or, Three Months at the South, in 1854.* Boston: T. R. Marvin, 1855.

Adger, John B. *My Life and Times, 1810-1899.* Richmond: Presbyterian Committeee of Publication, 1899.

Aleckson, Sam. *Before the War, and After the Union: An Autobiography.* Boston: Gold Mind Publishing Company, 1929.

Anderson, William J. *Life and Narrative of William J. Anderson, 24 Years a Slave.* Chicago: Daily Tribune Book and Job Office, 1857.

Andrews, Garnett. *Reminiscences of an Old Georgia Lawyer.* Atlanta: Franklin Steam Printing House, 1870.

Archer, Armstrong. *A Compendium of Slavery, as It Exists in the Present Day in the United States of America.* London: privately published, 1844.

Armstrong, Orland Kay. *Old Massa's People: The Old Slaves Tell Their Story.* Indianapolis: Bobbs-Merrill Company, 1931.

Aunt Sally; or, The Cross the Way of Freedom. A Narrative of the Slave-Life and Purchase of the Mother of Rev. Isaac Williams, of Detroit, Michigan. Cincinnati: American Reform Tract and Book Society, 1858.

Avirett, James Battle. *The Old Plantation: How We Lived in Great*

House and Cabin Before the War. New York: F. Tennyson Neely Co., 1901.

Bailey, Robert. *The Life and Adventures of Robert Bailey, from His Infancy up to December, 1821*. Richmond: privately published, 1822.

Ball, Charles. *Slavery in the United States: A Narrative of the Life and Adventures of Charles Ball*. New York: John S. Taylor, 1837.

Banks, Mary Ross. *Bright Days in the Old Plantation Time*. Boston: Lee and Shepard, 1882.

Bassett, John Spencer. *The Southern Plantation Overseer: As Revealed in His Letters*. Northampton: Smith College, 1925.

Battle, Kemp Plummer. *Memories of an Old-Time Tar Heel*. Ed. by William James Battle. Chapel Hill: University of North Carolina Press, 1945.

Bibb, Henry. *Narrative of the Life and Adventures of Henry Bibb, An American Slave*. New York: privately published, 1849.

Blassingame, John W., ed. *Slave Testimony: Two Centuries of Letters, Speeches, Interviews, and Autobiographies*. Baton Rouge: Louisiana State University Press, 1977.

Bremer, Fredrika. *The Homes of the New World; Impressions of America*. 2 vols. Trans. by Mary Howitt. New York: Harper and Brothers, 1853.

Brown, David. *The Planter: or, Thirteen Years in the South. By a Northern Man*. Philadelphia: H. Hooker, 1853.

Brown, John. *Slave Life in Georgia: A Narrative of the Life, Sufferings, and Escape of John Brown, A Fugitive Slave*. London: W. M. Watts, 1855.

Brown, Josephine. *Biography of an American Bondman, by His Daughter*. Boston: R. F. Wallcut, 1856.

Brown, William Wells. *My Southern Home: or, the South and Its People*. Boston: A. G. Brown & Co., 1880.

————. *Narrative of William W. Brown, A Fugitive Slave*. Boston: Anti-Slavery Office, 1847.

————. *Sketches of Places and People Abroad: The American Fugitive in Europe*. Boston: John P. Jewett, 1855.

Bruce, H. C. *The New Man: Twenty-Nine Years a Slave, Twenty-Nine Years a Free Man*. York, Pa.: P. Anstadt & Sons, 1895.

Buckingham, J. S. *The Slave States of America.* 2 vols. London:
    Fisher, Son & Co., 1842.
Burke, Emily P. *Reminiscences of Georgia.* n.p.: James M. Fitch,
    1850.
Burwell, Letitia M. *Plantation Reminiscences*, by Page Thacker,
    pseud. Owensboro (?), Ky.: n.p., 1878.
Carson, James Petrigru. *Life, Letters and Speeches of James Louis
    Petigru.* Washington, D.C.: W. H. Lowdermilk & Co., 1920.
Catterall, Helen Tunnicliff, ed. *Judicial Cases Concerning American
    Slavery and the Negro.* 5 vols. Washington, D.C.: Carnegie
    Institution, 1926-37.
Chesnut, Mary Boykin. *A Diary from Dixie.* New York: D. Appleton
    and Company, 1905.
Chester, Samuel H. *Pioneer Days in Arkansas.* Richmond: Presby-
    terian Committee of Publication, 1927.
Childs, Arney R., ed. *Rice Planter and Sportsman: The Recollec-
    tions of J. Motte Alston, 1821-1909.* Columbia: University of
    South Carolina Press, 1953.
Clarke, Lewis and Milton. *Narrative of the Sufferings of Lewis and
    Milton Clarke. . . .* Boston: Bela Marsh, 1846.
Clayton, Victoria. *White and Black Under the Old Regime.* Mil-
    waukee: The Young Churchman Co., 1899.
Clinkscales, J. G. *On the Old Plantation: Reminiscences of His
    Childhood.* Spartanburg, S.C.: Band & White Publishers, 1916.
Conyngham, Kate. *The Sunny South; or, the Southerner at Home.*
    . . . Ed. by J. H. Ingraham. Philadelphia: G. G. Evans, 1860.
Corning, Howard, ed. *Journal of John James Audubon Made During
    His Trip to New Orleans in 1820-1821.* Cambridge: Business
    Historical Society, 1929.
Cross, Eleanor P. and Charles B., eds. *Glencoe Diary: The War-
    Time Journal of Elizabeth Curtis Wallace.* Chesapeake, Va.:
    Norfolk County Historical Society, 1968.
Darby, James C. "On Planting and Managing a Rice Crop."
    Southern Agriculturist II (June, 1829), 247-54.
Davis, Edwin Adams, ed. *Plantation Life in the Florida Parishes of
    Louisiana, 1836-1846, as Reflected in the Diary of Bennet H.
    Barrow.* New York: Columbia University Press, 1943.

Davis, John. *Travels of John Davis in the United States of America, 1798 to 1802*. Ed. by John Vance Cheney. Boston: Bibliophile Society, 1910.

Davis, Varina Jefferson. *Jefferson Davis, Ex-President of the Confederate States of America: A Memoir by His Wife*. 2 vols. New York: Belford Company, Publishers, 1890.

Devereux, Margaret. *Plantation Sketches*. Cambridge: privately published, 1906.

Drew, Benjamin, ed. *A North-Side View of Slavery, the Refugee: or the Narratives of Fugitive Slaves in Canada*. Boston: John P. Jewett, 1856.

DuBose, John Witherspoon. "Recollections of the Plantation." *Alabama Historical Quarterly* I (Spring, 1930), 63-75; (Summer, 1930), 107-18.

Duke, Basil W. *Reminiscences of General Basil W. Duke, C. S. A.* Freeport, N.Y.: Books for Libraries Press, 1969 [New York, 1911].

Easterby, J. H., ed. *The South Carolina Rice Plantation as Revealed in the Papers of Robert F. W. Allston*. Chicago: University of Chicago Press, 1945.

"Eighteenth Century Slaves as Advertised by their Masters." *Journal of Negro History* I (April, 1916), 163-216.

Eppes, Mrs. Nicholas Ware. *The Negro of the Old South: A Bit of Period History*. Chicago: Joseph G. Branch, 1925.

Featherstonhaugh, G. W. *Excursion Through the Slave States*. 2 vols. London: John Murray, 1844.

Foby. "Management of Servants." *Southern Cultivator* XI (August, 1853), 226-28.

Foote, Henry S. *Casket of Reminiscences*. Washington, D.C.: Chronicle Publishing Company, 1874.

Ford, Arthur P. and Marion J. *Life in the Confederate Army and Some Experiences and Sketches of Southern Life*. New York: Neale Publishing Company, 1905.

Grandy, Moses. *Narrative of the Life of Moses Grandy, Late a Slave in the United States of America*. Boston: Oliver Johnson, 1844.

Green, William. *Narrative of Events in the Life of William Green*. Springfield, Mass.: L. M. Guernsey, 1853.

Greene, Jack P., ed. *The Diary of Colonel Landon Carter of Sabine Hall, 1752-1778.* 2 vols. Charlottesville: University Press of Virginia, 1965.

Grimes, William. *Life of William Grimes, the Runaway Slave, Brought Down to the Present Time.* New Haven: privately published, 1855.

Hall, Basil. *Travels in North America, in the Years 1827 and 1828.* 3 vols. Edinburgh: Cadell and Co., 1829.

Hall, Samuel. *47 Years a Slave: A Brief Story of His Life Before and After Freedom Came to Him.* Washington, Ia.: n.p., 1912.

Haviland, Laura S. *A Woman's Life-Work: Labors and Experiences of Laura S. Haviland.* Chicago: C. V. Waite & Company, 1887.

Hazzard, W. W. "On the General Management of a Plantation." *Southern Agriculturist* IV (July, 1831), 350-54.

Heard, William H. *From Slavery to the Bishopric in the A.M.E. Church: An Autobiography.* Philadelphia: A.M.E. Book Concern, 1924.

Henson, Josiah. *An Autobiography of the Rev. Josiah Henson ("Uncle Tom") from 1789 to 1881.* London, Ontario: Schuyler, Smith & Co., 1881.

―――. *Truth Stranger Than Fiction. Father Henson's Story of His Own Life.* Boston: John P. Jewett, 1858.

Holcombe, William H. "Sketches of Plantation-Life." *Knickerbocker* LVII (June, 1861), 619-33.

House, Albert Virgil, ed. *Planter Management and Capitalism in Ante-Bellum Georgia: The Journal of Hugh Fraser Grant, Ricegrower.* New York: Columbia University Press, 1954.

Hughes, Louis. *Thirty Years a Slave.* Milwaukee: H. E. Haferkorn, 1897.

Jacobs, Harriet Brent. *Incidents in the Life of a Slave Girl,* by Linda Brent, pseud. Ed. by L. Maria Child. Boston: privately published, 1861.

Jamison, M. F. *Autobiography and Work of Bishop M. F. Jamison, D.D.* Nashville: Publishing House of the M. E. Church, South, 1912.

Jones, Charles C. *The Religious Instruction of the Negroes in the United States.* Savannah: Thomas Purse, 1842.

Jones, J. Ralph. "Portraits of Georgia Slaves." *Georgia Review*

XXI (Spring, 1967), 126-32; (Summer, 1967), 268-73.

Jones, Thomas H. *The Experience of Thomas H. Jones, Who Was a Slave for Forty-Three Years*. Boston: Bazin & Chandler, 1862.

Jordan, Weymouth. "The Management Rules of an Alabama Black Belt Plantation, 1848-1862." *Agricultural History* XVIII (January, 1944), 53-64.

Kearney, Belle. *A Slaveholder's Daughter*. New York: Negro Universities Press, 1969 [1900].

Kellar, Herbert Anthony, ed. *Solon Robinson, Pioneer and Agriculturist*. 2 vols. Indianapolis: Indiana Historical Bureau, 1936.

Kemble, Frances Anne. *Journal of a Residence on a Georgian Plantation in 1838-1839*. New York: Harper and Brothers, 1863.

King, Jr., R. "On the Management of the Butler Estate, and the Cultivation of the Sugar Cane." *Southern Agriculturist* I (December, 1828), 523-29.

Knight, Henry C. *Letters from the South and West*, by Arthur Singleton, pseud. Boston: Richardson and Lord, 1824.

Lane, Lunsford. *Narrative of Lunsford Lane, Formerly of Raleigh, N.C.* Boston: J. G. Torrey, 1842.

Langston, John Mercer. *From the Virginia Plantation to the National Capitol*. Hartford: American Publishing Company, 1894.

Lanman, Charles. *Haw-Ho-Noo; or Records of a Tourist*. Philadelphia: Lippincott, Grambo and Co., 1850.

Latrobe, Charles Joseph. *The Rambler in North America*. 2 vols. London: R. B. Seeley and W. Burnside, 1836.

Leigh, Francis B. *Ten Years on a Georgia Plantation Since the War*. New York: Negro Universities Press, 1969 [London, 1883].

Lewis, G. *Impressions of America and the American Churches*. Edinburgh: W. P. Kennedy, 1845.

Loguen, Jermain W. *The Rev. J. W. Loguen, as a Slave and as a Freeman. A Narrative of Real Life*. Syracuse: Daily Journal, 1859.

Lyell, Charles. *A Second Visit to the United States of North America*. 2 vols. London: John Murray, 1850.

Mackay, Alexander. *The Western World; or Travels in the United States in 1846-47*. 3 vols. London: Richard Bentley, 1849.

Mallard, R. Q. *Plantation Life Before Emancipation*. Richmond: Whittet & Shepperson, 1892.

Martineau, Harriet. *Retrospect of Western Travel*. 3 vols. London: Saunders and Otley, 1838.

———. Society in America. 3 vols. London: Saunders and Otley, 1837.

Mason, Isaac. *Life of Isaac Mason as a Slave*. Worcester: privately published, 1893.

Meade, Anna Hardeman. *When I Was a Little Girl: The Year's Round on the Plantation*. Los Angeles: Fred S. Lang, 1916.

Miller, Randall M., ed. *"Dear Master": Letters of a Slave Family*. Ithaca: Cornell University Press, 1978.

"A Mississippi Planter." "Management of Negroes upon Southern Estates." *DeBow's Southern and Western Review* X (June, 1851), 621-27.

Mott, Alexander and Wood, M. S. *Narratives of Colored Americans*. New York: William Wood & Co., 1877.

Murat, Achille. *America and the Americans*. New York: William H. Graham, 1849.

Myers, Robert Manson, ed. *The Children of Pride: A True Story of Georgia and the Civil War*. New Haven: Yale University Press, 1972.

Nichols, Thomas L. *Forty Years of American Life*. 2 vols. London: John Maxwell and Company, 1864.

Northup, Solomon. *Twelve Years a Slave*. . . . Buffalo: Derby, Orton and Mulligan, 1853.

O'Ferrall, S. A. *A Ramble of Six Thousand Miles through the United States of America*. London: Effingham Wilson, 1832.

Olmsted, Frederick Law. *A Journey in the Back Country*. New York: Mason Brothers, 1860.

———. *A Journey in the Seabord Slave States, with Remarks on Their Economy*. New York: Mason Brothers, 1859.

———. *A Journey Through Texas: or, a Saddle-Trip on the Southwestern Frontier*. New York: Mason Brothers, 1859.

———. *The Cotton Kingdom: A Traveller's Observations on Cotton and Slavery in the American Slave States*. New York: Mason Brothers, 1861.

"An Overseer." "On the Conduct and Management of Overseers, Drivers, and Slaves." *Farmers' Register* IV (June, 1836), 114-16.

"Overseers at the South." *DeBow's Review* XXI (September, 1856), 277-79.

Parker, William. "The Freedman's Story." *Atlantic Monthly* XVII (February, 1866), 152-66.

Pearson, Elizabeth Ware. *Letters from Port Royal: Written at the Time of the Civil War.* Boston: W. B. Clarke Company, 1906.

Perdue, Jr., Charles L.; Barden, Thomas E.; and Phillips, Robert K., eds. *Weevils in the Wheat: Interviews with Virginia Ex-Slaves.* Charlottesville: University Press of Virginia, 1976.

Peterson, Walter F., ed. "Slavery in the 1850s: The Recollections of an Alabama Unionist." *Alabama Historical Quarterly* XXX (Fall and Winter, 1968), 219-27.

Phillips, Ulrich B., ed. *Plantation and Frontier Documents, 1649-1863.* Vols. I and II of John R. Commons, et al. *A Documentary History of American Industrial Society.* Cleveland: Arthur H. Clark, 1909-10.

Phillips, Ulrich Bonnell, and Glunt, James David, eds. *Florida Plantation Records from the Papers of George Noble Jones.* St. Louis: Missouri Historical Society, 1927.

Pickard, Kate E. R. *The Kidnapped and the Ransomed. Being the Personal Recollections of Peter Still and His Wife "Vina," after Forty Years of Slavery.* Syracuse: William T. Hamilton, 1856.

"A Planter." "Notions on the Management of Negroes, &c." *Farmers' Register* IV (December 1, 1836), 494-95.

Pollard, Edward A. *Black Diamonds Gathered in the Darkey Homes of the South.* New York: Pudney & Russell Publishers, 1860.

Pope-Hennessy, Una, ed. *The Aristocratic Journey: Being the Outspoken Letters of Mrs. Basil Hall Written during a Fourteen Months' Sojourn in America, 1827-1828.* New York: G. P. Putnam's Sons, 1931.

Pulszky, Francis and Theresa. *White, Red, Black: Sketches of American Society in the United States.* 3 vols. New York: Redfield, 1853.

Randolph, Peter. *From Slave Cabin to the Pulpit: The Autobiography of Rev. Peter Randolph.* Boston: James H. Earle, 1893.

Rawick, George P., ed. *The American Slave: A Composite Autobiography.* Series One and Two. 19 vols. Westport, Conn.: Greenwood Press, 1972, 1974.

SELECTED BIBLIOGRAPHY

SELECTED184

————. *The American Slave: A Composite Autobiography,* Supplement, Series One. 12 vols. Westport, Conn.: Greenwood Press, 1978.

Redpath, James. *The Roving Editor: or, Talks with Slaves in the Southern States.* New York: A. B. Burdick, 1859.

Riley, Franklin L., ed. "Diary of a Mississippi Planter, January 1, 1840, to April, 1863." *Publications of the Mississippi Historical Society* X (1909), 305-481.

Roper, Moses. *A Narrative of the Adventures and Escape of Moses Roper, from American Slavery.* London: Harvey and Darton, 1843.

Ruffin, F. G. "Overseers." *Southern Planter* XVI (May, 1856), 147-48.

Saxon, Lyle; Dreyer, Edward; and Tallant, Robert. *Gumbo Ya-Ya: A Collection of Louisiana Folk Tales.* Boston: Houghton Mifflin Company, 1945.

Scarborough, William Kauffman, ed. *The Diary of Edmund Ruffin.* 2 vols. Baton Rouge: Louisiana State University Press, 1972, 1977.

Schoolcraft, Mary Howard. *Plantation Life: The Narratives of Mrs. Henry Rowe Schoolcraft.* New York: Negro Universities Press, 1969 [Philadelphia, 1852, 1860].

Seabrook, Isaac DuBose. *Before and After or the Relations of the Races at the South.* Ed. by John Hammond Moore. Baton Rouge: Louisiana State University Press, 1967.

Sealsfield, Charles. *The Americans as They Are; Described in a Tour through the Valley of the Mississippi.* London: Hurst, Chance, and Co., 1828.

Shippee, Lester B., ed. *Bishop Whipple's Southern Diary, 1843-1844.* Minneapolis: University of Minnesota Press, 1937.

Smedes, Susan Dabney. *Memorials of a Southern Planter.* Baltimore: Cushings & Bailey, 1887.

Smith, Alice R. Huger. *A Carolina Rice Plantation of the Fifties.* New York: William Morrow and Company, 1936.

Smith, Daniel E. Huger; Smith, Alice R. Huger; and Childs, Arney R., eds. *Mason Smith Family Letters, 1860-1868.* Columbia, S.C.: University of South Carolina Press, 1950.

Smith, Harry. *Fifty Years of Slavery in the United States of America.*

Grand Rapids: West Michigan Printing Co., 1891.

Smith, James L. *Autobiography of James L. Smith*. Norwich: Press of the Bulletin Company, 1881.

Stevens, Charles Emery. *Anthony Burns: A History*. Boston: John P. Jewett, 1856.

Stevenson, Mary, ed. *The Diary of Clarissa Adger Bowen, Ashtabula Plantation, 1865*. Pendleton, S.C.: Foundation for Historic Restoration in Pendleton Area, 1973.

Steward, Austin. *Twenty-Two Years a Slave, and Forty Years a Freeman*. Rochester: William Alling, 1857.

Still, William. *The Underground Rail Road*. Philadelphia: People's Publishing Company, 1871.

Stirling, James. *Letters from the Slave States*. London: John W. Parker and Son, 1857.

Stroyer, Jacob. *My Life in the South*. Salem: Newcomb & Gauss, 1898.

Stuart-Wortley, Lady Emmeline. *Travels in the United States, etc. During 1849 and 1850*. New York: Harper and Brothers, 1855.

Sturge, Joseph. *A Visit to the United States in 1841*. Boston: Dexter S. King, 1842.

Tasistro, Louis Fitzgerald. *Random Shots and Southern Breezes*. 2 vols. New York: Harper and Brothers, 1842.

Thompson, John. *The Life of John Thompson, A Fugitive Slave*. Worcester: privately published, 1856.

Thomson, William. *A Tradesman's Travels in the United States and Canada, in the Years 1840, 41, & 42*. Edinburgh: Oliver & Boyd, 1842.

Tocqueville, Alexis de. *Democracy in America*. Ed. by J. P. Mayer and Max Lerner. Trans. by George Lawrence. New York: Anchor Books, 1969 [Paris, 1835, 1840].

Tower, Philo. *Slavery Unmasked: Being a Truthful Narrative of a Three Years' Residence and Journeying in Eleven Southern States*. Rochester: E. Darrow & Brother, 1856.

Webb, William. *History of William Webb*. Detroit: Egbert Hoekstra, 1873.

Weston, P. C. "Management of a Southern Plantation." *DeBow's Review* XXII (January, 1857), 38-44.

Whipple, Henry B. *Bishop Whipple's Southern Diary, 1843-1844*.

Ed. by Lester B. Shippee. Minneapolis: University of Minnesota Press, 1937.

Whittington, G. P., ed. "Concerning the Loyalty of Slaves in North Louisiana in 1863: Letters from John H. Ransdell to Governor Thomas O. Moore, dated 1863." *Louisiana Historical Quarterly* XIV (October, 1931), 487-502.

Williams, James. *Narrative of James Williams. An American Slave, Who Was for Several Years a Driver on a Cotton Plantation in Alabama.* New York: American Anti-Slavery Society, 1838.

Work Projects Administration. Savannah Unit, Georgia Writers' Project. *Drums and Shadows: Survival Studies Among the Georgia Coastal Negroes.* Athens: University of Georgia Press, 1940.

Work Projects Administration. Workers of the Writers' Program, State of Virginia. *The Negro in Virginia.* New York: Hastings House Publishers, 1940.

SECONDARY SOURCES, BOOKS

Alford, Terry. *Prince Among Slaves.* New York: Harcourt Brace Jovanovich, 1977.

Allan, William. *Life and Work of John McDonogh.* Baltimore: Isaac Friedenwald, 1886.

Aptheker, Herbert. *American Negro Slave Revolts.* New York: Columbia University Press, 1943.

———. *Nat Turner's Slave Rebellion.* New York: Humanities Press, 1966.

Ballagh, James Curtis. *A History of Slavery in Virginia.* Baltimore: Johns Hopkins University Press, 1902.

Bassett, John S. *History of Slavery in North Carolina.* Baltimore: Johns Hopkins University Press, 1899.

Berger, Max. *The British Traveller in America, 1836-1860.* New York: Columbia University Press, 1943.

Bettelheim, Bruno. *The Informed Heart: Autonomy in a Mass Age.* New York: The Free Press, 1960.

Blassingame, John W. *The Slave Community: Plantation Life in the Antebellum South.* New York: Oxford University Press, 1972.

Brackett, Jeffrey R. *The Negro in Maryland: A Study of the Institution of Slavery*. Baltimore: Johns Hopkins University Press, 1889.

Bridenbaugh, Carl. *Myths & Realities: Societies of the Colonial South*. Baton Rouge: Louisiana State University Press, 1952.

Bruce, Philip Alexander. *Economic History of Virginia in the Seventeenth Century*. 2 vols. New York: Macmillan and Co., 1896.

Butterfield, Stephen. *Black Autobiography in America*. Amherst: University of Massachusetts Press, 1974.

Cash, W. J. *The Mind of the South*. New York: A. A. Knopf, 1941.

Cohen, Elie A. *Human Behavior in the Concentration Camp*. New York: W. W. Norton & Company, 1953.

Coulter, E. Merton. *Thomas Spalding of Sapelo*. University: Louisiana State University Press, 1940.

Coyner, Jr., M. Boyd. "John Hartwell Cocke of Bremo: Agriculture and Slavery in the Ante-Bellum South." Ph.D. dissertation, University of Virginia, 1961.

Craven, Avery. *Edmund Ruffin, Southerner; A Study in Secession*. New York: D. Appleton and Company, 1932.

Curlee, Abigail. "A Study of Texas Slave Plantations, 1822 to 1865." Ph.D. dissertation, University of Texas, 1932.

David, Paul A., et al., eds. *Reckoning with Slavery: A Critical Study in the Quantitative History of American Negro Slavery*. New York: Oxford University Press, 1976.

Davis, Charles S. *The Cotton Kingdom in Alabama*. Montgomery: Alabama State Department of Archives and History, 1939.

DesPres, Terrence. *The Survivor: An Anatomy of Life in the Death Camps*. New York: Oxford University Press, 1976.

Eaton, Clement. *A History of the Old South*. New York: The Macmillan Company, 1949.

———. *The Mind of the Old South*. Baton Rouge: Louisiana State University Press, 1967.

Elkins, Stanley M. *Slavery: A Problem in American Institutional and Intellectual Life*. Chicago: University of Chicago Press, 1959, 1968, 1976.

Flanders, Ralph Betts. *Plantation Slavery in Georgia*. Chapel Hill: University of North Carolina Press, 1933.

Fogel, Robert William, and Engerman, Stanley L. *Time on the*

Cross, Vol. I: *The Economics of American Negro Slavery*. Boston: Little, Brown and Company, 1974.

———. *Time on the Cross*. Vol. II: *Evidence and Methods–A Supplement*. Boston: Little, Brown and Company, 1974.

Fry, Gladys-Marie. *Night Riders in Black Folk History*. Knoxville: University of Tennessee Press, 1975.

Furnas, J. C. *Goodbye to Uncle Tom*. New York: William Sloane Associates, 1956.

Gaines, Francis Pendleton. *The Southern Plantation: A Study in the Development and the Accuracy of a Tradition*. New York: Columbia University Press, 1925.

Gara, Larry. *The Liberty Line: The Legend of the Underground Railroad*. Lexington: University of Kentucky Press, 1961.

Garraty, John A., ed. *Interpreting American History: Conversations with Historians*. 2 vols. New York: The Macmillan Company, 1970.

Genovese, Eugene D. *In Red and Black: Marxian Explorations in Southern and Afro-American History*. New York: Pantheon Books, 1968.

———. *The Political Economy of Slavery: Studies in the Economy & Society of the Slave South*. New York: Pantheon Books, 1965.

———. *Roll, Jordan, Roll: The World the Slaves Made*. New York: Pantheon Books, 1974.

Goffman, Erving. *Asylums: Essays on the Social Situation of Mental Patients and Other Inmates*. Garden City, N.J.: Anchor Books, 1961.

Gray, Lewis Cecil. *History of Agriculture in the Southern United States to 1860*. 2 vols. Washington, D.C. Carnegie Institution, 1933.

Greene, Jack P. *Landon Carter: An Inquiry into the Personal Values and Social Imperatives of the Eighteenth-Century Virginia Gentry*. Charlottesville: Dominion Books, 1967.

Gutman, Herbert G. *The Black Family in Slavery and Freedom, 1750-1925*. New York: Pantheon Books, 1976.

———. *Slavery and the Numbers Game: A Critique of Time on the Cross*. Urbana: University of Illinois Press, 1975.

Hart, Albert Bushnell. *Slavery and Abolition, 1831-1841*. New York: Harper and Brothers, 1906.

Henry, H. M. *The Police Control of the Slave in South Carolina*. Emory, Va.: n.p., 1914.

Heyward, Duncan Clinch. *Seed from Madagascar*. Chapel Hill: University of North Carolina Press, 1937.

Huggins, Nathan Irvin. *Black Odyssey: The Afro-American Ordeal in Slavery*. New York: Pantheon Books, 1977.

Jackson, Margaret Young. "An Investigation of Biographies and Autobiographies of American Slaves Published Between 1840 and 1860: Based upon the Cornell Special Slavery Collection." Ph.D. dissertation, Cornell University, 1954.

Johnson, Charles S. *Shadow of the Plantation*. Chicago: University of Chicago Press, 1934.

Johnson, Guion Griffis. *A Social History of the Sea Islands*. Chapel Hill: University of North Carolina Press, 1930.

Jordon, Weymouth T. *Hugh Davis and His Alabama Plantation*. University: University of Alabama Press, 1948.

Jordan, Winthrop D. *White Over Black: American Attitudes Toward the Negro, 1550-1812*. Chapel Hill: University of North Carolina Press, 1968.

Kifer, Allen Francis. "The Negro Under the New Deal, 1933-1941." Ph.D. dissertation, University of Wisconsin, 1961.

Lane, Ann J., ed. *The Debate Over Slavery: Stanley Elkins and His Critics*. Urbana: University of Illinois Press, 1971.

Lester, Julius. *To Be a Slave*. New York: Dial Press, 1968.

Levine, Lawrence W. *Black Culture and Black Consciousness: Afro-American Folk Thought from Slavery to Freedom*. New York: Oxford University Press, 1977.

Loggins, Vernon. *The Negro Author: His Development in America*. New York: Columbia University Press, 1931.

Lovell, Caroline Couper. *The Golden Isles of Georgia*. Boston: Little, Brown and Company, 1932.

McColley, Robert. *Slavery and Jeffersonian Virginia*. Urbana: University of Illinois Press, 1964, 1973.

McDonald, William F. *Federal Relief Administration and the Arts*. Columbus: Ohio State University Press, 1969.

Mangione, Jerre. *The Dream and the Deal: The Federal Writers' Project, 1935-1943*. Boston: Little, Brown and Company, 1972.

Mesick, Jane Louise. *The English Traveller in America, 1785-1835*. New York: Columbia University Press, 1922.

Miller, Elinor, and Genovese, Eugene D., eds. *Plantation, Town, and County: Essays on the Local History of American Slave Society*. Urbana: University of Illinois Press, 1974.

Mooney, Chase C. *Slavery in Tennessee*. Bloomington: Indiana University Press, 1957.

Moore, John Hebron. *Agriculture in Ante-Bellum Mississippi*. New York: Bookman Associates, 1958.

Morgan, Edmund. *American Slavery, American Freedom: The Ordeal of Colonial Virginia*. New York: W. W. Norton & Company, 1975.

Mullin, Gerald W. *Flight and Rebellion: Slave Resistance in Eighteenth-Century Virginia*. New York: Oxford University Press, 1972.

Nichols, Jr., Charles Harold. "A Study of the Slave Narrative." Ph.D. dissertation, Brown University, 1948.

Oates, Stephen B. *The Fires of Jubilee: Nat Turner's Fierce Rebellion*. New York: Harper & Row, Publishers, 1975.

Owens, Harry P., ed. *Perspectives and Irony in American Slavery*. Jackson: University Press of Mississippi, 1976.

Patterson, Caleb Perry. *The Negro in Tennessee, 1790-1865*. Austin: University of Texas, 1922.

Penkower, Monty Noam. *The Federal Writers' Project: A Study in Government Patronage of the Arts*. Urbana: University of Illinois Press, 1977.

Phillips, Ulrich Bonnell. *American Negro Slavery: A Survey of the Supply, Employment and Control of Negro Labor as Determined by the Plantation Regime*. New York: D. Appleton and Company, 1918.

————. *Life and Labor in the Old South*. Boston: Little, Brown and Company, 1929.

Postell, William Dosite. *The Health of Slaves on Southern Plantations*. Baton Rouge: Louisiana State University Press, 1951.

Pringle, Elizabeth W. Allston. *Chronicles of Chicora Wood*. Boston: Christopher Publishing House, 1940.

Rawick, George P. *From Sundown to Sunup: The Making of the*

Black Community. Westport, Conn.: Greenwood Press, 1972.

Rose, Willie Lee. Rehearsal for Reconstruction: The Port Royal Experiment. Indianapolis: Bobbs-Merrill Company, 1964.

Rowland, Eron. *Varina Howell, Wife of Jefferson Davis*. 2 vols. New York: The Macmillan Company, 1927.

Rubin, Morton. *Plantation County*. Chapel Hill: University of North Carolina Press, 1951.

Scarborough, William Kauffman. *The Overseer: Plantation Management in the Old South*. Baton Rouge: Louisiana State University Press, 1966.

Sellers, James Benson. *Slavery in Alabama*. University: University of Alabama Press, 1950.

Sitterson, J. Carlyle. *Sugar Country: The Cane Sugar Industry in the South, 1753-1950*. Lexington: University of Kentucky Press, 1953.

Smith, Julia Floyd. *Slavery and Plantation Growth in Antebellum Florida, 1821-1860*. Gainesville: University of Florida Press, 1973.

Smith, Sidonie. *Where I'm Bound: Patterns of Slavery and Freedom in Black American Autobiography*. Westport, Conn.: Greenwood Press, 1974.

Stampp, Kenneth M. *The Peculiar Institution: Slavery in the Ante-Bellum South*. New York: A. A. Knopf, 1956.

Starling, Marion Wilson. "The Slave Narrative: Its Place in American Literary History." Ph.D. dissertation, New York University, 1946.

Stone, James Herbert. "Black Leadership in the Old South: The Slave Drivers of the Rice Kingdom." Ph.D. dissertation, Florida State University, 1976.

Sydnor, Charles S. *A Gentleman of the Old Natchez Region: Benjamin L. C. Wailes*. Durham: Duke University Press, 1938.

―――. *Slavery in Mississippi*. New York: American Historical Association, 1933.

Taylor, Joe Gray. *Negro Slavery in Louisiana*. Baton Rouge: Louisiana State University Press, 1963.

Thorpe, Earl E. *The Old South: A Psychohistory*. Durham: Seeman Printing, 1972.

Trexler, Harrison Anthony. *Slavery in Missouri, 1804-1865*. Baltimore: Johns Hopkins University Press, 1914.

Wall, Bennett Harrison. "Ebenezer Pettigrew, An Economic Study of an Ante-Bellum Planter." Ph.D. dissertation, University of North Carolina, Chapel Hill, 1946.

Wiley, Bell Irvin. *Southern Negroes, 1861-1865*. New Haven: Yale University Press, 1938.

Wood, Peter H. *Black Majority: Negroes in Colonial South Carolina from 1670 through the Stono Rebellion*. New York: A. A. Knopf, 1974.

Zinn, Howard, *The Politics of History*. Boston: Beacon Press, 1970.

SECONDARY SOURCES, ARTICLES

Bettelheim, Bruno. "Individual and Mass Behavior in Extreme Situations." *Journal of Abnormal and Social Psychology* XXXVIII (October, 1943), 417-52.

Blassingame, John W. "Black Autobiographies as History and Literature." *Black Scholar* V (December, 1973-January, 1974), 2-9.

———. "Using the Testimony of Ex-Slaves: Approaches and Problems." *Journal of Southern History* XLI (November, 1975), 473-92.

Botkin, B. A. "The Slave as His Own Interpreter." *Library of Congress Quarterly Journal of Current Acquisitions* II (November, 1944), 37-63.

Cade, John B. "Out of the Mouths of Ex-Slaves." *Journal of Negro History* XX (July, 1935), 294-337.

Ferris Jr., William R. "The Collection of Racial Lore: Approaches and Problems." *New York Folklore Quarterly* XXVII (September, 1971), 261-79.

Fleming, Walter L. "Jefferson Davis, the Negroes and the Negro Problem." *Sewanee Review* XVI (October, 1908), 407-27.

Fredrickson, George M., and Lasch, Christopher. "Resistance to Slavery." *Civil War History* XIII (December, 1967), 315-29.

Hofstadter, Richard. "U. B. Phillips and the Plantation Legend." *Journal of Negro History* XXIX (April, 1944), 109-24.

Kolchin, Peter. "Toward a Reinterpretation of Slavery." *Journal of Social History* IX (Fall, 1975), 99-113.

Kneebone, John T. "Sambo and the Slave Narratives: A Note on Sources." *Essays in History* XIX (1975), 7-23.

Lewis, Roscoe E. "The Life of Mark Thrash." *Phylon* XX (Winter, 1959), 389-403.

Menard, Russell R. "The Maryland Slave Population, 1658 to 1730: A Demographic Profile of Blacks in Four Counties." *William and Mary Quarterly* XXXII (January, 1975), 29-54.

Miller, Randall M. "The Man in the Middle: The Black Slave Driver." Paper presented at the Organization of American Historians' meeting, April 9, 1976, St. Louis, Missouri.

Moody, V. Alton. "Slavery on Louisiana Sugar Plantations." *Louisiana Historical Quarterly* VII (April, 1924), 191-301.

Murphree, Dennis. "Hurricane and Brierfield: The Davis Plantations." *Journal of Mississippi History* IX (April, 1947), 98-107.

Nichols, Charles H. "Slave Narratives and the Plantation Legend." *Phylon* X (3rd Quarter, 1949), 201-10.

———. "Who Read the Slave Narratives?" *Phylon* XX (Summer, 1959), 149-62.

Nichols, William W. "Slave Narratives: Dismissed Evidence in the Writing of Southern History." *Phylon* XXXII (Winter, 1971), 403-9.

Reddick, L. D. "A New Interpretation for Negro History." *Journal of Negro History* XXII (January, 1937), 17-28.

Scarborough, William Kauffman. "The Southern Plantation Overseer: A Re-evaluation." *Agricultural History* XXXVIII (January, 1964), 13-20.

Sitterson, J. Carlyle. "The William J. Minor Plantations: A Study in Ante-Bellum Absentee Ownership." *Journal of Southern History* IX (February, 1943), 59-74.

Stampp, Kenneth M. "Rebels and Sambos: The Search for the Negro's Personality in Slavery." *Journal of Southern History* XXXVII (August, 1971), 367-92.

Starobin, Robert S. "Privileged Bondsmen and the Process of Accommodation: The Role of Houseservants and Drivers as Seen in Their Own Letters." *Journal of Social History* V (Fall, 1971), 46-70.

Stephenson, Wendell Holmes. "A Quarter-Century of a Mississippi Plantation: Eli J. Capell of 'Pleasant Hill.' " *Mississippi Valley Historical Review* XXIII (December, 1936), 355-74.

Stuckey, Sterling. "Through the Prism of Folklore: The Black Ethos in Slavery." *Massachusetts Review* IX (Summer, 1968), 417-37.

Sydnor, Charles Sackett. "A Slave Owner and His Overseers." *North Carolina Historical Review* XIV (January, 1937), 31-8.

Taylor, Paul S. "Plantation Laborer Before the Civil War." *Agricultural History* XXVIII (January, 1954), 1-21.

Van Deburg, William L. "Elite Slave Behavior During the Civil War: Black Drivers and Foremen in Historiographical Perspective." *Southern Studies* XVI (Fall, 1977), 253-69.

———. "Slave Drivers and Slave Narratives: A New Look at the 'Dehumanized Elite.' " *Historian* XXXIX (August, 1977), 717-32.

———. "The Slave Drivers of Arkansas: A New View from the Narratives." *Arkansas Historical Quarterly* XXXV (Autumn, 1976), 231-45.

———. "Ulrich B. Phillips: Progress and the Conservative Historian." *Georgia Historical Quarterly* LV (Fall, 1971), 406-16.

Wall, Bennett H. "Medical Care of Ebenezer Pettigrew's Slaves." *Mississippi Valley Historical Review* XXXVII (December, 1950), 451-70.

Woodward, C. Vann. "History from Slave Sources." *American Historical Review* LXXIX (April, 1974), 470-81.

Yetman, Norman R. "The Background of the Slave Narrative Collection." *American Quarterly* XIX (Fall, 1967), 534-53.

index

Abbott, John S. C., on slave intelligence, 122

Abdy, E. S., 124

Abolitionists: and black autobiographies, 93, 95-97, 99, 112, 129-130, 131-132, 170; on character of slavery, xvii, 65; and travel accounts, 63

Abraham, slave driver, 97-98, 99

Adams, Nehemiah: on slavery, 64, 65; as traveler, 121

Adams, Will, 18

Adger, John Bailey, 21-22

Alcckson, Sam, 10, 98

Alexander, Archer, slave driver: and family separation, 18; as fugitive, 18, 105

Allen, Washington, 128-129

Allston, Benjamin, 28

Allston, Joseph, 58

Allston, Robert F. W., 58; on slave driver Orinoca, 54; on slave driver qualifications, 8

American Anti-Slavery Society, 96-97

American Negro Slavery (Phillips), 33

Andrews, Cornelia, 84

Andrews, Garnett, 24

Antebellum travelers. *See* Travelers

Antislavery movement. *See* Abolitionists

Association for the Study of Negro Life and History (ASNLH), 125, 127

Atlantic Slave Trade, The (Curtin), 77

Auctions. *See* Slave auctions, slave drivers involved in

"Aunt Janie," 89

Austin, slave driver, 47-48

Autobiographies. *See* black autobiographies

Avirett, James B., 46

Ball, Charles, slave driver, 95-96; *Slavery in the United States*, 95-96, 97

Beavers, Edmond, slave driver, 26

Behn, Aphra, *Oroonoko*, 129

Bell, Frank, 17, 18

Bell, Moses, slave driver: protects relatives, 17; separated from family, 18

Benjamin, Sam, slave driver, 28

Bernard, J. H., 51

Bettelheim, Bruno, on Kapos, 36-37

Betty, wife of slave driver, 70

Bibb, Henry, slave driver: as fugitive, 101; refuses to whip, 100, 102; on slaveholder Francis Whitfield, 102-103

Binns, Arrie, 28

Black autobiographies: development in American literature, 129-130, 163, 170; drivers as authors of, 99-100, 112; as rebellion against slavery, 112; relationship to oral history, 93, 94; use of by historians, 93-95, 97, 100, 130-131, 132-133

Bland, Henry, 15

Blassingame, John W., 42, 77; on black autobiographies, 100, 130-131, 132, 170; on elite slaves, 38-39; *Slave Community, The*, 38, 40-41; on *Slavery in the United States*, 97

Body, Rias, 128

Bondsmen. *See* Slaves
Boss man, 3. *See also* Slave drivers
Botkin, Benjamin A., 126; *Lay My Burden Down*, 94
Bremer, Fredrika: on slave driver cruelty, 67; on southern travel, 61
Brown, Abraham, slave driver, 27
Brown, Fred, 143-144
Brown, Henry, 27
Brown, Henry "Box," reenacts escape, 131-132
Brown, Lucy, 27
Brown, Molly, 84
Brown, William Wells, slave driver, 102; as author, 129
Bruce, Henry Clay, slave driver: criticized by master, 103; during Reconstruction, 28
Bu Allah, slave driver, 22-23
Buckingham, J. S., 121
Burwell, Letitia M. (pseud. Page Thacker), 45
Butler, Pierce M., 69-70
Byrd, Susie, 84

Cade, John B., and oral history, 124-125, 127-128
Cannon, Frank, 9
Carney, William, 98
Carolina, Albert, 86
Carter, Landon, 55, 58
Carter, Robert "King," 8, 55
Cavin, Freeman, slave driver, 18
Cheatam, Henry, 81
Chesnut, Mary Boykin, 20-21
Christianity, slave drivers reject, 21-23
Christians, slave drivers as, 20-21, 23, 105, 109
Civil War, slave drivers during, 25-27, 105
Claibourn, Ellen, 90
Clarke, Lewis, 98, 99, 100
Clayton, Victoria, 20
"Climate of opinion," influences historiography, 31, 44

Cliometricians, 42-44
Clinkscales, John, 48
Clothing, slave drivers', 43, 51, 96
Cocke, John Hartwell: forms Temperance Society, 56-57; and slave drivers, 57, 59
Cody, Elbert, slave driver, 88
Cohen, Eli, 36
Cole, Bill, slave driver, 21
Commandeur, 8. *See also* Slave drivers
Corn generals, slave drivers as, 24-25
Couper, J. Hamilton, 51
Coxton, Sam, slave driver, 15
Craftsmen. *See* Industrial crafts, slave supervisors in
Crew leader, 3. *See also* Slave drivers
Cruelty, of slave drivers: antebellum critics on, 7; in black autobiographies, 97-99; historians on, 35, 41-42, 114; in oral history, 80-82, 85-86, 91; in popular characterization, xv-xvii; travelers on, 66-68
Curtin, Philip D., *Atlantic Slave Trade, The*, 77

Dabney, Thomas S., 46
"Daddy Joe," slave driver, 10, 98
Davis, David Brion, 77
Davis, Jefferson, 28, 49
Davis, Joe, 28
Davis, Louisa, 87-88
Davis, Varina, 49-50
Davy, slave driver, 55
Defiance, of slave drivers, 26, 75, 90, 100, 102, 103, 107, 115. *See also* Fugitive slaves; Insurrection plots, slave drivers in
Dehumanization, slave drivers resist, 31, 88, 91, 112, 115-116
Demotion, of slave drivers, 59, 74, 96, 115
Des Pres, Terrence, on Kapos, 36-37
Dickey, Gilbert, slave driver, 103
Dirt, Rufus, slave driver, 29
"Display" slaves, slave drivers as, 65-66

Dortch, Charles, 87, 88
Dortch, Reuben, slave driver, 87, 88
Douglass, Frederick, 93-94
Dread, slave driver, 73-75
Drew, Benjamin, 98
Drivers. *See* Slave drivers
Duke, Basil, 46
Duties, slave driver, diversity of, 4, 5,
    11-14, 70, 87-88, 104, 114

Eaton, Clement, on black auto-
    biographies, 130
Education, of slave drivers, 12, 20, 22,
    88. *See also* Teachers, slave drivers as
Eliot, William G., 105
Elites: defined, xiii; and "New Left"
    history, xiv; slave drivers as, xiv;
    social science views of, xiii-xiv
Elkins, Stanley M.: on "infantilization"
    of slaves, 35-36, 37; on slave drivers,
    37; *Slavery*, 35, 77
Engerman, Stanley L., *Time on the
    Cross*, 42-44
Essex, slave driver, 48

Fallon, John, 17
Families, of slave drivers, 14-20, 70-71;
    separation of, 17-18, 26-27, 115
Featherstonhaugh, George, 68-69
Federal Emergency Relief Administra-
    tion (FERA), 125-126
Federal Writers' Project (FWP), 78,
    127; activities of, 126, 128, 169; black
    interviewers in, 83, 160; white inter-
    viewers in, 83-85. *See also* Oral
    history
Feldstein, Stanley, *Once a Slave*, 41
Fenmore, slave driver, 58
Fisk University, Social Science Institute,
    125, 127
Fogel, Robert William, *Time on the
    Cross*, 42-44
Food: as slave driver bonus, 51; slave
    drivers supply bondsmen with, 12,
    53-54, 70, 86, 103, 115, 162

Ford, Sarah, 80-81
Foremen, slave, 3. *See also* Slave drivers
Frank, slave driver, 69-71
Franklin, John Hope, on historians'
    source materials, 127
Fraser, slave driver, 82
Frazier, E. Franklin, and oral history,
    127
Fredrickson, George M., 78
Free blacks, as slave supervisors, 4, 90,
    138
Free labor supervisors, slave drivers
    compared to, xiv, 3, 32
Freeman, Mittie, 26
From Sundown to Sunup (Rawick), 41
Fugitive slaves: slave drivers as, 18, 90,
    96, 101, 103-105, 108, 109, 111-112,
    115; slave drivers capture, 14
Furnas, J. C., 31

Gabe, slave driver, 86
Gang system, slave drivers used in, 5
Genovese, Eugene D., 42; *Roll, Jordan,
    Roll*, 39-41; on slave historiography,
    39, 113
George, slave driver, 58
Gillard, Jim, 16
Gilmore, Mattie, 5
Gist, July, slave driver, 87
Glasgow, slave driver, 9
Goffman, Erving, 36
Goodman, Andrew, slave driver, 26
Goodrum, John, 27
Goodwater, Thomas, 86, 162
Gould, William Proctor, 56
Gresham, Harriet, 15-16
Grimball, John Berkley, 59
Grimes, William, 98, 99
Gullins, David Goodman, 87
Gutman, Herbert G., on *Time on the
    Cross*, 43-44

Hall, Basil: describes slave sale, 17-18;
    tours plantation, 121-122
Hall, Margaret: on *negro funk*, 123;

tours plantation, 121-122
Hamlin, Susan, 83
Hammon, Briton, *Narrative*, 129
Hammond, James Henry: boosts slave
  drivers' image, 50; rewards drivers, 51
Hanover, Jim, slave driver, 29
Harris, Aaron, slave driver, 165
Harris, Newit, 165
Hart, Albert Bushnell, 3, 34
Hazzard, W. W., grants drivers exten-
  sive disciplinary powers, 142-143
Head man, 3. *See also* Slave drivers
Henderson, Celia, 84
Henry, Jefferson Franklin, 90
Henry, slave driver, 52-54
Henson, Josiah, slave driver, 109, 111-
  112, 129
Heyward, Duncan Clinch: on origin of
  slave driver, 136-137; on planters, 47
Heyward, Nathaniel, 136
Hicks, Edward, 98
Higgerson, Joseph, 89
Hildreth, Richard, *Slave, The*, 95, 96
Historiography. *See* Slavery, histori-
  ography of
Hofstadter, Richard, 127
Horry, Ben, 82
Housing, of slave drivers, 15, 16, 43, 88
Humanity, slave drivers maintain. *See*
  Dehumanization, slave drivers resist
Hunter, John Linguard, 20

Indentured servants, as labor super-
  visors, 4
Industrial crafts, slave supervisors in, 6
Inside View of Slavery, An (Parsons),
  73-75
Insurrection plots, slave drivers in,
  72-73, 165-166
Isaac, slave driver, 72-73
Islamic faith, drivers practice, 22-23

Jackson, Margaret, 94
Jackson, Martin, 85
Jake, slave driver, 80-81
Jamison, Monroe F., 98, 99

Johnson, Charles S., 85, 125
Johnson, James H., 28
Johnston, James C., 53
Jones, George Noble, 58
Jones, J. Ralph, 128-129
Jones, Lewis, slave driver, 104
Jones, Richard, 86-87
Jones, Thomas H., 97-98, 99

Kapo, as slave driver-figure, 36-37
Kearney, Belle, 47
Kemble, Frances Anne (Fanny): observes
  slave driver family, 69-71; on slaves,
  123-124; as traveler, 121
King, Roswell, Jr., 50-51, 70
Krump, Betty, 84

Larkin, Patsy, 86
Lasch, Christopher, 78
Laws relating to slave drivers, 7, 138,
  156
Lay My Burden Down (Botkin), 94, 126
Leading man, 3. *See also* Slave drivers
Legree, Simon, xvii
Lemon, Jim, 87
Lester, Julius, 77
Lewis, Roscoe, 78-79
Library of Congress Project, 126
Little, John, 94
Logan, Miriam, 84
Loguen, Jermain W., slave driver, 106,
  109, 110; separated from family, 18;
  on whites' religion, 23
Loyalty, slave driver, 35, 48-49, 65-66,
  114, 115, 153; during Civil War,
  25-26, 105
Lubbar, Jack, slave driver, 55-56

McCormick, Andrew Phelps, 46-47
McCormick, Joseph, on slave driver
  faithfulness, 153
Mackay, Alexander: on slave intelli-
  gence, 122; on travelers, 61
Macks, Richard, 16
Mappin, John, slave driver, 87

Marriage, of slave drivers. *See* Families, of slave drivers
Masters. *See* Slaveholders
Meade, Anna Hardeman, 47-48
Merchants, slave drivers' dealings with, 12, 14, 114
Ministers, slave drivers as. *See* Preachers, slave drivers as
Monroe, Prince, slave driver, 153
Montgomery, Benjamin T., slave driver, 28-29
Montgomery, Jane, 26
Morgan, Charles, slave driver, 21-22
Moses, slave driver, 52-54
Muslim slave drivers, 22-23

Narrative of . . . Briton Hammon (Hammon), 129
Narrative of James Williams (Williams), 96-97, 164
Nelson, Jim, slave driver, 20-21
Newby, Idus A., 34
"New Left" history, xiv, 127
Nichols, Charles H., 132
Nichols, Christopher, 98
Nichols, Thomas, 62
Northup, Solomon, slave driver, 9, 105-106, 107; as autobiographer, 93, 129, 166

O'Ferrall, Simon A., 67-68
Oliver, Caesar, slave driver, 88
Olmsted, Frederick Law, 8; on "display" slaves, 65; on slave character, 123; as traveler, 63
Once a Slave (Feldstein), 41
Oral history: collection of, 124-126, 169; recorded by black interviewers, 83, 160; recorded by white interviewers, 82-85; relationship to black autobiographers, 93, 94; use by historians, 77-78, 79-80, 82, 85, 91, 126-128, 129. *See also* Federal Writers' Project
Orinoca, slave driver, 54
Oroonoko (Behn), 129

Overdriver, 3. *See also* Slave drivers
Overlooker, 3. *See also* Slave drivers
Overseers: black, 137; described by Charles Ball, 96; Edmund Ruffin on, 10; in history books, 34; laws relating to, 7, 138, 156; in oral history, 85; relationship to slave drivers, 5-6, 7, 10-11, 50, 58, 89, 90; white, compared to slave drivers, 124
Owens, Leslie Howard, 31

Parsons, C. G., *Inside View of Slavery, An,* 73-75
Peculiar Institution, The (Stampp), 34-35, 37, 77
Pemberton, James, slave driver, 49
Prequisites of office, slave driver. *See* Rewards, slave drivers receive; Sexual privileges, slave drivers granted
Pettigrew, William Shepard; instructs slave drivers, 12, 14, 51-54; on slave driver attributes, 8, 9
Phillips, Ulrich B.: on black autobiographies, 130, 166; influence on historiography, 32-34; on oral history, 77, 79-80; on slave drivers, 32; on slavery, 32, 35, 44; on twentieth-century blacks, 33
Planters. *See* Slaveholders
Political Economy of Slavery, The (Genovese), 39
Politics of History, The (Zinn), 79
Pompey, slave driver, 69
Preachers, slave drivers as, 20-21, 27
"Pride of place," as slave driver trait, 32, 33, 34, 50-51
Prince, slave driver, 58
Proctor, Jenny, 81-82
Psychological pressures, slave drivers experience, 89-90, 112. *See also* Dehumanization, slave drivers resist
Punishment, of slave drivers, 26, 50, 72-73, 74-75, 89, 98, 103, 105, 115. *See also* Demotion, of slave drivers
Pyles, Henry, 25

Quarters: slave drivers' cabins in, 16; slave drivers supervise, 11, 14, 16. *See also* Slave community

Quimbo, slave driver, xv-xvii, 34, 114

Randolph, Peter, 19

Ransdell, John H., 25

"Rascality," slave drivers accused of, 54-59

Rawick, George P., 77, 128; *From Sundown to Sunup*, 41

Reconstruction, slave drivers during, 26-29

Reddick, Lawrence D.: on historiography, 126-127; and oral history, 125-126, 128

Redpath, James, 71-72

Reed (ex-slave), on oral history, 77

Religion, of slave drivers. *See* Christianity, slave drivers reject; Christians, slave drivers as; Muslim slave drivers

Renty (slave), 71

Resistance, slave driver. *See* Defiance, of slave drivers; Dehumanization, slave drivers resist; Fugitive slaves; Insurrection plots, slave drivers in

Rewards, slave drivers receive, 15, 16 34, 35, 43, 51, 73, 88, 103, 114, 162. *See also* Sexual privileges, slave drivers granted

Rice growing, use of slave drivers in, 5

Richard, slave driver, 59

Robertson, Irene, 84

Robin, Claude, 67

Robinson, Solon, 64

Role model, slave driver as, xiv, 40, 150

Role playing: slave drivers engage in, 69, 106, 108; slaves engage in, 66

Roll, Jordan, Roll (Genovese), 39-40

Roper, Moses, 129

Ruffin, Edmund, 10

Ruffin, F. G., 50

Runaways, drivers as. *See* Fugitive slaves

Sam, slave driver, 20

Sambo, slave driver, xiii, xv-xvii, 34, 114; compared to Elkins' "Sambo," 149

"Sambo" stereotype, 35; compared to Stowe's "Sambo," 149

Sanford, Joseph, slave driver, 104-105

Scott, Robert, slave driver, 90

Sealsfield, Charles, 124

Selection, of slave drivers, 4, 6, 8-11, 49, 65, 90

Self purchase, slave drivers negotiate, 106, 108, 111

Settle, Ophelia, 125, 128

Sexual privileges, slave drivers granted, 16, 143-144

Sheppard, Morris, 27

Sitterson, J. Carlyle, 31, 149-150

Skipwith, George, slave driver, 57, 59

Slave, The (Hildreth), 95

Slave auctions, slave drivers involved in, 17-18, 144

Slave community: slave drivers as protectors of, 17, 53-54, 58, 86, 115; slave drivers' commonality with residents of, 30, 75, 103, 115; slave drivers' role in, 11, 12, 14, 16, 19, 20, 23-25, 115. *See also* Slaves

Slave Community, The (Blassingame), 38

Slave courts, 6

Slave drivers: age of, 9; capture fugitive slaves, 14; as Christians, 20-22, 23, 105, 109; during Civil War, 25-27, 105; clothing of, 43, 51, 96; commonality with bondsmen, 30, 75, 103, 115; compared to free labor supervisors, xiv, 3, 32; as corn generals, 24-25; criticized, 6-7, 47-48, 54-58, 59, 74-75, 103; cruelty of, xv-xvii, 7, 35, 41-42, 66-68, 80-82, 85-86, 91, 97-99, 114; defy whites, 26, 75, 90, 100, 102, 103, 107, 115; demotion of, 59, 74, 96, 115; as "display" slaves, 65-66; duties of, 4, 5, 11-14, 70, 87-88, 104, 114; education of, 12, 20, 22, 88; as elites, xiv; fake whippings, 40, 86, 115; families of, 14-20, 69-71; female,

6; forced to whip, 19, 86, 99; as fugitives, 18, 90, 96, 101, 103-105, 108, 109, 111-112, 115; housing of, 15, 16, 43, 88; in gang system, 5; in industrial crafts, 6; in insurrection plots, 72-73, 165-166; laws relating to, 7, 138, 156; limitation on authority of, 11-12, 89; loyalty of, 35, 48-49, 65-66, 114, 115, 153; method of selection, 4, 6, 8-11, 49, 65, 90; as Muslims, 22-23; number of, in South, 40, 42; number of slaves supervised, 7-8; physical characteristics of, 8-10; popular characterization of, xv-xvii, 114; as preachers, 20-21, 27; "pride of place" of, 32, 33, 34, 50-51; protect slaves, 17, 53-54, 58, 86, 115; psychological pressures on, 89-90, 112; punishment of, 26, 50, 72-73, 74-75, 89, 98, 103, 105, 115; "rascality" of, 54-59; during Reconstruction, 26-29; relationship to merchants, 12, 14, 114; relationship to overseers, 5-6, 7, 10-11, 50, 58, 89, 90; relationship to slaveholders, 50, 59, 67, 80-81, 88, 89, 90, 109; resist dehumanization, 31, 88, 91, 112, 115-116; rewards given to, 15, 16, 34, 35, 43, 51, 73, 88, 103, 114, 162; role in slave community, 11, 12, 14, 16, 19, 20, 23-25, 115; as role models, xiv, 40, 150; role playing of, 69, 106, 108; sale of, 17-18, 115, 144; self direction of, 14, 23, 53, 103; self purchase of; 106, 108, 111; separation from families, 17-18, 26-27, 115; sexual privileges of, 16, 143-144; slaves' attitudes toward, 20, 23-25, 34, 86-87; in slave trade, 68-69, 102-103; supply slaves with food, 12, 53-54, 70, 86, 103, 115, 162; in task system, 5; as teachers, 86-87; term defined, 3-4, 6, 136-137; term of service, 4; theft committed by, 55, 103; in *Uncle Tom's Cabin*, xv-xviii; whips of, 11-12

Slaveholders: attachment to drivers, 49-51; boost slave drivers' image, 50-51; as Christian examples, 21-22, 23; consult with slave drivers, 49, 50, 51-54; influence travelers, 62-63, 65-66, 157; limit slave drivers' authority, 11-12, 89; in oral history, 85; relationship to slave drivers, 50, 59, 67, 80-81, 88, 89, 90, 109; use of slave drivers criticized, 6-7
Slave Narrative Collection, 126, 128
Slave revolts. *See* Insurrection plots, slave drivers in
Slavery (Elkins), 35, 77
Slavery, historiography of: during 1950s, 34-38; during 1960s, 39; during 1970s, 38-44, 113; during Phillips era, 32-34, 44
Slavery in the United States (Ball), 95-96, 97
Slaves: attitudes of, toward slave drivers, 20, 23-25, 34, 86-87; role playing of, 66, 69, 106, 108; stereotypes of, 32, 47, 63, 64, 67, 122-123. *See also* Dehumanization, slave drivers resist; "Display" slaves, slave drivers as; Slave community; Slave drivers
Slave supervisors. *See* Free blacks, as slave supervisors; Overseers; Slave drivers
Slave trade, 18; slave drivers in, 68-69, 102-103
Smedes, Susan Dabney, 46
Smith, Boyd, 56
Smith, Harry, 9
Snipes, Charlie, slave driver, 87
Socialist Scholars Conference, 39
Solomon, slave driver, 121-122
Spalding, Thomas, 22
Stamper, Billy, 86
Stampp, Kenneth M.: on oral history, 78; *Peculiar Institution, The*, 34-35, 37, 77; revises Phillips, 34-35, 37-38; on slavery historiography, 79, 127
Starling, Marion, on black auto-

biographies, 133, 163
Starobin, Robert, 41-42
Stereotypes, slave. *See* Slaves (stereo-
    types of)
Stewart, slave driver, 56
Still, Peter, slave driver, 106, 108
Stirling, James, 121
Stowe, Harriet Beecher, 34, 114;
    Uncle Tom's Cabin, xv-xvii, 136
Straw boss, 3. *See also* Slave drivers
Stuart-Wortley, Lady Emmeline, 62-63
Sutton, Samuel, 84
Sybert, Jordan, slave driver, 28
Sydan, Nancy, 104
Sydan, Thomas, 104

Tasistro, Louis, 66
Task system, slave drivers used in, 5
Taylor, Zachary, 62
Teachers, slave drivers as, 86-87
Thacker, Page. *See* Burwell, Letitia M.
Theft, slave driver, 55, 103
Thomas, Richard, 10
Thompson, John, 10
Thomson, William: on blacks, 120-121,
    123; on slavery, 64; on slave theft, 123
Thorpe, Earl, 68
Thrash, Mark, 78-79
Time on the Cross (Fogel and Enger-
    man), 42-44
Tocqueville, Alexis de, 124
Tower, Philo: on travelers, 62; on
    whippings, 158
Trammel, Robert, 90
Trash gang, slave drivers in, 6
Travelers: accounts used by historians,
    119-120; as authors, 61, 119; influ-
    enced by slaveholders, 62-63, 65-66,
    157; interests of, 117-118; interpre-
    tive problems of, 61-66, 120-124;
    itineraries of, 119; number of, 117-
    118; objectivity of, 64, 119; and slave
    punishments, 64-65, 67-68
Turner, Nat, 165
Tuskegee Institute, and oral history, 83

"Uncle Paul," slave driver, 9
"Uncle Philip," slave driver, 9
Uncle Tom's Cabin (Stowe), xv-xvii,
    136
Underdriver, 3, 70. *See also* Slave
    drivers

Vaughan, John C., 72, 73

Walker, James, 102
Wall, Bennett, 78
Walton, Sol, 10-11
Washington, George, 54-55
Watson, Andrew P., 125
Webster, Daniel, 73
Weeks, David F., 56
Weld, Theodore D., 63
Whip, slave drivers', 11-12
Whipping boss, 3. *See also* Slave drivers
Whippings: slave drivers fake, 40, 86,
    115; slave drivers forced to give, 19,
    86, 99
Whipple, Henry B., 120
Whitfield, Francis, 102-103
Whittier, John Greenleaf, 96, 97
Williams, Harry, slave driver, 26
Williams, Isaac, slave driver, 103
Williams, James, *Narrative of James
    Williams,* 96-97, 164
Williams, Nancy, 19-20, 90
Women, as slave drivers. *See* Slave
    drivers (female)
Woodson, Carter G.: on black auto-
    biographies, 163; on oral history, 125;
    on Ulrich B. Phillips, 33
Woodward, C. Vann, on oral history,
    80, 83, 160
Works Progress Administration (WPA),
    83, 126, 128, 129

Yetman, Norman, 77

Zinn, Howard, 79

——————ABOUT THE AUTHOR——————

WILLIAM VAN DEBURG is Assistant Professor of Afro-American Studies at the University of Wisconsin in Madison. His articles have appeared in such journals as the *Historian*, *Negro History Bulletin*, and the *Journal of the American Academy of Religion*.